RELIGION IN PRACTICE

RELIGION
IN PRACTICE

BY

SWAMI PRABHAVANANDA

WITH AN INTRODUCTION BY
CHRISTOPHER ISHERWOOD

VEDANTA PRESS
HOLLYWOOD, CALIFORNIA

PRINTED IN GREAT BRITAIN

PREFACE

The lectures in this book were originally delivered at the temples of the Vedanta Society of Southern California. They were later edited and published in our magazine, *Vedanta and the West*. I am grateful to all those who helped in their editing.

I am greatly indebted to Clive Johnson, a monastic member of the Vedanta Society of Southern California, for undertaking the task of final revision and arrangement. He has done everything possible to arrange the contents of this book in a way that conforms to its title.

I am also grateful to my dear friend Christopher Isherwood for writing an introduction to it.

Part I, 'The Problem', sets the stage, as it were, by acquainting the reader with the basic principles of religion and how they relate to modern man and his search for meaning in life. The thoughtful man has always been asking, 'Who am I? Where am I going?' These are questions expressing the dilemma of existence. I have tried to show that there is an eternal truth which can, once we overcome ignorance, be known and experienced by every genuine spiritual aspirant.

Part II, 'The Goal', concerns the objectives of religion; that is, the 'ends' as distinct from the 'means'. Although the ultimate goal of spiritual life is the realization of God, there are a great many intermediate goals – some ethical and others experiential. All of them are essential aspects of the religious life.

The third section, 'The Methods', is practical in its emphasis. This section treats the various disciplines and aids that can help lead man to God. I am afraid I cannot offer any 'chemical' short-cuts to those who seek a higher life. Nor any easy path. But those who are sincere and, above all, *yearn* for Him, will find their struggle greatly lessened.

The next part, 'The Exemplars', contains four lectures I gave on Buddha, Christ, Vivekananda, and Sri Ramakrishna. I think we may safely say that the world, or a major portion of it, regards these men as outstanding examples of spiritual greatness. It is they who provide us with the inspiration to continue the struggle for ultimate truth.

Part V is devoted to questions that have been asked me over a period of several years and my answers to them.

I should perhaps add one final comment. I hope that the reader will bear with the number of repetitions of scriptural passages, similes, and parables which appear in many places throughout the text. There is a simple reason for this. I delivered these lectures over a period of more than a decade. It was only natural, therefore, for me to refer frequently to those passages which I considered particularly significant.

S.P.

CONTENTS

Religion in Practice

PART V VITAL QUESTIONS ON
RELIGION ANSWERED

INTRODUCTION

Question: 'How would you define mysticism?'

Answer: 'Mysticism is the essence of religion. It is the conviction that God can be seen; that he can be directly known and realized; and that to have this realization is the only purpose of life.'

This is Swami Prabhavananda's answer to a question put by one of his students. It gives you a fair sample of the 'tone of voice' which he uses in these lectures; a tone which is direct and simple but never oversimplified. He never talks down to his hearers – as some preachers are apt to, because their way of urging us to improve ourselves is to remind us that we are miserable sinners. Prabhavananda isn't in the least naive about sin. He is well aware that most of us are blocking our own enlightenment by idiotically repeated acts of desire, vanity, violence and untruth; but, as a Vedantist, he urges us to improve ourselves by looking up rather than down, toward the inspiring belief that our nature, despite all its apparent blemishes, is essentially of God.

Prabhavananda's tone of voice is simple because his approach to religion is so practical. As he has proved in his book *The Spiritual Heritage of India*, he thoroughly grasps and can lucidly explain the subtleties of Hindu philosophy. But he isn't interested in philosophy as an intellectual exercise or an artform, and he only discusses philosophic theory in its relation to practice.

Those of us who first turn to religion when we are already adults usually do so because we have become aware of a lack in our lives, an absence of purpose, a need for a kind of security which no insurance company can offer. We long to believe that such security can be found, yet we are naturally afraid of yielding to mere superstition. We have been told so many lies and have met so many crooks in our professional world that we enter the world of religion with deep misgivings – and rightly so, for lies and crooks abound there also. We are right to demand intellectual reassurance, right to question the character of our prospective teacher, right to heckle him with such questions as: 'If God is all good, how do you account for evil?' 'What part does sex play in religion?' 'Suppose we want to do

God's will, how can we be certain what it is?'

Prabhavananda is able and willing to answer these and many other questions of a like kind; he does so in this book. But each reader will have to weigh the answers for himself and decide whether or not they solve his personal problems. If they don't, there is really nothing more to be said; the dissatisfied seeker must look elsewhere. Truth is one, but the kind of language you use to impart it is necessarily individual. If a teacher happens not to speak your language, this doesn't of itself prove that he is a charlatan or that you are wallowing in invincible ignorance. The loud evangelist may make you shudder with distaste. The teacher of spiritual discrimination may repel you by his stern refusal to appeal to your emotions. Always remember that they have been able to help many others.

Let us suppose, however, the reader is satisfied by the way his questions have been answered here—hasn't he thereby taken a big step forward into the religious life? Yes and no. Rational acceptance of a teacher's propositions is a first step forward, certainly; but there is still a danger that this step may also be the seeker's last. There are many sad characters who wander around the borders of religion, listening to all the teachers, reading all the books, accepting everybody and everything – and doing nothing about it. A wide, agnostic no-man's land stretches between intellectual assent and the beginnings of emotional conviction; it can only be crossed when the seeker starts practising religion instead of just reading and hearing about it and saying cautiously, 'That much sounds reasonable, that much I can agree to . . .'

The nature of the seeker's difficulty, as Prabhavananda analyses it, is this: Religion must not contradict reason, certainly, for religion without reason is mere superstition; and if our reason can destroy that superstition so much the better for us, we are better off without it. On the other hand, however, religion cannot be confined within the limits of reason. Reason is the signpost, pointing out the direction we should follow; but the practice of religion necessarily takes us beyond reason, since the aim of religion is to obtain supra-rational knowledge. When the seeker says at the beginning of his search: 'I am ready to agree that I, an apparently separate individual, must logically be a part of the Universal Consciousness, and therefore I am going to try to make contact with this Consciousness within myself' – that is a rational statement. When the seeker says at the end of his search, 'I have made contact, and therefore I now *know* that I am essentially this Consciousness, and that you are essentially this Consciousness, and that nothing else really exists' – that is a supra-rational statement.

All religious teachers are agreed that this supra-rational knowledge is to be obtained through regular practice of one kind or another – daily prayer and meditation, or the ritual cult of an embodied ideal, or the service of one's fellow human beings performed as worship of God within man. The importance of regularity is always stressed; it is far better to keep to the amount of practice that is within our everyday capacities than to alternate between violent effort and total omission, according to our mood.

But regularity is very hard to maintain; it is so easy to give way to boredom and discouragement. What is to keep us practising when the mood is wrong? Reason tells us to persevere; but its voice, in most of us, isn't persuasive. At such times, reason is a bore, too. We need a much stronger, more exciting inspiration.

What we need, in fact, is someone to inspire us to action by his example. He may or may not be a scholar or a philosopher, but he must speak out of his own experience; he must have made at least some definite progress in the practice of religion and gained some empirical knowledge. He must never pretend (this is of the utmost importance) to know more than he knows. We have got to be able to believe in this man's knowledge, even if it is only partial, strongly enough to want to follow his example, face the tediousness of regular practice, and thus find that knowledge for ourselves.

But how are we to recognize such a man, if we are lucky enough to meet him?

If we are going to join a gymnasium, we expect the instructor to be healthy and adequately muscular, to look as if the exercises he teaches have done him good. You can see a physical instructor's muscles at first glance, but a spiritual instructor's powers are not so easily measured. It may even be misleading to pay too much attention to his apparent moral virtues; some very sinister individuals wear a thick mask of humility, patience and nonaggression. It is true that spiritual growth must change a man's character for the better. But when we speak of character, even at its noblest, we are still speaking of the ego-personality; and spiritual knowledge has no concern with the ego.

Igor Stravinsky was once asked about the composition of one of his greatest works, *Le Sacre du Printemps*, 'The Rite of Spring'. He answered, 'I heard and I wrote what I heard. I am the vessel through which *Le Sacre* passed.' Stravinsky's use of the word 'vessel' has tremendous significance. He is speaking, without the least vanity or false modesty, of something which is other and greater than himself, the music. 'I heard and I wrote what I heard' – he does not cling to the honour of being its composer, in the usual egotistical sense. He is proud only to have been its chosen vessel.

In the same manner, I think, we can judge a teacher by his attitude towards his own spiritual experiences. If he regards them as his personal achievement and the due reward of his efforts, then he is really claiming merit for his ego-personality and we should mistrust him. The truly spiritual man knows that he is only a vessel; however great his efforts may have been, they cannot command the coming of experience, for that is always a gift of grace. The most he can do is to purify the vessel so that it is ready to receive the gift at any time – and to purify, in this sense, is to break the bonds of personal attachment and subdue the ego, not to exalt it. To return to my analogy from the life of the arts, one can put it that Stravinsky had to break the bonds of musical tradition and the prejudices of contemporary theory before he was ready to receive artistic grace in the form of *Le Sacre*.

If, having read through this book, the reader finds himself seriously impressed and intellectually convinced by its statements, he is now forced to ask himself, 'Could Swami Prabhavananda perhaps be the person I am looking for to inspire me to begin trying to practise religion?'

My own answer to that question has been 'yes'; I have been the Swami's disciple for the past twenty-eight years. My attitude is therefore not impartial. I wish that everyone who opens this book might end by accepting him as a teacher.

Allowing for my partiality, I think I can safely say this

much: If those of you who have never met Prabhavananda could hear him lecture and, better still, ask him questions, listening to the tone of his voice, studying his face and manner and all those tiny psychophysical clues by means of which, without being aware of how we do it, we form our opinion of a human being, then I am quite sure that very many of you, certainly the majority, would say to yourselves, 'This man does know something – I can trust him.'

Much of the Swami's quality seems to me to come through, as one reads these pages, but something, admittedly, is lost in the transfer from live voice to print. So I will try to supplement your impressions as a reader by adding a few facts about Prabhavananda himself and the influences which have worked upon him to make him what he has now become. In introducing a book of this sort, one can't venture any assumptions as to the reader's previous knowledge of the subject. I must risk boring many of you by starting with some familiar history.

In 1855, a youth of nineteen, later to be known as Ramakrishna, was engaged as an assistant priest at a temple which had just been built beside the Ganges, not far from Calcutta. The temple had been paid for by a very pious and wealthy widow lady, who was a devotee of Kali, the Mother of the Universe. The youthful priest was well versed in the scriptures, and he had been thoroughly trained in the performance of ritual worship by his elder brother, who was also a priest. He was sweet-natured, charming in appearance and well liked by all who knew him; indeed he seemed ideally suited for his new position.

Nevertheless, this youth was soon to scandalize his patroness and the other members of the temple staff; not long after his arrival he began to behave in the most unorthodox manner. He behaved, that is to say, as though the goddess Kali whom they all worshipped were literally present within the shrine; he addressed her three-foot image as though it were a live being, chiding her, coaxing her with food, joking with her, questioning her, pleading with her tearfully for enlightenment!

At first they naturally thought he must be mad. Doctors were sent for to examine him. But he was not mad – little by little they had to admit this to themselves and to face the fact that they were in the presence of something far more extra-

ordinary, disconcerting and unpredictable than a mere madman: a man of God.

The eruption of a volcano is the most awe-inspiring of
physical phenomena. We are suddenly made aware of the
appalling power which exists always beneath the seemingly
firm foundations of our world; it bursts forth with thunder
and fire. The spiritual phenomenon called Ramakrishna produced an altogether different but equally awe-inspiring kind
of eruption; through the vessel of his fragile body a tremendous power was continuously discharging itself into our world
from an unknown Beyond. This power manifested itself
variously from hour to hour, throughout the day; sometimes
Ramakrishna was withdrawn into profound contemplation,
sometimes he spoke with the serene certainty of experience,
sometimes he danced and sang the praises of God in an ecstasy
of delight. Now he seemed an inspired seer, now a disconcert-
ingly candid, utterly innocent, child, full of jokes and play.
People came to see him in increasing numbers, and the power
which issued from him changed the lives of many.

After Ramakrishna's death in 1886, a group of his disciples
formed a monastic order in his name. Its leaders were Vivekananda and Brahmananda, two young men who had been
school friends since their boyhood. The Ramakrishna Order
was tiny and poor at first; but, as the years passed, it grew and
began to flourish. Land was bought for a monastery at Belur
on the Ganges, not far from the temple where Ramakrishna
had spent his adult life; monasteries of the Order were opened
in other Indian cities, together with medical service-stations
and schools. Meanwhile, Vivekananda had travelled and
preached in America and Europe, founding a few centres at
which monks of the Order could reside and teach. He died in
1902 at the Belur Monastery. Thereafter, his room was kept
exactly as it had been during his physical occupancy of it.
Devotees came there daily to bow down before the bed on
which he had slept and sit for a while in meditation.

One day, in 1911, an eighteen-year-old student named
Abanindra Nath Ghosh was among those who visited the
Vivekananda Room. Outside the room, which is on the upper
floor of the building, there is a balcony overlooking the
Ganges. When Abanindra came out on to this balcony, he

found himself, for the first time in his life, face to face with Swami Brahmananda.

Brahmananda was then in his late forties. He had been head of the Ramakrishna Order for more than ten years. The gentle, sensitive boy whom Ramakrishna had regarded as his spiritual son had become a figure of benign but absolute authority. Indeed, his brother monks, the senior swamis of the Order, deferred to his judgment without question, calling him 'Raja', their king, because they believed that he, along with Vivekananda, had inherited Ramakrishna's full spiritual power. Even Brahmananda's physical presence and movements sometimes reminded them of their Master.

Abanindra was a lively young man, fond of sports and a bit of a dandy; but he was also seriously eager to find the meaning of life and to speak with those who might be able to teach him. He had been born not far from Ramakrishna's birthplace, he had been inspired by the writings of Vivekananda, and he had already sought out and met two other members of Ramakrishna's inner circle. But never until this moment had he felt himself overwhelmed by contact with another human being. 'I was immediately drawn to him,' he said later, 'as if to a long-lost friend.' And Brahmananda's first words to Abanindra were, 'Haven't I seen you before?'

This kind of spiritual recognition is indeed a mysterious thing. What is it that is recognized, and by whom? Perhaps something within oneself – the indwelling Presence of which we are so seldom aware – is glimpsed like a mirror-image when we recognize that Presence dwelling, so much more evidently, within a man of God. For Abanindra, this glimpse was accompanied by an intense emotion of love, such as he had never experienced before in his life. Brahmananda, he later explained, was not merely lovable in a personal sense. Brahmananda had realized God, who is love; so Brahmananda *was* love.

Abanindra could not forget that meeting. He yearned to see Brahmananda again. A few months after this, when he was a student at the City College of Calcutta, he impulsively spent the money he had been given for tuition fees on a ticket to Hardwar in the north of India, because he knew that Brahmananda had gone to visit a monastery there. He arrived in the middle of the night, unannounced. But Brahmananda did not seem at all surprised to see him. He allowed Abanindra to stay a month, accepted him formally as his disciple, and then sent him back to Calcutta to continue his education.

At college, Abanindra came under other influences, however; for organized militant opposition to the British rule was now beginning in earnest, and many students were among the revolutionaries. Abanindra, who was courageous and aggressive by nature, as well as idealistic, began to tell himself that his duty was to devote himself to the national cause. He resolved never to marry until India won her freedom – thus becoming, as it were, a political monk. He also joined a terrorist organization, for which he wrote subversive pamphlets and hid revolvers under his bed, without being quite sure how to shoot with them. Abanindra was chosen to hide the revolvers because of his youthfully innocent appearance; but this was no child's play. He and his friends were literally risking their lives. One of them, Rash Bihari Bose, threw a bomb at Lord Harding, the Viceroy, and had to fly the country and go to Japan. Another was arrested and died in prison; the police called it suicide, of course.

At the age of twenty, Abanindra graduated from the City College and entered the Calcutta University College. He was studying philosophy and often went to the Belur Monastery because one of the swamis there could instruct him in the teachings of Shankara. It was then that the second great event of Abanindra's life took place. Here is Prabhavananda's description of it in his memoir of Brahmananda, *The Eternal Companion*. (Brahmananda is referred to in this passage as 'Maharaj', a title of respect which was commonly used in speaking of him.)

'Although Maharaj initiated me while I was still a college student, I had no intention of entering the Order. However, during one Christmas vacation, I went to live for a few days at the monastery. Swami S— used to urge me to become a monk. But I would argue with him. I thought the monastic life was lazy. I wanted to devote myself to political activities, believing that India must be freed from the domination of the British. An old man, who was also a guest at the monastery, used to be present during these arguments. Swami S. could never convince me. One morning, as usual, I went to prostrate before

Maharaj. This old man was also in the room. Suddenly he asked Maharaj: "When is this boy going to become a monk?" Maharaj looked me up and down, and his eyes had an unforgettable sweetness as he answered quietly: "When the Lord wills." That was the end of my political plans and ambitions. I remained at the monastery.'

Prabhavananda goes on to say that many politically-minded young men who came into contact with Brahmananda began to realize that the awakening of India would never come through political action but only through an intensification of the nation's spiritual life. This is no doubt an accurate summary of the opinions which Abanindra and others formed later, to justify their change of life. But opinions are not reformed in an instant. And it seems impossible to explain in logical terms the scene described above. The effect of Brahmananda's seemingly casual reply is even more astonishing than Jesus of Nazareth's summoning of the two fishermen to be his disciples, for Brahmananda did not even summon Abanindra. As for Abanindra himself, if he had merely acted on impulse in deciding so abruptly to join the monastery, he would almost certainly have regretted it and probably returned to his terrorists in the long run.

What in fact happened was that Abanindra remained in the Order from that day onward, and devotedly attended Brahmananda whenever he was allowed to, which was not often, because the Swami travelled a great deal from place to place in the course of his administrative duties. Brahmananda was with Abanindra, however, at his third great moment – when in the autumn of 1921 he took his final vows and received the Swami's blessing as Swami Prabhavananda.

The next year, Brahmananda died. And now Prabhavananda faced a severe test. His own inclinations were toward a contemplative life; he wanted to remain at a monastery in the Himalayas and practice intensive meditation. But in 1923 he was told by his seniors that an assistant swami was needed at the San Francisco centre. To Prabhavananda the prospect of going to work in the United States must then have seemed like spiritual exile; and for the work itself he felt utterly unprepared. As he now says, 'I was barely thirty, I looked like twenty, and I felt even younger than that.'

The senior swamis reproved him for his lack of confidence. How could he dare to say that he couldn't teach – he who had known Brahmananda! Wasn't that inspiration enough? And how could he presume to imagine that success or failure depended on his own efforts? Didn't he have faith that Maharaj would be beside him?

At Prabhavananda's second lecture in San Francisco he found himself at a loss for words and had to walk out of the room. But this was only a temporary setback. Within two years he had shown himself so well fitted for his duties that he was sent to Portland, Oregon, to open a new centre there. In 1929 he moved south to open a centre in Los Angeles. He has been here ever since.

Speaking of Brahmananda, Prabhavananda has told us: 'After his passing away, I felt no void. As long as Maharaj was in the physical body, there was a barrier. Afterwards the barrier was gone. Now I know that Maharaj is still living – and helping all of us.'

I do believe that Prabhavananda knows this; his life proves that he does, he himself is a living proof of it. Until that day when I too can say 'I know', I hold firmly to my belief in Prabhavananda's knowledge. It is all the reassurance and all the inspiration that I need.

CHRISTOPHER ISHERWOOD

PART I

THE PROBLEM

I

IS VEDANTA FOR
WESTERN MAN?

We are living in an age when time and space have been narrowed to such an extent that distant countries with different cultures, different ideologies, and different religions have become next-door neighbours. We are, in short, one world. As races and nations have come into closer contact, conflict has increased, and even culminated in atomic warfare. Moreover, modern man's personal life has become fraught with tension and chaos. Yet it is the natural desire of all mankind to live in harmony and peace.

How can we establish this peace in our individual lives and the lives of the nations on earth? This is the chief problem of Western man today, as it has been the main concern of all mankind throughout the history of the world. Let us analyse the principal trends in the cultural history of the West, examine the progress made as well as the mistakes, and see what contribution Vedanta can make toward ensuring harmony, individually and collectively.

Three basic influences have moulded Western civilization. First, the spirit of science and rationalism, which we find in Greek thought. Secondly, what may be called humanistic ethics, which are also based upon Greek heritage. The third influence has been national politics. With the exception of Platonic and Pythagorean thought, devotion to the city-state became the religion of the Greek people. And strange as it may seem, there are nations even today which are still trying to supplant the urge for religion by a narrow nationalism; as yet they have not even progressed to the idea of a commonwealth of nations.

During the Middle Ages we find an adjustment taking place

in Western thought as a result of the influence of two great religions: Judaism and Christianity. The first indication of this religious influence was an insistence on the insufficiency of intellect and reason. The Greeks had taught that all knowledge of man and the universe could be obtained by the rational mind through scientific experiment. Through such knowledge, they claimed, the hunger of the body would be satisfied and the powers of the mind developed. Judaism and Christianity, on the contrary, emphasized the existence of a truth which the human mind cannot reach. Both religions took their stand on revelation: God reveals his laws and his will to his lawgivers and prophets whose words must be accepted on faith.

Unfortunately they stopped at this point and did not insist that we must seek these revelations for ourselves. No attempts were made to reconcile faith with reason nor to show that although revelation is beyond and above reason, it cannot contradict reason. Whenever an individual, a nation, or a people have practised righteousness, not for the sake of righteousness, but authority, the result has been fanaticism. We read of instances in the history of the world, especially of Christianity, that when blind faith in acceptance of religion was insisted upon, free intellectual inquiry was stifled, bigotry increased, and the face of the earth was polluted with blood in the name of God.

The Renaissance brought to the West a simultaneous growth in political freedom, economic prosperity, intellectual advancement, and social reform. Worldly life became once more the object of existence, and religion was made subservient to it. The Greek spirit of science and rationalism developed into predominance during this period and eventually led to the great progress in scientific investigation and research which has characterized the life of Western man from the Renaissance to the present age.

Today, confronted by jet planes and hydrogen bombs, an increasing number of earnest and thoughtful people feel that science cannot solve their basic problems and that the knowledge it gives does not bring lasting peace. They are coming to believe that religion alone can end the present crisis in the life of modern man. But what kind of religion? We have seen fanaticism, persecution, and war when free inquiry is banned and reason stifled to uphold a religion, a religion that teaches acceptance of authority on blind faith. Moreover, how many contending sects there are! And each claims that it alone has the key to the truth of God. Which are we to choose? The answer is that if we continue to live on the surface of life and hold on to the external manifestations of cultures, ideologies, and religions, we shall never find any harmony or peace. The fundamental truth as taught by all religions is that man has to transform his base human nature into the divine that is within him. In other words, he must reach the deeper strata of his being, wherein lies his unity with all mankind. Vedanta can help us discover that truth which unfolds our real nature – the divinity lying hidden in man.

Vedanta is not a particular religion, but a religion which includes the basic truth of all religions. It teaches that man's real nature is divine; that it is the aim of man's life on earth to unfold and manifest the hidden Godhead within him; and that truth is universal. In the oldest scripture of the world, the Upanishads, we find a sage declaring: 'I have known that truth, that great light, which is beyond all darkness. You also, having known that truth, will attain to immortality.' The truth of God exists eternally. Each one of us has to discover this truth within his own heart. Is our hunger appeased if someone else eats for us? Similarly, it is not by accepting a prophet or by believing in a dogma that we are saved, but by experiencing the truth of God for ourselves as did Christ, Buddha, and Ramakrishna. This Vedantic teaching does not contradict the teachings of Jesus. For, where did Christ's authority come from? Christ realized his perfection, his divinity, within himself. Then he said: 'Ye shall know the truth and the truth shall make you free.' And, 'Be ye therefore perfect even as your Father which is in heaven is perfect.'

Moreover, Vedanta is not antagonistic to the Western spirit of science and rationalism, because the revelation of truth does not contradict another truth. Although reason cannot reach that knowledge, this does not mean that reason and intellect are to be stifled. On the contrary, reason and intellect are elevated and expanded through the practice of spiritual disciplines. It is then the truth of God becomes revealed. Swami Vivekananda has pointed out:

'All religion is going beyond reason, but reason is the only guide to get there. . . . Stick to your reason until you reach something higher, and you will know it to be higher because it will not jar with reason. . . . First hear, then reason and find out all that reason can give about the Self; let the flood of reason flow over it, then take what remains. If nothing remains, thank God you have escaped a superstition. When you have determined that nothing *can* take away the Self, that it stands every test, hold fast to this. . . .'

The Western ideal of humanistic ethics cannot be ignored. The welfare of body and mind must be taken into account. But consider what man really is and what his *dharma* is. Man is not a conglomeration of body, senses, and mind that communicates with an extra-cosmic being which is God. He is fundamentally Spirit and has a body and mind. Thus Vedanta emphasizes and directs our minds toward the same truth which was also taught by Moses and Christ – that the kingdom of God is within. And we have to enter into that kingdom and unfold our latent divinity. We are one in spirit. The differences between man and man are only differences in the degree to which the Godhead is manifest. In the words of Vivekananda: 'Each soul is potentially divine. The goal is to manifest this divinity within by controlling nature: external and internal. Do this either by work, or worship, or psychic control, or philosophy – and be free. This is the whole of religion.'

A widespread misunderstanding exists in the West with regard to Vedanta in its emphasis upon meditation. People often say that it is all right for Orientals to close their eyes and try to find God within, but that Western minds are different and it is not possible for them to meditate. Many sincere and earnest people are of this opinion. But Vedanta and Christianity both emphasize the truth that meditation is essential. St Paul taught his followers to 'pray without ceasing'. Where is the truth of our being? Within ourselves. Yet how can we find that which is within by looking outside? Thus meditation is fundamental in spiritual life. It is nonsense to say that the Western mind cannot meditate, for the West could not have its progress in science or any other field of life without meditation. No sense pleasure, no economic or cultural success is possible without concentrated thought. But there is a difference. In the West, the end is outward achievement. As a result of making external accomplishments the goal, we live in fear of a nuclear holocaust. True, we must satisfy our bodily desires, we must develop our mental powers, but for what purpose? To realize God. He must be made the end, not the means. Christ taught: 'Lay not up for yourselves treasures upon earth, where moth and rust doth corrupt, and where thieves break through and steal: But lay up for yourselves treasures in heaven, where neither moth nor rust doth corrupt, and where thieves do not break through nor steal.' Our attitude must change. We must be active, we must work; but let us work for God and dedicate our actions to him. Eventually, through meditation and selfless actions the law of our being becomes revealed to us, and we become fearless. That is the state of attainment each one of us can reach.

The question may arise: What about the creeds, dogmas, and rituals of the various religions? Should they be discarded? No, Vedanta says. Have as many creeds, dogmas, and rituals as you like, but consider whether they are helping you to realize God. If not, discard them. Doctrines, books, temples, and symbols are only secondary details. The main thing is to realize God. Whatever helps you to unfold the divinity within you is right; whatever keeps you from realizing your true nature is wrong.

Each individual has a particular path to follow, depending on his stage of development; but the goal, the divine unfoldment, is the same for all. This is true for nations as well as individuals. From ancient times it has been taught in the Vedas: 'Truth is one, but its expressions are many.' If we can understand this principle and apply it in our everyday life, we will have co-operation instead of competition. This truth of Vedanta does not conflict with the ideals of Western man. Only the Western tendency to insist on one path for all, whether in the field of material or spiritual culture, must be eradicated. If we assimilate the Vedantic concept of unity in variety, we can learn to live together harmoniously with different cultures, different ideologies, and different religions. Let there be variety in every department of life. At the same time let us recognize the underlying oneness in spirit. That is the only way to find peace.

Thus Vedanta preaches a universal message, the message of harmony. In its insistence on personal experience of the truth of God, on the divinity of man, and the universality of truth it has kept the spirit of religion alive since the age of the Vedas. Even in our time there have been great souls like Ramakrishna, Vivekananda, and Gandhi. The modern apostle of Vedanta, Swami Vivekananda, in speaking of the harmony of religions, said:

'It has been proved to the world that holiness, purity, and charity are not the exclusive possessions of any church in the world and that every system has produced men and women of the most exalted character. In the face of this evidence, if anybody dreams of the exclusive survival of his own religion and the destruction of the others, I pity him from the bottom of my heart, and point out to him that upon the banner of every religion will soon be written, in spite of their resistance: "Help and not fight", "Assimilation, and not destruction", "Harmony and Peace and not dissension".'

This 'sum total' of all religions does not mean that all people on earth have to come under the banner of one prophet or worship one aspect of God. If Christ is true, Krishna and Buddha are also true. Let there be many teachers, many scriptures; let there be churches, temples, and synagogues. Every religion is a path to reach the same goal. When the goal is reached, the Christian, the Jew, the Sufi, the Hindu, and the Buddhist will realize that each has worshipped the same Reality. One who has attained this knowledge is no longer a follower of a particular path or a particular religion. He has become a man of God and a blessing to mankind.

2

MYSTICISM AND MYSTIC EXPERIENCES

When we study the religions of the world, we find they have one factor in common: each is based, fundamentally, upon revelation. The truth of God cannot be experienced through our senses or even through our reason. Revelation means supersensory experience, and claim is made that there have been sages and prophets to whom such revelations were given. These revelations are recorded in the different scriptures of the world; thus, we find Christianity is based upon the Bible – the revelations of the prophets and of Christ. The Koran is the revelation of Mohammed, and the Tripitaka contains the revelations of Buddha. Each religion has a scripture of its own, and that scripture is said to be the word of God.

As a general rule, the followers of the different religions of the world claim that true revelation is contained only in their respective scriptures. But Hindus do not make such a claim. When they describe the Vedas, their scriptures, as beginningless and endless, they do not limit revelation to certain pages of a particular scripture. Books have an origin and books have an end, but revelation is eternal.

When we accept the idea that revelation is confined to a particular scripture, and do not insist upon the evidence of personal experience, we accept those revelations on faith alone. But when religion is confined to mere faith, and that faith does not urge us to act and strive to realize the same truths for ourselves, then religion becomes barren. Life on earth becomes the be-all and end-all of existence. In the scriptures we find certain moral principles or laws which must govern mankind. When we try to follow these moral and ethical principles without attempting to realize the truth of God for ourselves, we may become good men on earth it is true; but that is not enough. It is only the vision of God that can transform our lives. Thus, in order that we can follow a religion, we must experience the same revelations for ourselves. For instance, you may believe that God exists; but until you have known God, until you have seen him, he remains a theory. A mere theory cannot transform your life. The great seer-philosopher Shankara pointed out that scriptures are not the only authority for the truth of God. The real proof is one's personal experience. Truth is eternal. If that truth was revealed to sages and prophets in the past, it can be revealed to any individual who follows the path of spirituality.

If we go to the very source of any religion and leave aside theological dogmas, we find the same insistence upon personal experience. Christ said: 'Ye shall know the truth, and the truth shall make you free.' A great Upanishadic seer also declared: 'Hear all ye children of immortal bliss, I have known that truth which is beyond darkness. You also, having realized that truth, go beyond death.' It is said in the Buddhist scripture: 'Like a beautiful flower, full of colour but without scent, are the fair but fruitless words of him who does not act accordingly.'

A man may be versed in the scriptures, but unless he exemplifies the scriptural truths in his life, his words are fruitless. 'Like a beautiful flower, full of colour and full of scent, are the pure and fruitful words of him who acts accordingly.'

Sri Ramakrishna used to ask those teaching the word of God, 'Do you have the commission?' What this means is: Have you seen God? Have you known and realized him? You cannot appease your own hunger if somebody else eats for you. It is the same with religion. In order to be fruitful, religion must transform our lives and lead us to the level of spirituality where pure joy and pure consciousness are experienced. A passage in the Upanishads reads: 'From joy springs this universe, in joy exists this universe, unto joy goes back this universe.' To experience God is the very essence of religion; therefore, religion is identical with mysticism. What is mysticism? Mysticism has no creed, no theory, no dogmas; mysticism says that you can see God, you can talk to him, you can have the unitive knowledge of the Godhead. There have been mystics in all ages, and there will be mystics in the ages to come. It is the mystic, the saint to whom God has revealed himself, that keeps the truth of the scriptures alive.

Why is it that man seeks religion? Buddha approached this question from a psychological standpoint. He did not concern himself with theories or theological doctrines; he looked into the very depth of the human heart, and saw that sorrow and misery are universal experiences. Every individual feels the urge to overcome suffering and to go beyond the limitations of the body. That is the beginning of religion. As long as we think that we can avoid suffering and misery by any means other than God-realization, we remain within the relative domain of happiness and misery. There can never be unalloyed joy unless one transcends the world of duality, the opposites of life. In the words of the great philosopher Kapila, the ideal of life is the 'complete cessation of suffering and misery', complete liberation from disease, old age, and death.

When Buddha renounced the pleasures of the world, he went in search of the truth. He saw the three miseries that come to everyone – disease, old age, and death. He sought a way to escape these miseries, not for himself merely, but for all mankind. The man who attains *nirvana*, or spiritual illumination, is freed from all suffering and misery. This same truth has been taught not only by Buddha, but also by Christ, Krishna, and all the great prophets of the world.

Man, no doubt, is the measure of all things. In his nature are contained and reflected all levels of truth, from that of matter to God. Man is composed of body, mind and spirit. He may choose to look upon himself as a physical being, a mental being, or a spiritual being. If man considers himself a physical being, he sees everything in the universe as physical. If he regards himself as a mental being, his interest remains in the intellectual plane. But when man knows himself as a spiritual being, and has his eye of the Spirit opened, he sees everything as Spirit, as God. As long as we regard ourselves as either physical or mental beings, so long do we remain subject to duality. As long as we identify ourselves with the mind, we will experience both happiness and sorrow. Fundamentally, man is the Spirit, the Self. He has a body and mind only in order that these may help him realize that he is Spirit. It is only when he has that realization that he transcends all limitations.

Let us examine some of the objections that have been raised against mysticism. One great objection has been that mysticism is escapism. But is escapism really so wrong? If your house is on fire, should you not attempt to escape from it? If mysticism does provide an escape, it is from the limitations and sorrows of life. And who would not like to escape? Moreover, in his escape from suffering and misery, the mystic does not seek liberation solely for himself. One who attains illumination works to free others from the bonds of ignorance; he is the truly unselfish man. The Vedantic ideal is salvation for oneself and for the good of mankind.

Another objection immediately arises: Is life itself evil? Indeed, Buddha called this life evil, and so did Christ. 'He that loveth his life shall lose it.' But what did they mean? Life on earth is not evil in itself; it becomes evil only when we consider it as the ultimate end of existence. Nobody can say that an egg in itself is evil. But if an egg stays too long as an egg, how quickly it becomes rotten, noxious, and evil. This life is necessary in order that we may transcend it and attain eternal life. Christ said: 'Except a man be born again, he cannot see the kingdom of God.' But we need not die to attain that birth. We must struggle to be reborn in spirit, to attain superconscious knowledge in this very life.

A third objection is that mysticism is opposed to reason. It is not. It transcends reason. It leads us to the 'peace that passeth understanding'. No one maintains that knowledge must be based on sense experience alone; the scientist, for instance, finds it necessary to use instruments to make observations that cannot be made by his own senses. Reason, too, operates within only a limited domain, when it is forced to take data from sense experiences. And revelations, though they may not be 'seen' with physical eyes, are valid experiences. It is not an experience exclusive to a few individuals. Anyone who is able to transcend his senses and have his divine sight opened can experience truth. One to whom truth has been revealed is known as a 'seer'.

This question now arises. How can we discriminate between a valid spiritual experience and a figment of the imagination? Suppose, for instance, someone has hallucinations. He claims that these are supersensuous experiences. What are to be the criteria for our judgment? First, the revelations must be something that cannot be known through any other method or means. This excludes psychic powers. Clairvoyance or clair-audience, for example – seeing or hearing from a distance – merely reveal facts that others know who are in proximity to the scene of happening. (Television and radio perform the same function as the psychic – and more accurately.) Secondly, the revelation must not contradict any other rational proof. If I have a revelation which contradicts another experience, it is not a valid revelation.

Three steps have been given which lead to the attainment of revelation. First, one hears about the truth, from the scriptures and from an illumined soul in whom that truth has become revealed. But one does not accept truth on blind faith. Many people have faith in the words of the scriptures without knowing what those words mean. Therefore, the second step is to reason upon the truth. Through reason one gains understanding. The third step is meditation upon the truth. Every science has a method of its own. If I want to learn chemistry, I must experiment in the laboratory. Similarly, to experiment with the truth of God is an important part of religion. But again, one can only experiment under certain conditions, by following certain disciplines. A great sage was asked: 'What is the path?' His answer was: 'The path that has been trodden by the sages of old.' Let us assume I want to study physics. I go to the physicist and explain that because I come from the Orient, and Orientals are 'inward' people, I feel I must meditate in order to learn physics. I shall never become a physicist with that attitude. To learn physics one must follow a particular discipline. It is the same with religion. There is the path trodden by the sages of old. Follow that path.

What is that path? It can be summarized as self-mastery and devotion to God. We must learn to control our minds and give them to God. Prayer, concentration, and meditation are the means. They form the nucleus of spiritual disciplines.

With the practice of these disciplines, the spiritual aspirant's consciousness expands, and he becomes increasingly aware of the true nature of man and the universe. He learns there is a physical body, which includes the mind, the senses, and the intellect; and a causal body, which we call the ego. Beyond these is spirit, the true Self. And spirit is encased in these physical, subtle, and causal sheaths. When he transcends these sheaths, the aspirant reaches *Turiya*, the Fourth, the realm where pure consciousness is experienced.

Similarly, there is this physical universe, which may be said to be the body of *Brahman*, of spirit. Next is the subtle universe, the psychic plane. Beyond that is the causal sheath of *Brahman*, the realm of the personal God – the creator, preserver, and destroyer of this universe. And beyond this sheath is the impersonal Reality, *Brahman* Itself.

The macrocosm exists in the microcosm. This is corroborated by the scientists of today. Within a drop of water, exists the entire solar system. What is in the universe is within man. As the aspirant enters into the spiritual realm, new visions open to him. With our physical eyes we see this physical universe, but as we dive deep within ourselves another plane reveals itself – the psychic plane. In that psychic plane one sees, one hears, and perhaps may get, certain powers. There are psychic temptations in the psychic universe as there are physical temptations in the physical universe. But if one who possesses occult powers makes use of them, his spiritual growth is blocked. However, not everyone passes through this stage.

Beyond this, in the causal plane, one sees the personal aspect of God. In this plane one may have the vision of symbols or *mantras*, sacred words given by the teacher to the disciple. Then again, the forms of God may melt away, the universe disappears, and an ocean of light with waves of bliss touch every fibre of our being. One becomes God-intoxicated.

Beyond this realm is the Absolute, the impersonal Reality, *Brahman*. Ego vanishes and there is an experience of the unitive knowledge of the Godhead.

These states can be experienced whether one is a Hindu, a Christian, or a Buddhist. That is why a true religion is universal; it does not claim that its path is the only path, but recognizes that all paths are true. Whether you follow the path of Christ or Krishna, when you dive deep within yourself you find that Christ and Krishna are one and the same Reality.

Mysticism and Mystic Experiences

Whatever one's path may be, remember always that the goal is not to be a Christian, a Hindu, or a Buddhist. The ideal is to be a man of God.

3

MAN AND GOD

What is God? What is man? What is the relationship between them? These questions are discussed in almost every religion and philosophy; and we find from them a wide variety of answers. By classifying the various schools of thought, we discover three divisions: dualism, qualified non-dualism, and non-dualism.

Dualism considers man as the creature and God as the creator; and as such, separate from one another. The qualified non-dualist accepts God as the whole and man as a part of his being; whereas the non-dualist regards man as identical with God. There are definite statements in every scripture of the world – whether the Bible, the Koran, the Upanishads, or the Zend-Avesta – supporting the truth of each of these schools of thought.

Although they are apparently contradictory, these three schools of thought can be reconciled. It is impossible to establish that harmony from the standpoint of a theologian. A theologian is concerned with dogmas, creeds, and doctrines; he is interested in particular statements that support his own theory. It is only from the standpoint of a mystic, one who tries to experience God, that the reconciliation can be found.

Religion is primarily mysticism. And what is mysticism? Mysticism asserts that God is not a theory, not an opinion, not an idea, but Reality itself. God *is*. And if God exists, he can be known and realized. One may, through reason, establish a conception of God as an Absolute Being, as did the great German philosopher Hegel. But what proof have we that his *idea* of the Absolute and the Absolute itself are in conformity? Idea and fact are never similar. For instance, you may read books about a country and form an idea about it. When you go and see the country for yourself – what a difference! Thus, the mystic urges that God must be known and realized.

Of course, nobody can see God with these eyes. Nobody can hear the voice of God with these ears; and yet the mystic claims that you can see him, you can hear his voice, you can realize your oneness with him. Religion, therefore, is super-normal. If we consider our own lives, we find that it has to be so. In everyone there is the urge for perfection, in whatever way we may be seeking it; that is why mysticism came into existence. That perfection has been attained, not in the so-called world of the senses or the normal plane, but by transcending this normality. God is realized in the transcendental consciousness.

How is God realized? First, we find that there are different stages of experience. The highest stage is known as *nirvikalpa samadhi*, which means unified knowledge. In that state there is no division between the knower and the object of knowledge. For as long as there is a division between the knower and the object known, the knowledge is not perfect. The object still remains unknown. How do I know an object? The object gives me certain sensations and I form an idea of the object. That idea and the object itself remain separate. It is only when this division is eliminated that the thing-in-itself can be known. It is not known in the ordinary sense; one becomes That. There is an identity, the unitive knowledge of the Godhead. In this experience the universe of name and form disappears. There is no longer a separate knower or ego, nor an object of knowledge – such as God. Creator and creation have disappeared. There is only oneness. From that standpoint this universe is illusory.

Having experienced that *samadhi*, the great seers and sages become silent; they cannot express this experience in words. Sri Ramakrishna used to say that 'everything has been defiled by the lips of man, but the truth of God has never been defiled because nobody can express it'. Even the scriptures are expressions; and no expression is final. When the Upanishads declare 'Thou art That', or when Christ says, 'I and my Father are one', the actual experience is not conveyed because the sense of 'That' and 'thou', of 'I' and 'Father' has returned. From a strictly philosophical standpoint Buddha was a perfect philo-

sopher. Yet because of his philosophy he was misunderstood.
When he was asked, 'Do I understand you to say that there is
no *Brahman?*' he answered, 'Did I say that?' Another asked,
'Do I understand you to say that there is *Brahman?*' And
Buddha answered, 'Did I say so?' Even to say that God
is is to limit him. When we say one, we have the sense of
duality. Therefore the non-dualists try to express the truth of
God in negative terms as 'not this, not that'. This is neither
agnosticism nor nihilism. The only positive way the Vedantists
try to express the truth of God is by saying '*Brahman* is *Sat-
chit-ananda*' – immortal existence, pure consciousness, and
infinite love and joy. It is pointed out, however, that this does
not mean that God exists, or God is conscious, or God is
loving; but that he is Existence itself, he is Consciousness
itself, he is Love itself. These are just words to us. The mind
cannot grasp this truth; it must be assimilated and experienced
within one's own heart.

There also exist lower stages of realization, where the ego
remains, and we tell ourselves, 'I consciously know the love
of God.' This mystic experience is called *savikalpa samadhi*.
Here one experiences God as a personal being with attributes
and qualities. This state is described in the Upanishads: 'As
the spider weaves its thread, lives on it, and withdraws this
thread unto himself, so God out of himself issued forth this
universe, in this universe he exists, and unto himself he withdraws this universe.'

Now again, this personal being may be experienced as
having form or not having form. There are many aspects of
God seen by the mystics. They are not imagined by human
minds, but actual facts. Sri Ramakrishna used to give the
illustration of the 'formless' ocean, which, through intense
cold, at times assumes the shape of icebergs of various shapes
and sizes. Then again, a mystic sees the forms of God in divine
incarnations – those of Christ, Krishna, Buddha, and Ramakrishna are still alive for many. It is not self-hypnosis when a
St Francis of Assisi sees Christ. God came as Christ, and that
form is an eternal form. And not only a Christian sees Christ;
other saints see him. Sri Ramakrishna and Swami Brahmananda
saw Christ. Again, a Christian may see Ramakrishna. As a
man enters into the domain of *savikalpa*, he may see many

forms. That is why a true mystic – whether he is a Christian,
a Hindu, a Buddhist, or whether he belongs to no particular
religion at all – will never be a narrow sectarian. When the
door to the vision of God opens, the mystic sees him in many
aspects.

This experience of *savikalpa* is expressed in philosophical
terms as qualified monism: 'I am a part of God, distinct from
him but not separate.' In that state there is ecstasy; love, union,
and varied forms and attributes of God are experienced. God
is seen as the repository of all blessed qualities and attributes.
Christ expressed this standpoint when he said, 'I am the vine,
ye are the branches.' The illustration can be given of the ocean
and the waves. The waves themselves are not the ocean, but
they are in combined form. Similarly, the whole universe,
with all its varied names and forms, makes up the total God or
Brahman.

The mystic sees these various forms of God; again these
forms melt away into the formless. As Sri Ramakrishna said,
'When the sun of knowledge strikes the icebergs, they melt
away.' Through the intense devotion of a spiritual aspirant,
God assumes forms; but as the sun of knowledge rises, these
forms melt away into the formless.

When a man who has experienced these mystic states
returns to the normal plane, he still sees this universe, but with
this difference: he sees it as the play of God. For he has only
the semblance of an ego. At times he lives as a dualist. In this
state he assumes various relationships with God – as father or
mother, as friend or beloved, or as a child. We also find that
a devotee can establish more than one of these relationships
with God. Christ, for instance, taught us to pray to the Father
in heaven, and said to his disciples, 'Ye are my friends.'

Rama, who was regarded as a divine incarnation, at one time
asked his great devotee Hanuman, 'How do you look upon
me?' Hanuman's beautiful answer reconciles the three schools
of dualism, qualified non-dualism, and non-dualism. He said:
'As long as I possess physical consciousness, I consider you
as my master and I as your servant. When I consider myself
as an individual soul, you are the whole, I am thy part. And
when I consider myself as the *Atman*, I am one with thee.'
At different stages different moods prevail. Actually, one must

reach the highest stage in order to find a perfect harmony between these three schools of thought. In a lower stage, especially when we have been brought up in a theological school of thought with its doctrines and dogmas, we may think it blasphemous if we hear anybody say, 'I and my Father are one.' But from the Vedantic standpoint a spiritual aspirant from the very beginning finds a reconciliation between these schools of thought. He practices in his life all the three attitudes at different times.

What is really the principle behind the attainment of illumination? It is to free ourselves from the sense of ego. What hides our vision of God? Our sense of independent ego. Actually this ego has no independence at all; it is a shadow, and the shadow thinks it is real. Somehow we must merge that shadow in the Light. As a dualist or a qualified non-dualist you feel that the shadow is real, the sense of 'I' persists. Let the ego remain as a child of God. Think of yourself as pure and divine. Then surrender yourself completely to God.

There are practical disciplines that lead to the realization of God. We must practice these different attitudes in meditation. Consider yourself as a temple of God. God dwells within you, he is your very Self. No matter how you think of God, whether with or without form, he is immanent and he is the all-pervading Existence. Of course you have the sense of ego in you. But let your individual self be like a candle flame, and merge this flame in the great Light. Then there remains only the great Light, and you will find 'I and my Father are one.' Then try to feel that you are issuing forth from Him, and that you are worshipping him and meditating on him. Again, when you are working or eating or sleeping, take the attitude that you are a child of God. You may also meditate on the idea that 'I am Brahman, one with God. I am one with the universe,' renouncing that shadow of an ego.

Combine in your life the path of devotion and the path of knowledge. Use your heart and emotion, learn to love God, and at the same time feel your unity with the Godhead. In every one of your meditation periods use a harmonious combination of all the spiritual disciplines. Then will the door to the vision of God open.

4

THE PROBLEM OF EVIL

Every religion or system of philosophy has to deal with the problem of evil – and unfortunately it is a problem which is usually explained away rather than explained. 'Why,' it is asked, 'does God permit evil, when he himself is all goodness?'

One of two answers is usually given to this question by Western religious thought. Sometimes we are told that evil is educational and penal. God punishes us for our sins by visiting us with war, famine, earthquake, disaster, and disease. He employs temptation (either directly or through the agency of the devil) to test and strengthen the virtue of the good. This is the answer given by the Old Testament. It repels many people today and has become unfashionable – although, as we shall see in a moment, it contains a certain degree of truth, according to the philosophy of Vedanta.

The other answer – now more generally accepted – is that evil does not exist at all. If we view life *sub specie aeternitatis*, we shall know that evil has no reality; that it is simply a misreading of good.

Vedanta philosophy disagrees with both these answers – with the second even more radically than with the first. How, it asks, can evil be changed into good, merely by viewing it in a special manner? Pain and misfortune may be borne more easily if we fix our minds upon God – but they are very real experiences nevertheless, even though their duration is limited. Vedanta agrees that evil, in the absolute sense, is unreal. But it reminds us that, from this standpoint, good is unreal also. The absolute Reality is beyond good and evil, pleasure and pain, success and disaster. Both good and evil are aspects of *maya*. So long as one remains in bondage to *maya* and in ignorance, one is subject to this dual experience of life. Within *maya* they are real enough.

43

The question, 'Why does God permit evil?' is, in fact, most misleadingly phrased. It is as absurd as if one were to ask, 'Why does God permit good?' Nobody today would ask why rain 'permitted' a catastrophic flood; nobody would blame or praise fire because it burns one man's house and cooks another man's dinner. Nor can it be properly said that *Brahman* is 'good' in any personal sense of the word. *Brahman* is not 'good' in the sense that Christ was 'good' – for Christ's goodness was within *maya*; his life expressed the light of Reality reflected upon the relative world. The Reality itself is beyond all phenomena; even the noblest. It is beyond purity, beauty, happiness, glory or success. It can be described as 'good' only if we mean that absolute consciousness is absolute knowledge, and that absolute knowledge is absolute joy.

But perhaps the question does not refer to *Brahman* at all. Perhaps, in this connection, 'God' means *Iswara*, the personal aspect of God, the ruler of *maya*. If this is granted, can Vedanta agree with the Old Testament that God is a law-giver, a stern and somewhat unpredictable father, whose ways are not ours, whose punishments and rewards often seem un-merited, who permits us to fall into temptation? The answer is yes and no. The Vedanta doctrine of *karma* is a doctrine of automatic justice. The circumstances of our lives, our pains and our pleasures, are all the result of our past actions in this and countless previous existences, from a beginningless time. Viewed from a relative standpoint, *karma* is quite pitiless. We get exactly what we earn, no more, no less. If we cry out against some apparent injustice, it is only because the act that brought it upon us is buried deep in the past, out of reach of our memory. To be born a beggar, a king, an athlete or a help-less cripple is simply the composite consequence of the deeds of other lives. We have no one to thank but ourselves. It is no use trying to hold *Iswara* responsible for our troubles. It is no use inventing a devil as an alibi for our weaknesses. *Karma* is what we make of it.

Viewed from a relative standpoint, this world of appearance is a bleak place, and as such it often drives us to despair. The seers, with their larger knowledge, tell us otherwise. Once we become conscious, even dimly, of the *Atman*, the Reality within us, the world takes on a very different aspect. It is no longer a court of justice but a kind of gymnasium. Good and evil, pain and pleasure, still exist, but they seem more like the ropes and vaulting-horses and parallel bars which can be used to make our bodies strong. *Karma* is no longer an endlessly revolving wheel of pain and pleasure but a ladder which can be climbed to consciousness of the Reality. From this standpoint, fortune and misfortune are both 'mercies' – that is to say, opportunities. Every experience offers us the chance of making a constructive reaction to it – a reaction which helps to break some chain of our bondage to *maya* and bring us that much nearer to spiritual freedom. Shankara distinguishes between two kinds of *maya* – *avidya* (evil or ignorance) and *vidya* (good). *Avidya* is that which causes us to move further away from the real Self, and veils our knowledge of the Truth. *Vidya* is that which enables us to come nearer to the real Self by removing the veil of ignorance. Both *vidya* and *avidya* are transcended when we pass beyond *maya* into consciousness of the absolute Reality and become freed from the effects of all deeds.

It has been said already that the principle of *maya* is the superimposition of the ego-idea upon the *Atman*, the real Self. The ego-idea represents a false claim to individuality, to being different from our neighbours as well as from *Brahman*. It follows therefore, that any act which contradicts this claim will bring us one step back toward right knowledge, to consciousness of the inner Reality. If we recognize our brotherhood with our fellow men; if we try to deal honestly, truthfully, charitably with them; if, politically and economically, we work for equal rights, equal justice, and the abolition of barriers of race and class and creed, then we are in fact giving the lie to the ego-idea and moving toward awareness of the universal, non-individual existence. All such actions and motives belong to what is known as ethical goodness – just as all selfish motives and actions belong to ethical evil. In this sense, and in this sense only, goodness may be said to be more 'real', or more valid, than evil – since evil actions and thoughts involve us more deeply in *maya*, while good thoughts and actions lead us beyond *maya*, to consciousness of the Reality.

The words 'sin' and 'virtue' are somewhat alien to the spirit of Vedanta, because they necessarily foster a sense of possessiveness with regard to thought and action. If we say, 'I am good', or 'I am bad', we are only talking the language of *maya*. 'I am *Brahman*' is the only true statement any of us can make. St François de Sales wrote that 'even our repentance must be peaceful' – meaning that exaggerated remorse, just as much as excessive self-congratulation, simply binds us more firmly to the ego-idea, the lie of *maya*. We must never forget that ethical conduct is a means, not an end in itself. Knowledge of the impersonal Reality is the only valid knowledge. Apart from that, our deepest wisdom is black ignorance and our strictest righteousness is all in vain.

5

HARMONY OF RELIGIONS

None of us today can properly maintain that we live within the boundaries of one religion, one nation, or one culture. Thanks to the progress of modern science, we find ourselves in a world in which time, space, and geographical limitations have greatly changed. This has forced us to become intensely aware of the cultural habits and characteristics of other peoples of the world; it has opened our eyes to the existence of other faiths and customs. Unfortunately, there is still a large number of people who persist in believing that their religion is the only true religion. But it is heartening to know that there is a growing willingness on the part of many others to attempt some sort of sympathetic understanding among the religions of the world.

From a beginningless time, India has preached the harmony and universality of all religions. This was recently demonstrated by the Hindu people during the remarkable visit of Pope Paul VI. I think we may say, in all humility, that His Holiness learned a great lesson from this visit. Let us quote from the Pope's encyclical, published prior to his trip to India: 'Indeed honesty compels us to declare our conviction that there is but one true religion, the religion of Christianity. It is our hope that all who seek God, and adore him, may come to acknowledge its truth.' We, too, acknowledge that Christianity has the truth, *but not exclusively*. Did not St Augustine say: 'That which is called the Christian religion existed among the ancients, and never did not exist from the beginning of the human race until Christ came in the flesh, at which time the true religion, which already existed, began to be called Christianity.' This ancient religion is still a living religion; but it is not only known as Christianity, but also as Hinduism, Judaism, Zoroastrianism, Mohammedanism, and Buddhism.

Let us call it the Eternal Religion, beginningless and endless.
For God and his truth are infinite, beginningless and endless.

Now let us read Pope Paul's statement delivered after his
return from India, which is very gratifying to us. I quote from
the *India News*, January 1, 1965:

'Pope Paul VI, on December 22nd, described his visit to Bom-
bay early this month as "full of incomparable human value for
us". The Pontiff in his Christmas message to the world said:
"We might well have stayed there [in Bombay] like a
stranger, isolated, and surrounded only by our brothers in
faith . . . but, on the contrary, we met an entire people." He
added: "It represented, it seemed to us, immense crowds of the
vast Indian territory and those also of all Asia."

' "This country is not Catholic," Pope Paul said, "but what
courtesy, what opening of spirit, what an avid desire to get a
glance, or a word from this strange traveller from Rome!"
The Pontiff said: "That was a moment of understanding, of
community of mind. We do not know what these rejoicing
crowds saw in us, but we saw in the crowds a humanity of
great nobility, identified with its millennial cultural traditions.
These crowds were not all Christians, but they were pro-
foundly spiritual, and in so many ways so good and winning." '

Pope Paul was not aware of the attitude of the Hindu masses
in regard to religion or spiritual life. They came to see in Pope
Paul VI not a Christian, or a man belonging to any sect or
religion, but *a man of God*. To them it made no difference
whether he was a Hindu, a Christian, a Buddhist, a Mohammedan, or a Jew. A man of God is a man of God. The Hindus
accept such a man as they would accept a Hindu saint. Therefore, I believe India has something to offer. In her spirit of
acceptance, she has the key to the harmony of the world's
religions.

Before we discuss the ground on which harmony can be
built, let us point out certain facts testified to by time and
history.

There are six major religions in the world: Hinduism or
Vedanta, which is the most ancient of living religions;
Buddhism, Judaism, Christianity, Islam, and Zoroastrianism.

These six major religions in turn are divided into many sects. Christianity and Mohammedanism are the most militant of the group. Many Christians still believe their objective is to Christianize and to convert the entire world. But what can really be achieved by such a conversion? Will this bring peace to man? If men become Christians, will they be instilled with a greater love for God and their fellow man? Can one really *give* to the men and women of the world that 'peace which passeth understanding' of which St Paul speaks? It is also written: 'Jesus spoke as having authority, not as the scribes and pharisees.' Is it not true that Christ taught us we must enter into the Kingdom of Heaven in this life? Can conversion help people enter that Kingdom here and now? Why then does Christianity extend toward people a mere hope for the future, a heaven only after death? Where is that heaven? Christ said, 'within'.

Let us all – Hindus, Christians, Buddhists, Mohammedans, Jews, Zoroastrians – stand together and rather than 'Christianize' or 'Hinduize' the world, let us *spiritualize the world.*

How many dream of unifying the universe by converting the world to one faith! But all have failed; and they will continue to fail. The Hindus, too, seek universality, but in a different way. This is beautifully described by Swami Vivekananda:

'If there is ever to be a universal religion, it must be one which will have no location in place or time; which will be infinite like the God it will preach, and whose sun will shine upon the followers of Krishna and of Christ, on saints and sinners alike; which will not be Brahminical, or Buddhist, Christian, or Mohammedan, but the sum total of all these, and still have infinite space for development; which in its catholicity will embrace in its infinite arms, and find a place for every human being, from the lowest grovelling savage, not far removed from the brute, to the highest man, towering by the virtues of his head and heart almost above humanity, making society stand in awe of him and doubt his human nature. It will be a religion which will have no place for persecution or intolerance in its polity, which will recognize divinity in every man and woman, and whose only scope, whose whole force, will be centred in aiding humanity to realize its own true, divine nature.'

If we put aside dogmatism and take a common-sense view, we find in all religions a tremendous life power; for not one of the great religions has died. They are all living and will continue to live, because they have truth in them.

Vedanta and Buddhism are the most ancient of living religions. Vedanta, from Vedic times to the present, has recognized religious liberty for all mankind. Buddhism has also held this attitude. Again, may I quote Swami Vivekananda:

'It has been proved to the world that holiness, purity, and charity are not the exclusive possessions of any church in the world and that every system has produced men and women of the most exalted character. In the face of this evidence, if anybody dreams of the exclusive survival of his own religion and the destruction of the others, I pity him from the bottom of my heart, and point out to him that upon the banner of every religion will soon be written in spite of their resistance: "Help and not Fight." "Assimilation and not Destruction." "Harmony and Peace and not Dissension." '

Sri Krishna in the *Bhagavad-Gita* says: 'I am the thread that runs through all these pearls.' Each pearl is a religion and the Lord, the Lord God of all, is the thread that unites them.

Now, before we consider this concept of unity, let us note also the differences that exist. In this way we can perhaps determine where harmony lies. Every religion is divided into three parts: philosophy (or theology), which presents the scope and sets forth basic principles; mythology, which is philosophy made concrete by legends and lives of saints; and ritualism, which is symbolism. Let us consider each one.

First, can you imagine that there could be one common philosophy or theology? Impossible! Within Christianity, for instance, there are today many fine theologians who do not agree with one another. For religious opinions will always differ, and any attempt to alter such opinions, forcing them to conform to one philosophy or theology, will fail. It is the diversity of ideas which creates thought, for motion occurs when two forces meet in opposition. Diversity means life growth. There will be differences in religious concepts as long as mankind thinks.

As for a common mythology, where shall we meet? When we speak of 'our' mythology, we refer to it as history; it is 'yours' that is mythology; and when you speak of 'your' mythology, you say it is history, and 'ours' is mythology. So, we can find no common ground there.

What of ritualism? Do we find agreement here? Let us cite two examples. It has been said, again and again, by non-Hindus that the Hindus worship the phallic symbol. But the Hindus do not regard it as a phallus; they see in it merely a representative symbol of creation. Let us consider the Christian sacrament of Holy Communion. For many Christians it has become a wonderful and significant ritual, instilling in them the feeling that they are partaking of the body and blood of Christ. But by many non-Christians, it could be construed as cannibalism!

Is there then no common ground for the religions of the world? Is there not some holy personality who can draw them together in worship? Many Christians believe this possible. Let us quote Visser T. Hooft, secretary-general of the World Council of Churches. He says: 'We have a new opportunity to make it very clear that we really mean what we say and that our only motive is that the world may believe that in Jesus Christ, God reconciled the whole world to Himself.' Now as a Hindu, and especially a follower of Ramakrishna, I can say that I accept Jesus Christ, wholeheartedly, but I do not accept Him as the *only* Incarnation of God.

Despite Jesus's saying, 'I and my Father are one,' many Christians regard the Son of God as not being one with the Father. A well-known Christian theologian pointed out to me that Son and Father are not one. But when a Hindu accepts Jesus Christ, he sees in him God incarnated – that is, he sees him as a manifestation of God in human form. We read in the *Bhagavad-Gita*:

> 'When goodness grows weak
> When evil increases,
> I make myself a body.
> In every age I come back

51

To deliver the holy,
To destroy the sin of the sinner,
To establish righteousness.'

Let us compare what some of these divine incarnations have
said: *Jesus:* 'I am the way, the truth, and the life.' 'Come unto
Me, all ye that labour and are heavy-laden, and I will give you
rest.'

Krishna: 'Give me your whole heart, love and adore Me,
worship Me always, bow to Me only, and you shall find Me.
. . . Lay down all duties in Me, your refuge, fear no longer,
for I will save you from sin and bondage.'

In this present age, *Sri Ramakrishna:* 'I am the sanctuary. If
a man gathers his whole mind and fixes it on Me, then indeed,
he achieves everything.'

I firmly believe in all these statements because each of them
serves as a door, a door to reach the Ultimate Reality. In the
words of a Hindu saint:

'The eternal Vedantic religion opens to mankind an infinite
number of doors for ingress to the inner shrine of Divinity
and places before humanity an almost inexhaustible array of
ideals, there being in each of them a manifestation of the
eternal One. With the kindest solicitude, the Vedanta points
out to aspiring men and women the numerous roads hewn out
of the solid rock of the realities of human life by the glorious
sons or human manifestations of God in the past and in the
present, and stands with outstretched arms to welcome all, to
welcome even those that are yet to be, to that home of truth
and that ocean of bliss, wherein the human soul, liberated from
the net of Maya, may transport itself with perfect freedom,
and with eternal joy.'

Religion is the ultimate concern of human life. But what is
that ultimate concern? It is the search for the Ultimate
Reality. And how can we define Ultimate Reality? In the
Upanishads, the oldest scriptures of the world, it is defined as
'the eternal amongst the noneternals of life, the highest abiding
joy in the midst of the fleeting pleasures of life'. Call that God
or Christ or *Brahman* or *Allah*; what difference does it make?

It is one and the same Reality. In Him we are all one. The Hindus and Buddhists have held to this idea: that religion is *realization* and *experience* of God. You may believe in God, another may not believe in God; it makes no difference. Until you see Him, talk to Him, reach your union with Him, your belief has no validity. Every religion, every scripture, is based upon revelation: the Bible, the Vedas, the Koran, the Zend-Avesta, the Tripitaka. And what is that revelation? Direct vision of God.

The Hindus accept the four Vedas as their revealed word of God, just as the Christians accept the Bible. But the Hindus give a different meaning to their acceptance. They say the Vedas are beginningless and endless. But by this they do not mean just those four books; they mean that the truth of God is eternal, that wherever and whenever there is revelation the truth of the Vedas is to be found. So what Christ attained, what Buddha attained, is revelation; it is this the Hindus readily accept. What is most important is that all our seer-philosophers, all our spiritual teachers, tell us one thing: you have no religion until you personally experience the truth of God. Intellectual acceptance of the truth of the scriptures is not adequate. You must experience it directly. In the Vedas, a great seer says: 'I have known that truth which is beyond all darkness.' Then he adds: 'You also, having known that truth, attain to immortal bliss.'

If you study the history of world religions you will find that from the Vedic age on, various seers and saints as well as the great god-men – Krishna, Buddha, Christ, Ramakrishna – each in his own time, had the experience of God; and they insisted that every human being must have that experience. Buddha said: 'Experiment with the truth to experience it.' Christ said: 'Ye shall know the truth, and the truth shall make you free.' Mohammed gave this apt illustration: 'A man who is a scholar in the scriptures, but has no vision of God, is like an ass carrying a load of books.' Direct revelation is the test of truth in every religion; and we find that Hindus, Christians, Buddhists, Mohammedans, and Jews have produced saints and seers who walked with God, who talked with God, and who reached their union with God. There are such men of God in every age. Swami Vivekananda said, 'God is the centre of all religions, and each of us is moving toward Him along one of the radii – and all must reach that one centre where all radii meet, and all our differences will cease.'

Sri Ramakrishna demonstrated this truth in his own life. Stressing the mystic experience, in his unique approach to various religions, Ramakrishna harmonized the conflicting concepts of God. His method was pragmatic, for he accepted no path as valid until he himself had followed it and proved its efficacy. With simplicity and sincerity, Sri Ramakrishna applied the teachings and methods of the divergent Hindu sects and found that they all led to the same divine realization. But that was not enough for him. Mohammedanism was active in India, and Christianity was well known. He practised the disciplines of these religions also and verified the statement of the ancient seers: 'Truth is one; sages call it by various names.' In Sri Ramakrishna's words: 'So many religions, so many paths to reach one and the same goal.'

In defining this goal, Sri Ramakrishna was of course at one with all his spiritual ancestors. It was simply to realize God within one's own soul. Shankara, the great seer-philosopher of Vedanta, had declared that 'study of the scriptures is fruitless so long as *Brahman* has not been experienced'. 'He is born to no purpose,' said Sri Ramakrishna, 'who, having the rare privilege of being born a man, is unable to realize God.'

To quote Sri Ramakrishna again:

'I have practised Hinduism, Islam, Christianity, and in Hinduism again, the ways of the different sects. I have found that it is the same God towards whom all are directing their steps, though along different paths.

'The tank has several ghats. At one, Hindus draw water and call it *jal*; at another Mohammedans draw water and call it *pani*; at a third Christians draw the same liquid and call it water. The substance is one though the names differ, and everyone is seeking the same thing. Every religion of the world is one such ghat. Go with a sincere and earnest heart by any of these ghats and you will reach the water of eternal bliss. But do not say that your religion is better than that of another.'

What is the first requirement of any religion? The urge for God-realization. In other words, there must be a restlessness in you to find God. 'Seek and ye shall find; knock and it shall be opened unto you.' This is the one condition: longing for God, yearning for the truth of God. Whenever anybody asked Sri Ramakrishna how to find him, he said: 'Yearn for Him with a longing heart, and you are sure to find Him.'

And where is He? 'Know ye not that ye are the temple of God and that the Spirit of God dwelleth in you?' Where else would you seek but in your own heart? Are we to seek him in churches, in temples, in books? 'You will not find God until you find him within your own soul,' my master, Swami Brahmananda, pointed out to me one time when I was restless and wanted to go to some place of pilgrimage. I thought I would find God that way, but my master said, 'Find him here (pointing to the heart) and you will find him everywhere. If you do not find him here, you will find him nowhere.'

And when we find God, when we realize him, we shall be able to say, with Swami Vivekananda:

'Our watchword, then, will be acceptance, and not exclusion. Not toleration, for so-called toleration is often blasphemy, and I do not believe in it. I believe in acceptance. Why should I tolerate? Toleration means that I think that you are wrong, and I am just allowing you to live. Is it not blasphemy to think that you and I are allowing others to live? I accept all religions that were in the past and worship with them all; I worship God with every one of them, in whatever form they worship Him. I shall go to the mosque of the Mohammedan; I shall enter the Christian's church and kneel before the crucifix; I shall enter the Buddhistic temple, where I shall take refuge in Buddha, and in his law. I shall go into the shrine, and sit down in meditation with the Hindu, who is trying to see the Light which enlightens the heart of everyone.

'Not only shall I do all these, but I shall keep my heart open for all that may come in the future. Is God's book finished? Or is it still a continuous revelation going on? It is a marvellous book, these spiritual revelations of the world. The Bible, the Vedas, the Koran, and all the other sacred books, are but so many pages, and an infinite number of pages remain yet to be unfolded. I would leave it open for all of them. We stand in the present, but open ourselves to the infinite future. We take in all that has been in the past, enjoy the light of the present and open every window of the heart for all that will come in the future. Salutations to all the prophets of the past, to all the great ones of the present, and to all that are to come in the future.'

It is perhaps natural to emphasize that India has engaged herself in an age-old effort to reconcile various faiths. Not only has she attempted to harmonize the many Hindu schools of thought, but when confronted by Mohammedanism and Christianity, she has maintained her role of peacemaker among the creeds. It is probably by continuing this effort on an international scale that she is doing most to advance the spiritual welfare of mankind. To bring together against rampant evil the great religions of the world is no doubt a gigantic task, but it is one for which India has a special qualification. She strives for unity, not by calling for a common doctrine, but only by pointing to a common goal, and by exhorting men to its attainment. The path, she assures us, matters little; it is the goal that is supreme. And what is the goal? It is to realize God.

PART II

THE GOAL

6

THE GOAL OF LIFE

Before we can understand the kind of a life we must live, we must know the end, the goal, and the purpose of life and living. In regard to the end or the goal of life, all religions are in complete agreement. Jesus says: 'Be ye perfect even as the Father in Heaven is perfect.' St Paul explains this goal by saying: 'Ye are complete in Godhead.' The Upanishads declare: 'Blessed is he who realizes God in this life; if not, he has lived in vain.' 'There is no happiness in the finite, the Infinite alone *is* happiness.' Shankara says: 'A man is born not to desire life in the world of the senses, but to realize the bliss of a free soul in union with God.'

To attain perfection in union with Godhead and thereby enjoy the bliss of a free soul is the one goal of human life. Your life and achievement on earth will determine your life after death. The degree to which you have unfolded the divine qualities in this life will determine the degree to which you will enjoy union with God after death. There is an erroneous idea prevalent in the mass mind that heavenly felicity is to be attained only after death. But the many scriptures of many religions and the illumined seers of God in every age and in every country point out very definitely that the heaven is within ourselves and that it has to be attained here and now. 'Ye shall know the truth and the truth shall make you free.' 'Marvel not that I said unto thee, Ye must be born again.' And this birth in spirit is to be had here and now. The Upanishads emphasize, 'Attain liberation *here* and *now, not after the fall of the body*.'

There is a proverbial saying amongst the Hindus, 'If the husking machine goes to heaven, what will it do there but husk!' If we have not been able to overcome hatred, jealousy, passions in this life, we shall not be able to overcome them after

59

death; for we carry the same quality of the mind to the other world. What we have to earn we must earn here on earth. We must reach the unitive knowledge of Godhead and enjoy the bliss of heaven even in this life.

According to the Hindu theory of evolution, nothing is super-added in the course of evolution, but what is only potentially existing becomes unfolded. The whole of the tree potentially exists in the seed. Now if we study the process of evolution in the universe we find in one extreme what we may call dull, dead, inert matter, and in the other extreme a Christ, a Buddha, a Ramakrishna, children of light, light themselves. These have become one with God. God, whom we see unfolded in these children of light, is also existing potentially in the minutest atom. Swami Vivekananda rightly defined religion as the manifestation of divinity already in man. To unfold this divinity already existing within is the end of evolution and the goal of life.

Through the process of evolution God, *Sat-chit-ananda*, existence, consciousness, bliss absolute, God who dwells everywhere, becomes unfolded. Shankara by his subtle logic proves that existence, consciousness, and bliss absolute are not attributes of God, but identical with God, nor are they different from one another. God is existence *itself*, and that which is existence is also consciousness and bliss *itself* as well. We shall not enter into that subtlety of his reasoning. But let us simply state the fact that God who is existence, consciousness, and bliss absolute, *is everywhere*. 'The light shineth in darkness but the darkness comprehended it not.' Though He shines everywhere, He is not comprehended by all because of darkness.

Take the mineral kingdom, for instance. There is God there; there is life, and there is consciousness. But this life and consciousness remain covered by the darkness of so-called matter. In the vegetable kingdom we find, though darkness of matter predominates, that there is a certain release of life and consciousness. Within the past forty years, a Hindu scientist, J.C. Bose, conclusively demonstrated that the plant can breathe, has life and consciousness, and does act and react. In the lower animal kingdom we find consciousness predominates, but there is no evolved self-consciousness. In man, self-consciousness

is unfolded but man again is a slave to matter. In the illumined
seer, in a Christ or a Buddha or a Ramakrishna, we see that
infinite consciousness infinitely expressed. They have become
one with God. For a God-man transcends the sense of ego,
the ego which limits the infinite consciousness or God in man.
Sri Ramakrishna used to say, 'When the ego dies, all troubles
cease.'

To transcend this ego and unfold the infinite consciousness
is what Christ would call 'the birth in spirit', and Buddha
would call 'the awakening'. The *Mandukya Upanishad* speaks
of it as 'Turiya, the Fourth, the transcendental consciousness'.

The condition for the birth in spirit, for the inner awakening, is in the words of the Bible: 'And thou shalt love the
lord thy God with all thy heart, and with all thy soul, and
with all thy mind, and with all thy strength.' In other words,
we must devote ourselves completely and wholeheartedly to
loving contemplation of God. Our consciousness becomes
matter-bound or released to infinity according to the object of
consciousness, the object of our love. If we devote our mind
to worldly objects, our mind remains clouded by the darkness
of matter, and if we devote ourselves to the inner light, to God,
the covering of darkness is removed, and the light shines forth.

The natural tendency of the mind, however, is to run outward toward objects of sense. The senses are drawn naturally
to objects and the mind is attached to the senses because of
ignorance of the inner light.

Why does the mind become attached to the senses and the
objects of the senses? It is because through ignorance it accepts
the shadow of life, the appearance of the world as real.

There is the infinite God, the inner light, within each one
of us. There is also the covering of darkness. The mind receives
the reflection of the inner light, gets the fragrance, as it were,
of God – existence, consciousness, and bliss absolute; does not
know wherefrom the fragrance comes; seeks to find fulfilment in the objective world by running after the shadows of
life. Thus the mind becomes externalized. In the *Yoga Sutras* of
Patanjali, the causes of our bondage to life are said to be first,
avidya, the universal ignorance which covers the face of
reality. From this ignorance, or forgetfulness of the presence
of the Divine Reality within, there arises next the sense of ego.

Then there come in man *attachment* to pleasing things of the world, *aversion* to unpleasant things, and lastly, *thirst for life*.

Swami Vivekananda used to say, if a room is dark, you cannot remove the darkness by crying aloud, 'It is dark! It is dark!' But bring the light and the darkness will vanish. Our mind is darkened by ignorance. To remove the ignorance, we must look to the inner light that shines in spite of the covering of darkness. In short, contemplation of God is the direct means to reach the Inner Light of God.

This does not mean, however, that we must give up activity, or that we should neglect our duties. On the other hand, duties must be performed in order that we may practice detachment through action and rise above the sense of ego, the obstacle to the uncovering of the inner light. In the words of Sri Krishna in the *Gita*:

'Let him who would climb
In meditation
To heights of the highest
Union with Brahman
Take for his path
The Yoga of action.'

Work in the spirit of egolessness is a means to contemplative life.

In this connection, let me emphasize once more that in regard to a goal, all religions are in complete agreement. That goal is a life in union with God. Contemplative life is a stage in our progress that we arrive at through selfless action. Action is not the end, but only a means. But unfortunately the modern man, if he makes any concession to contemplative life, will regard it only as a means to greater urge to action and achievement in the external world. The modern man, through his progress in the knowledge of science and his outward achievements in the external world, has come to believe in a sort of millennium; he thinks that with a greater progress of machines, man will also have greater moral and spiritual progress. Instead of making the attempt to reach the unitive knowledge of Godhead, instead of trying to live a life of inner check and a life in union with God, he is busy in achieving progress in the external world by trying to bring more cash and comfort to mankind.

History, however, has proved again and again that Utopia can never be reached in the external world; that it is like a dog's curly tail. Straighten it out; it will curl up again. To quote the words of the great American poet-philosopher Ralph Waldo Emerson:

'There are two laws discrete
Not reconciled, –
Law for man, and law for thing;
The last builds town and fleet,
But it runs wild,
And doth the man unking.'

Unfortunately again, the professed Christians also have begun to believe that by bringing progress in the outward world through action they can bring heaven down to earth, and that God needs the help of man to achieve this millennium. I was once told by a professor of theology that God has not yet reached His fullness and infinitude and that we as human beings must help God to achieve His fullness! What an ego-centric theology that is! I thought to myself. Just the very opposite of what Jesus has taught! No, on the contrary, *we need God*. We need to forget ourselves, and wipe out all sense of ego, in love for God and in His contemplation.

The ideal, the end of life, is the unitive knowledge of God-head – this must never be forgotten. The modern man in the name of practicality often regards a man with the spiritual ideal as a queer creature, a dreamer. Suppose you see a man walking with a heavy burden on his shoulders. You ask him, 'What is this burden you are carrying?' He answers, 'I don't know.' 'Where are you going?' 'I don't know.' If these were the answers you were to receive from such a person, what would you think of him? Would you consider him a practical man? Yet, such is the irony of this age that he who tries to find an answer to such questions is considered a dreamer.

True it is that everyone tries to form some ideal, some end ne may strive to achieve. But until a man learns the spiritual ideal, he cannot find the exact purpose of life and living, and in the words of the *Gita*, 'his will wanders in all directions, after innumerable aims'.

We must understand the spiritual ideal; then our will, in the words of the *Gita*, 'must be directed singly towards one ideal'. No compromise can be made with this ideal; only then it is possible to 'develop that concentration of the will which leads a man to absorption in God'.

Contemplative life, absorption in God, is a stage in our development. To achieve that we must be active. Work is a means and not the end. To quote the words of the *Gita* which teaches absorption in God:

'Nobody can become perfect by merely ceasing to act. A man who renounces certain physical actions but still lets his mind dwell on the objects of his sensual desire, is deceiving himself. He can only be called a hypocrite. The truly admirable man controls his senses by the power of his will. All his actions are disinterested. All are directed along the path to union with Brahman. The world is imprisoned in its own activity, except when actions are performed as worship of God. Therefore you must perform every action sacramentally and be free from all attachment to results.'

What is the secret of worshipping God through actions? Try to understand that behind our surface life and our outward consciousness there is the deeper life, the inner consciousness which is identical with God. The appearance of a world cannot exist without some ground as support. That Ground is *Brahman* – God – Reality. Learn therefore to see God within yourself and in the universe. Then act with your senses and let your work be the worship of God. To quote the words of the *Gita* again:

'If a man sees Brahman
In every action,
He will find Brahman.'

7

PURITY

What is purity? Purity is generally understood to mean the observance of the moral and ethical laws of life. But do we become pure by merely *observing* such principles? No. The criterion of purity is whether a man has attained the vision of God. For did not Christ say: 'Blessed are the pure in heart for they shall see God?'

In another vein, Christ spoke of ethics: 'And, behold, one came and said unto him, "Good Master, what good thing shall I do, that I may inherit eternal life?" And he said unto him, "Why callest thou me good? There is none good but one, that is God." ' This is significant, for by refusing to be called good, Jesus proclaims himself a man – not God – because his questioner regarded him as a man. Goodness belongs to God alone. There are many good and ethical men on earth, but unless they have the vision of God or union with Him, they cannot be called good in the sense that Jesus means. It is needless to say that Jesus, having attained his union with God, was God himself. He was truly good.

Jesus's teachings to the young man continue: 'Thou knowest the commandments, "Do not commit adultery. Do not kill. Do not steal. Do not bear false witness. Do not defraud. Honour thy father and mother." And Jesus looked upon him and loved him, and said to him, "You lack one thing; go sell what you have and give to the poor, and you will have treasure in heaven; and come, follow me." '

What did Christ mean when he said, 'Follow me?' He meant renunciation of all attachments and devotion to God alone. Sri Ramakrishna used to say: 'A wet match does not ignite, however hard you may strike it; it only smokes. But a dry match lights at once, even with the slightest rubbing. The heart of the true devotee is like the dry match; the slightest

E   65

mention of the name of the Lord kindles the fire of love in his heart, while the mind of the worldly man, soaked in lust and attachment for wealth, resists all warmth like the moistened match.' As long as a single worldly desire persists, God cannot be found.

This total renunciation, which leads us to the love of God, is expressed in Sri Ramakrishna's prayer to the Divine Mother: 'Here is Thy ignorance and here is Thy knowledge; take them both and give me pure love for Thee. Here is Thy virtue and here is Thy sin; here is merit and demerit; here is good and evil; take them all and give me only pure love for Thee.' This pure love is synonymous with that purity which gives us the vision of God. It transcends both good and evil. It rises above the sense of duality.

Does this mean that we should not observe the moral and ethical laws of life? We most certainly must observe them. They are the very foundation of spiritual life. Problems arise when spiritual life becomes identified with rules and customs, and the ideal of union with God is forgotten; then the spirit of religion is lost. On the other hand, just to be moral is not enough. Look at the cow grazing in the field. She is very moral. She does not steal, she does not lie, she does not commit murder; but the cow remains a cow.

But man is different. A man may commit a heinous crime, and later the same man may become a knower of God. This does not mean, of course, that we can do as we please and still unfold our inner divinity. The observance of ethical laws is a step toward union with God. Therefore, in the beginning of our spiritual life we must discriminate between good and evil. Later we come to a stage of spiritual unfoldment when the mind becomes absorbed in the love of God, and all sense of duality vanishes naturally. In that state we cannot do any evil; the heart has become so pure that not even an impure thought can arise.

There are very few aspirants who from the very beginning of spiritual life have discrimination and love of God for love's sake, knowing him to be the one and only Reality. Most devote themselves to God in order to be freed from the troubles and miseries of life or to satisfy some unfulfilled desire. This does not matter. As Sri Krishna pointed out in the

Bhagavad-Gita, all aspirants, no matter why they seek God, are noble indeed. But of those who know the vanity of the transitory world and seek God for God's sake only, he said, 'They are my very Self; they are dear to me.' In the course of our spiritual progress, there comes a stage when we learn to love God for love's sake without any ulterior motive.

There are two characteristics of purity: the first is to rise above the sense of duality, of relativity; and the other is to love God for love's sake and thus to enter into his kingdom. Examine yourself and test your purity. Try to think of God. What do you find? Your concentration lasts for a fraction of a second, and then distracting thoughts arise. These distractions are not necessarily evil thoughts. Though they may be good and unselfish, they reveal that your mind is not attached to God and your heart has not yet become pure.

What are these distractions that come to us? They are the impression of thoughts and actions, not only of this life but of past lives as well, which are stored in the subconscious mind. Thus again, purity is synonymous with Patanjali's definition of *yoga*: the control of the thought waves or impressions of the mind. When the mind becomes like a calm lake without any ripples or waves, then God, who dwells in the innermost recesses of your heart, becomes revealed to you.

How do we calm the mind and free it from the thought waves? It is not done, as some people believe, by making the mind blank or unconscious. When we are in deep sleep, for instance, there is no wave of thought or content of consciousness. We are unconscious. But what do we achieve? When we awake from that state we find that we still have the same bundle of old impressions and thoughts. That calmness we must attain is not unconsciousness but the highest form of activity. Imagine a carriage, drawn by four powerful horses, poised on the edge of a cliff. The driver, tightly holding the reins, maintains perfect control over the horses. This perfect control is the state of a mind freed from distractions. It can only be achieved by a complete house-cleaning of the dirt and dust that have accumulated in the mind. St Paul expressed the same truth: 'Be ye transformed by the renewing of your mind.'

In order that there can be a complete renewing of the mind,

we must find the root-causes of the distracting impressions. Patanjali, the great psychologist of India, pointed out that there are five root-causes, namely: ignorance, egoism, attachment, aversion, and the desire to cling to life. Of these, ignorance is the mother. This ignorance is universal, affecting the educated as well as the illiterate. Encyclopedic knowledge is not wisdom. True wisdom comes when that being within ourselves, the ultimate Reality of the universe, is revealed.

What is the nature of this ignorance which is said to be universal? It has two functions: first, it makes us forget our true being; secondly, it creates something that does not really exist. For instance, all the great saints and prophets taught that the fundamental Reality, our true nature, is one with God. Christ said, 'I and my Father are one.' The Vedic seers proclaimed, 'That Thou art.' But are we conscious that our very nature is pure, perfect, and divine? Ignorance has made us forget what we really are; furthermore, it has created a sense of ego in every one of us. It is this sense of ego which separates us from God and from one another. The Hindu psychologists define this ego as something that arises from the identification of our true being with our body, mind, senses, and discriminative faculty. In reality, these are separate from us. They are so many sheaths or coverings which hide our real Self. If you examine what this sense of ego is, you will find it has no reality. Sri Ramakrishna gave the illustration of an onion. You peel one layer after another from it; finally, there is nothing left. In the same way, if we analyse ourselves we find that we are not the body, not the mind, not the senses, not the intellect; nor are we a combination of these sheaths. For these sheaths change, and yet we still retain the consciousness that I am 'I'. However, mere analysis does not help. We still cling to our ego. And with the sense of ego there arise attachment, aversion, and the desire to cling to life.

Why do we become attached? Because something gives us pleasure. Why does aversion arise in us? Because something gives us pain. However, pleasure and pain are not in the objects, themselves, but in our attitude towards them. An ancient psychologist has given the illustration of a beautiful young woman. She gives pleasure to her husband, but she rouses envy in other women. She gives pain to men who may desire her, but creates only indifference in a self-controlled man. Therefore, happiness and unhappiness depend on our reactions to objects and experiences.

Lastly, there is the desire to cling to life, which Buddha called *tanha*, or thirst for life. Christ referred to it when he said, 'He that loveth his life shall lose it.' Our love for our present life is so intense that if someone wished to give us illumination, we would shrink from it. St Augustine used to pray that he might be freed from lust, and then he would say, 'But not yet, Lord, not yet.' It is the same with most of us.

How are we to overcome the impressions in the mind? The great *yogis* Patanjali and Sri Krishna have pointed out practice and dispassion as the means. Impressions are caused by habit. Therefore we have to create new habits and free ourselves from attachment and aversion. We thus gain purity, and the vision of God arises.

The root cause of distracting thought waves is ignorance. What is this ignorance? It is forgetfulness of the divinity within us. Therefore, we must practice one-pointed concentration on God, on our Chosen Ideal. Although we do not know God, although we do not see Him, we must realize that He is the Self within. He is there. He is real.

Purification of the mind may be compared to washing ink from a bottle attached to a desk. How is this accomplished? You pour clean water into the bottle until all the ink has been emptied and replaced by pure water. Similarly, in order to overcome our tendencies and past impressions we must keep pouring crystal-clear, pure thoughts of God into our minds. Thus we renew the subconscious and unconscious mind, and find eternal life. Practice the presence of divinity within your heart. Of course, you cannot become perfect immediately; but you can think of God for a moment. Frequently people practice spiritual disciplines for a while and then give up. That is wrong. With patience and perseverance we must continually cudgel our minds until we reach the very root of ignorance, the sense of ego. This ego we then surrender to God. Identify yourself with the divinity within by knowing that you are not the body, nor the mind, nor the senses, nor any of the sheaths covering your true being.

Since we are subject to attachment and aversion, we must

gather only pure food. In the Upanishads we read: 'Pure food brings purity of heart. Purity of heart results in constant recollectedness of God. Constant recollectedness of God brings us union with God.' Now what is the meaning of 'pure food'? Food does not mean merely what we eat, but what we gather through all our senses. How do we gather this pure food? By learning to see God everywhere. Be conscious of the presence of God wherever the senses lead you.

God is joy and love. By practicing constant recollectedness of Him we gradually taste the joy of spiritual life. Love arises in our hearts and the desire to cling to the surface life, to this normal consciousness, vanishes. We become free souls while living on this earth.

8

FAITH

In a popular dictionary we find this definition of faith: 'The assent of the mind or understanding to the truth of what God has revealed.' This definition expresses the Western attitude towards faith, that the mind must accept the truth of God as he reveals it. Now let us see how the Vedantist philosopher Shankara defines faith. He says faith is 'a firm conviction, based upon intellectual understanding, that the teachings of the scriptures and of one's master are true – this is called by the sages the faith which leads to realization of the Reality'.

These are differences in interpretation and emphasis between the Western and Eastern conceptions of faith. But it is more important that we try to understand the principle which is common to both points of view, the principle which is accepted by all the great religions of the world – an insistence upon faith in the scriptures, because they contain the revealed words of God.

What exactly are the scriptures? And why are they regarded as authoritative? Before we inquire further into these questions, we must understand that three kinds of proof exist. The first kind is that of sense perception. I see an object before me; my senses perceive it. The second kind of proof is inference. An inference is a truth drawn from another which is admitted to be true. For instance, I see smoke, therefore I conclude that there must be a fire. From past observation I have learned that wherever there is smoke there is fire. And the third kind of proof is revelation – transcendental knowledge, or superconscious vision.

Although it may sound strange to Western ears, I must point out here that two kinds of truth exist. One kind of truth is perceived by the senses; and the other kind of truth, which cannot be perceived by the senses, is discovered through the subtle, supersensuous power of *yoga*.

Take, for instance, the truths of God, soul, and immortality. Nobody can perceive these truths through the senses. Once a doctor, trying to disprove the immortality of the soul, remarked that he had seen hundreds of people die yet never saw a soul come out of a body. Obviously, such an argument is meaningless, because no believer in spiritual concepts claims that the soul can be seen with physical eyes. Religious truths can be perceived only supersensuously, through revelation.

Now, what are the scriptures? They are revelations given to sages, seers, or divine incarnations like Christ, Buddha, or Ramakrishna. Furthermore, these great teachers are not unique in the sense that they alone were able to perceive the truth of God. You and I, or anyone who develops that supersensuous power, may do so. And that is the point we must try to understand. Why should we have faith in the words of the scriptures? Because they are revelations. The truth of God was revealed to Christ, Krishna, Moses, Mohammed, and other world teachers. And these teachers have pointed out that every individual at a certain stage of spiritual unfoldment can experience this same truth.

As I have already mentioned, the truth of God cannot be known by any means other than revelation. Of course, we find that attempts have been made and are still being made to establish the existence of God by reasoning. But all such attempts are futile. For example, the great philosopher Hegel proved with logic and reason that an absolute reality exists. Other philosophers, by the use of logic and reason, can refute his arguments. But let us suppose that Hegel's arguments prevail. What guarantee is there that his idea of the Absolute corresponds to the Reality which he tries to prove? What can a philosopher prove, after all? Only his *idea* of a Reality, his *idea* of an Absolute. And that is why one often hears people say, 'I don't believe in God.' What is it that they do not believe in? Certain ideas of God, which do not appeal to them. Reason, therefore, although it has an important place in spiritual life as we shall see later, is insufficient to prove the existence of God. The only real proof of his existence is to see him.

You may ask: Suppose the truth of God was revealed to

Christ, or Moses, or Ramakrishna; and suppose it is revealed to me? But what is the criterion of the truth of God? The criterion is that this truth is absolute. This means that it must be *trikala abadhittva*, not contradicted by time – past, present or future.

All other truths are known through the senses or through inference; and they are only relatively true. For instance, I see a table in front of me. It exists in the present; it did not always exist in the past, nor will it always exist in the future. Moreover, when the Reality is revealed to me, the table will disappear; and everything will be seen as *Brahman*.

Or take the dream experience. While we are dreaming, our dreams have a relative reality; but our dreams are contradicted by the waking experience. When we wake up, they vanish.

Brahman, Pure Consciousness, is present in all three states of ordinary awareness – waking, dreaming, and dreamless sleep. It is the ground of everything we experience in these three states. But *Brahman* in its total reality is experienced only in transcendental consciousness. When we attain that consciousness, our waking experience also is contradicted. But the transcendental experience is never contradicted by any other experience. Therefore it has a greater reality than either sense perception or inference.

Is there any other criterion of transcendental knowledge? How can we distinguish, for instance, between transcendental truth and psychic phenomena? Before any revelation is recognized as genuinely transcendental, it must be related to *arthe anupalabdhe* – something which is otherwise unknown and unknowable.

If I have psychic power, for example, I can look at you and guess correctly how many dollars you have in your coat pocket. But that is not transcendental knowledge, because I can get this information in other ways. I can ask you how much money you have with you, or I can threaten you with a gun and search your coat pocket.

Transcendental revelation, on the other hand, is not a revelation of things normally perceived, nor of truths apprehended through the ordinary instruments of knowledge.

In the Upanishads we read: 'Words cannot reveal *Brahman*; unable to reach Him, the mind comes away baffled. How then

73

save through those who know him, can he be known?' We can learn of God only through those who have had direct experience of God. This means faith in the scriptures, because the scriptures have been revealed to the seers and sages.

But, according to Vedanta, faith in the scriptures is not enough. We must also have faith in the words of the *guru*, the living teacher, in whom the truth has been revealed. There must be living exemplars of the scriptural truths, otherwise the scriptures will be misunderstood or become forgotten.

Even to believe in the words of the scriptures and of the *guru* is not enough. Our faith – as we learn from Shankara's definition – must lead to the realization of God. Belief must be translated into action. This is true even in worldly matters. For a medical student to read and have faith in his medical books is insufficient. He must become an intern in a hospital, and through personal experience with patients learn how to diagnose and prescribe. Similarly, reading the scriptures and believing in them is only the beginning of spiritual aspiration. One must experiment with the truth of God and experience it for oneself.

To quote the Upanishads again: 'The truth of the Atman must be heard about, reasoned upon, and meditated upon.' First, we must learn about the truth of the *Atman*, the Self within, from the scriptures and from the lips of a teacher who has experienced the truth himself.

The second step is reasoning. Having heard about the truth, we must not accept blindly, without understanding it. We must test it, and question the teacher. Our reason must be satisfied. Although revelation is beyond and above reason, it does not contradict it. Thus Vedanta, though having its foundation in supernormal revelation, gives a legitimate place to reason.

The third step is meditation. Once we have become intellectually convinced of the truth of God, what will we do? We will want to realize it. Unless a man acts on the basis of his intellectual understanding, unless he tries to reach the transcendental consciousness, his faith is mere lip faith. Mohammed compared such a man to a donkey carrying a load of books.

In order to illustrate the inadequacy of mere scholarship, Sri Ramakrishna used to tell the following parable:

Faith

Some men were crossing the Ganges in a boat. Among them was a pundit who was proud of his learning. He was telling his fellow passengers how familiar he was with the six systems of philosophy. He questioned one of the men: 'Do you know Vedanta?'

'No, revered sir.'

'How about Sankhya and Yoga?'

'No, revered sir.'

'Haven't you read any philosophy at all?'

'No, revered sir.'

When the boat reached the middle of the river, a storm arose. The boat was on the point of capsizing when one of the passengers asked the pundit: 'Sir, do you know how to swim?'

'No,' was his answer.

The passenger remarked, 'I don't know Sankhya or Yoga; but I do know how to swim.'

Religion is very pragmatic. It is not mere book learning. We must learn to swim across this ocean of worldliness and reach the other shore, where we are safe, where we are freed from all limitations, and where there is no sorrow.

But the difficulty is that we have so little interest in God. Faith in him is rare. Emerson said: 'There is faith in chemistry, in meat and wine, in wealth, in machinery, in the steam engine, galvanic battery, turbine wheels, sewing machines, and in public opinion, but not in divine causes.' As the *Gita* describes it: 'Who cares to seek for that perfect freedom? One man, perhaps, in many thousands.' When Sri Rámakrishna told his young disciple Naren that few people have faith in God, the boy objected, saying that he knew many who were believers. Then Sri Ramakrishna replied: 'Suppose a thief knows that just beyond the wall there is a great treasure. Would he rest quietly? No, he would struggle with all his might to get hold of it!'

The intensity of our struggle then is the test of our faith. We must practice spiritual disciplines; we must make repeated efforts to realize our true nature, which is divine and one with God. Ignorance of our divinity is an immediate experience; another immediate experience – revelation, or supersensuous vision – is needed to dispel the ignorance.

75

The necessity of self-effort and practice is pointed out by Shankara:

'A buried treasure is not uncovered by merely uttering the words, "Come forth". You must follow the right directions, dig, remove stones and earth from above it, and then make it your own. In the same way, the pure truth of the Atman, which is buried under maya and the effects of maya, can be reached by meditation, contemplation, and other spiritual disciplines such as a knower of Brahman may prescribe – but never by subtle arguments.'

Now what are the fundamental truths or principles upon which we must base our faith? First of all, we must have faith that *God is*. Even if we do not have this faith to begin with – if we are seekers after truth and follow certain spiritual disciplines, we will gradually become convinced of the existence of God.

Secondly, we should have the faith that *God can be realized*. Merely to be convinced that he exists is not enough. We must have the confidence: 'Others have realized him, and so can I.'

Finally we must be convinced that *to realize God is the supreme goal of human existence*. Why? Because in God alone there is complete fulfilment.

What is the way to achieve this ultimate purpose of life? A Christian mystic pointed out: 'God's light dwells in the Self; it shines alike in every living being, and one can see it with one's mind steadied.' And the Indian saint Ramprasad said: 'Fix your heart in God, then love will awaken within; and faith is the root of all.'

How to steady the mind and fix the heart in God is explained in greater detail in the *Gita*: 'Patiently, little by little, a man must free himself from all mental distractions with the aid of the intelligent will. He must fix his mind upon the Atman, and never think of anything else. No matter where the restless and unquiet mind wanders, it must be drawn back and made to submit to the Atman only.'

You may fail many times in your efforts to direct the mind singly to God and to keep it in his presence. Don't become discouraged. With perseverance continue your spiritual practices. Sri Ramakrishna said: 'Countless are the pearls lying hidden in the sea. If a single dive yields you none, do not conclude that the sea is without pearls. Similarly, if after practising spiritual disciplines for a little while you fail to have the vision of God, do not lose heart. Practise the disciplines with patience, and at the proper time you are sure to obtain grace and God will reveal himself to you.'

If you continue your practices patiently and faithfully, you will one day have a tangible feeling of the presence of God. Until you come to this stage, you may doubt the existence of God. Occasionally doubts arise even after God's presence has been experienced; but these are healthy doubts and they make the aspirant struggle harder and in this way further his spiritual growth. As the living presence of God is experienced, a sweetness is felt within and love for God grows in your heart. Then comes constant recollectedness of his presence. A current in your mind flows continually toward Him. When you reach this stage of unfoldment, there arises *prajna* – illumination, or the vision of God.

Prior to illumination, the kind of faith we have may be termed 'working faith'. This kind of faith is the root of spiritual life. But after illumination a different kind of faith comes, a lasting faith, which is the fruit of God-realization.

In this connection, I am reminded of something M., the compiler of Sri Ramakrishna's *Gospel*, told me many years ago, when I asked his blessings before leaving for America. On this occasion I inquired, 'What is the greatest thing you achieved by coming to Sri Ramakrishna?' M.'s answer was: 'Faith.' As M. was an intimate disciple of Sri Ramakrishna and an illumined soul, I knew he meant the faith that follows God-vision.

My master, Swami Brahmananda, referred to this same kind of faith, when he said, on his deathbed: 'I am floating on the leaf of faith on the ocean of Brahman.'

What is the nature of a man who has found this deeper faith? How does it manifest in him? In the sixth chapter of the *Gita* we find a description of the illumined soul and his state of attainment:

'When, through the practice of yoga, the mind ceases its restless movements, and becomes still, he realizes the Atman. It satisfies him entirely. Then he knows that infinite happiness which can be realized by the purified heart but is beyond the grasp of the senses. He stands firm in this realization. Because of it he never again wanders from the truth of his being.

'Now that he holds it he knows this treasure above all others: faith so certain shall never be shaken by heaviest sorrow. . . .

'Released from evil, his mind is constant in contemplation. The way is easy. Brahman has touched him; that bliss is boundless.'

9

HAPPINESS

—————

I think we can safely assume that man, whether he is Christian, Hindu, Buddhist, Jewish, Moslem, or even agnostic, is in search of a common goal. What might that goal be? Kapila, the great philosopher who lived perhaps fourteen centuries before Christ, described it as the 'complete cessation of suffering and misery'. What causes suffering and misery? Although Kapila admitted a great number of causes, he classified them under three headings. The first is *adhyatmika*, which refers to suffering that is closely related to one's self. For instance, suffering from sickness and disease that attack the body; and fears or worries that attack the mind. A second cause of suffering is known as *adhibhautika*, caused by extraneous circumstances, either involving one's own family and friends or strangers. Something unfortunate happens to your family; or somebody hurts you, talks harshly to you, is jealous of you, envious of you, and so on. The third cause of suffering is *adhidaivika*, which might be termed supernatural, which insurance companies refer to as 'acts of God', for example, flood, fire, earthquake, etc.

All these are different sources of misery to mankind; and everyone, whether he believes in God or not, wants to be freed from them. It is true there are persons who remind us that if we get sick we usually get healed; and there undoubtedly exist temporary means and methods by which we can free ourselves from pain. Yet, is this really adequate? One gets sick and is healed; but he gets sick again. And then, inevitably, there is death. 'Nobody,' Buddha said, 'can escape death.' And so the ideal which, it must be admitted, seems utopian, is a complete cessation of suffering and misery. And Kapila says it can be done.

Now I am not such a pessimist as to believe that there is only misery in life. Life is not merely suffering. It also has its joys, pleasures, and happiness. In the Upanishads we read: 'Who could live and breathe a moment if there were no happiness at all?' Yes, there is happiness. One gets thirsty or hungry; he drinks or eats, and he is happy. He has passions and appetites; he satisfies them, and he is happy. But a spiritually discriminating soul wisely points out: 'Yes, there is happiness, but it is not lasting.' In the *Bhagavad-Gita* we read: 'Senses also have joy in their marriage with things of the senses, sweet at first but at last how bitter! Steeped in rajas that pleasure is poison.'

Why do spiritual aspirants regard pleasures in such a way? Because their very fulfilment suggests an inadequacy. Somehow, no matter what we gain, it is not enough. As one mystic said: 'The terrible thing is that we can never make ourselves drunk enough.' The fact is that man is so constituted that his hunger cannot be satisfied by anything that is finite. Lower animals do not have many cravings; they have a few fundamental wants and, with the satisfaction of these, they are quite happy. However, man is so constituted that nothing of the finite can satisfy him completely; because in him dwells the infinite God; self-consciousness has evolved in him, and it is only in the infinite that man will find complete happiness.

Again, we are confronted with worldly-wise people who would tell us, 'Yes, there is suffering and misery, there is happiness also; but the concept of God and the infinite are idealistic. Instead, let us make the most out of life. Religion only gives a post-mortem happiness. Therefore, let us fully enjoy ourselves while living on earth.'

Kapila, as well as the great spiritual teachers – Buddha, Christ, Krishna, Ramakrishna – were aware of this attitude. But they taught that we can completely end suffering and misery in this life. The sages declared that there is a positive experience which can be realized: 'From joy springs this universe, in joy dwells this universe, unto joy goes back this universe.'

Still, you might ask, have the great ones really gone beyond pain? Christ was crucified and apparently suffered on the cross, so much so that he cried out: 'My God, my God, why hast thou forsaken me?' However, it is not wise to judge a divine incarnation by external appearances. Christ knew he was not the body, and he was capable of withdrawing his mind from the physical plane. Sri Ramakrishna gave this illustration: When a coconut is green and you drive a nail into it, the nail will injure both the shell and meat; but when the coconut becomes ripened, the meat and shell easily separate, so whatever you may do to the shell, it does not affect the meat; similarly, when the *Atman* (the Self within, or God) becomes realized, nothing can disturb the saint who has realized the *Atman*.

In this connection, let me relate one incident in the life of Ramakrishna. He was suffering from cancer of the throat. A young disciple came to visit him, and Ramakrishna said, 'Oh, look how I am suffering!' The disciple looked at him and said: 'Holy Sir, you say that you are suffering, but I see only that you are immersed in the ocean of bliss.' Then Ramakrishna said with a smile, 'This rascal has found me out!'

These great teachers are the exemplars in life; they are the embodiments of victory over pain. Here I shall quote to you what the Western philosopher Spinoza said about the cause of suffering and the attainment of infinite joy and blessedness:

'For the things which men, to judge by their actions, deem the highest good, are riches, fame, or sensual pleasure. Of these, the last is followed by satiety and repentance, the other two are never satiated; the more we have, the more we want; while the love of fame compels us to order our lives by the opinions of others. But if a thing is not loved, no quarrels will arise concerning it, no sadness will be felt if it perishes, no envy if another has it; in short, no disturbances of the mind. All these spring from the love of that which passes away, but the love of a thing eternal and infinite fills the mind wholly with joy, and is unmingled with sadness. Therefore, it is greatly to be desired and to be sought with all our strength.'

Where is this infinite to be realized? Where is God to be realized? That is the most important question for every human being. Religion means finding the answer to that question. Religion is not theological dogma or belief; it is something which touches life, gives us infinite bliss, frees us from suffering and misery. No belief, no theology can do that. Only when we experience God, when he know our true Self, our true Being – then is it that we can call ourselves religious. And the most important, the most wonderful truth which has been taught by all the great religions of the world – when we go to their very source – is that 'the kingdom of heaven is within'. These words of Christ have been emphasized by the teachers, prophets, and illumined souls of the world. Yet, unfortunately, in the Christian world this fundamental truth is misunderstood. Many have even sought to explain it away by various far-fetched interpretations. But Christ truly meant that within each human soul is hidden the Lord himself. This is the truth that each of us has to learn first and foremost.

Let me quote what Swami Vivekananda learned from his own experience and realization:

'After long searches here and there, in temples and in churches, on earth and in heaven, at last you come back, to your own soul, completing the circle from where you started, and find that He whom you have been seeking all over the world, for whom you have been weeping and praying in churches and temples, on whom you were looking as the mystery of all mysteries, shrouded in the clouds, is the nearest of the near, is your own Self, the reality of your life, body, and soul.'

One time I remember my Master (Swami Brahmananda), finding me restless, said, 'Look here, if you find Him within yourself you will find Him everywhere; if you don't find Him within, you will find Him nowhere.'

So this is the truth we must learn: 'Know ye not that ye are the temple of God?' When you go to pray and meditate, do not look towards the sky; look within, to the shrine of your own heart. His presence is there. I am talking to Him, He knows it. You are listening, He knows it. I could not breathe, I could not speak, I could not move, without that Presence.

But what is His nature? You will find that there are many descriptions of God – many of them contradictory – in almost every book on theology. One time, in fact, Sri Ramakrishna was asked, 'How is it that God has been defined in so many ways, and these ways are so contradictory?' He replied, 'They are *apparently* contradictory, but if you go to the neighbour-

hood of God, you will find that in him all contradictions meet.'
Then he affirmed the fact that no definition of God is possible,
because to define is to limit. He said, 'Never try to limit the
limitless and infinite God by saying he is this and cannot be
that.' Sri Ramakrishna gave the illustration of the bee, which
makes a great deal of noise before it sits on the flower. But
when the bee finally settles and begins to suck the honey, it
becomes silent. Becoming intoxicated by drinking that honey,
it flies again and makes a sweet humming sound. Similarly,
before we enter into the realm of God we talk about him, and
we attempt to establish our idea of God as the only idea; but
as we become spiritual aspirants, as we sit and begin to drink
the honey, the sweetness that is in God, we become silent.
Then becoming God-intoxicated, we describe him in many
ways: He is the Absolute, the Impersonal; he is also the Personal. He is beyond all ideas and thoughts and conceptions; he
is without form, without attributes; he is also with attributes
and with form.

Most important, he can be known, he can be felt, he can be
experienced; and not only that: the experience of the ultimate
reality is unitive. The knowledge of God is more than knowledge of any objective thing, or knowledge of persons and
places and objects. Philosopher Immanuel Kant wrote, 'As
long as there is the least demarcation between the knower and
the object of knowledge, the thing-in-itself remains unknown.'
The same truth was brought out in the Upanishads and by the
great seer-philosopher, Shankara, who said that the subject and
object can become united. He calls it technically *triputi-
bheda*: the untying of the three knots of knowledge. The
result is unified consciousness, or *samadhi*. In *samadhi* you
realize your oneness with God. You are That, and ignorance is
removed.

In the *Gita* we read: 'Who knows the Atman knows that
happiness, born of pure knowledge, the joy of sattwa. Deep his
delight, after strict schooling: sour toil at first, but at last what
sweetness, the end of sorrow.' It *is* sour toil at first, but in the
end, in this very life, both wisdom and sweetness come.

It is a hard struggle only because we do not have longing
for Him. Whenever Sri Ramakrishna was asked, 'What is the
way?', he would answer: 'Yearn for Him with a longing

heart.' The craving for God, the desire for God, the longing for God, is the one condition necessary for spiritual attainment. But it does not come because we have so many other cravings and desires. Sri Ramakrishna noted, 'Everybody is interested in the creation; how few are interested in the Creator?' St John of the Cross said: 'The more the soul cleaves to created things, relying on its own strength, by habit and inclination, the less is it disposed for this union, because it does not completely resign itself into the hands of God that He may transform it supernaturally.'

When we try to meditate and pray, we find all kinds of distractions arising. Why? Because we have so many other desires and thoughts. Our minds are scattered. They have to be brought back, brought under control. This takes time. It is 'a sour toil', but it can be achieved. That great longing for Him will come at last. You may have many desires and cravings, but as you meditate on God, as you practice from day to day, you will go deeper – you are bound to as you persist in your practice – and you will begin to feel the breeze of grace, as it were; you begin to find that sweetness. Then the desires commence to lose their hold on you. There are, of course, many disciplines in spiritual life which, if followed, make it easier to contemplate and meditate, but the main principle is to bring the mind under control and fix it on God.

My master, Swami Brahmananda, used to call this *sahaja-yoga* ('easy yoga') – keeping recollectedness of God as continuously as possible. You do not have to sit and close your eyes in order to meditate; you can meditate upon God with your eyes open by feeling His presence within and around you. When you see people, see God in them first. Practice, practice, practice! Brother Lawrence said: 'In order to know God we must often think of him, and when we come to love him we shall then also think of him often, for our heart will be with our treasure.' So, psychologically, you begin to think of Him; then as you begin to think of Him, love grows in your heart. And that is the greatest achievement: to love God. It is the Bible's first commandment: 'Love the Lord thy God with all thy heart, and with all thy soul, and with all thy mind, and with all thy strength.' We must do that as human beings in this life (not after we grow wings and go elsewhere!). We have a saying in India that if the husking machine goes to heaven, what will it do? Husk! So we have to achieve love for God here and now. And what is the way? Practice! Whenever we would go to our master and complain, his answer was, 'Practice, practice, practice.'

We read in the *Bhagavad-Gita*: 'When can a man be said to have achieved union with Brahman? When his mind is under perfect control, and freed from all desires, so that he becomes absorbed in the Atman, and nothing else.' If you meditate and feel that presence within the shrine of your own heart and become even once absorbed in him, you have arrived at the goal. 'The light of a lamp does not flicker in a windless place; that is the simile which describes a yogi of one-pointed mind who meditates upon the Atman.' Steadiness! It must be like oil poured from one vessel to another – continuous, uninterrupted thought. 'When through practice the mind ceases its restless movement and becomes still, it realizes the Atman.' If the vagaries of your mind can be stilled, your true Self becomes revealed to you. Then, 'It satisfies him entirely; then he knows that infinite happiness which can be realized by the purified heart but is beyond the grasp of the sense.'

You cannot imagine with your senses the nature of this joy, this happiness. It is incomparable. It is nothing like the pleasures and joys of the world. St Paul called it 'the peace of God which passeth all understanding'. And the *Gita* relates: 'He stands firm in this realization; because of it, he can never again wander from the inmost truth of his being.' Once you have realized God you have reached the end and purpose of life. You have attained what Christ taught: 'Be ye perfect, even as the Father which is in heaven is perfect.'

How can man be perfect, you ask? He cannot. But a man of realization is no longer a man. He appears to react like any other human being, but has become God. Thus do we read in the Upanishads: 'A knower of Brahman becomes Brahman.' A knower of God has become God. And each one of us has to become God.

Again, the *Gita* says, 'Now that he holds it, he knows this treasure above all others. Faith so certain shall never be shaken by heaviest sorrow. To achieve this certainty is to know the real meaning of the word *yoga*. It is the breaking of contact with pain. You must practice this yoga resolutely, without losing heart.'

It is worth the greatest struggle. If you practice a few days, or a few months, or a few years, and still you seem to be getting nowhere, do not lose heart. Stick to it. You may seem to get nowhere, your mind is still restless, but in the midst of the storm and stress that you may be going through in your meditation, something will suddenly happen. The darkness is gone; the light is shining. One day in your life, through the grace of God, this ignorance will vanish – in a moment. Darkness may accumulate for centuries in a room; but one strike of a match, and it is gone. But you must persist. 'You must practice this yoga resolutely without losing heart,' the *Gita* advises, 'patiently, little by little, a man must free himself from all mental distractions with the aid of the intelligent will.' Many times during meditation you will lose contact with the object of concentration; after three-quarters of an hour you suddenly wake up to realize you have not been thinking of God. That is not meditation. You must use this intelligent will and try to control the vagaries of your mind. Swami Vivekananda gave the illustration: 'A carriage, drawn by four powerful horses, is moving down the hill. The rider draws in the reins tightly; the horses want to run, but the carriage stands still.' That is meditation. The mind wants to run here and there like restless horses, but you are firmly holding the reins. The mind is fixed in one place – at the feet of God.

The *Gita* continues: 'He must fix his mind upon the Atman, and never think of anything else. No matter where the restless and unquiet mind wanders, it must be drawn back and made to submit to the Atman only.'

That is the secret; that is the gateway to contemplation and happiness. That is the key to everlasting joy. 'Utterly quiet, made clean of passion, the mind of the yogi knows that Brahman; his bliss is the highest.'

10

PERFECTION

'Be ye therefore perfect, even as your Father which is in heaven is perfect.' In this sentence, Christ has stated the whole purpose of man's life. For if we go to the source of any religion, we find the same theme: Realize God! Seek perfection! For in him alone is to be obtained perfection.

But what is meant by perfection? None of us can have a definite conception of what perfection is, because it is absolute. We live in the relative world, under the limitations of time, space and causation. All that we know of perfection is that it refers to a state where nothing is lacking – all is abiding peace and fulfilment. In a way, each one of us seeks perfection. The sick man seeks it in his struggle for perfect health. The poor man yearns for the 'perfection' he thinks wealth will bring him. In every field of life we crave perfection – the artist in his creation, the scientist in his experiments, and so on. But whether we have health or wealth, beauty or secular knowledge, we still cannot be satisfied. A certain lack – the sense of imperfection – continues to haunt us and drive us on in a fruitless search for fulfilment – which ultimately ends in disappointment and frustration.

Of course, it is perfectly true that the world can temporarily satisfy our cravings. We can have some measure of pleasure and success. But we always forget this fact: it does not last. We simply cannot have success without failure, pleasure without pain. They are like two sides of the same coin.

Kapila, the ancient Hindu philosopher, expressed the state of perfection in a negative way, defining it as the 'complete cessation of misery'. Expressed positively, the Vedic seers called it *sat*, immortal life; *chit*, infinite consciousness or wisdom; and *ananda*, infinite love and bliss. Behind every human effort there is the desire – though usually unconscious

87

– to find *Sat-chit-ananda*, or what one may call God. But since
most of us are not aware that God-realization is our real purpose in life, we continue to repeat the same enjoyments and
sufferings over and over again. We squander our energies in
ephemeral achievements, hoping against hope to find infinite
reward in the finite. Only after countless disappointments and
hardships does spiritual discrimination awaken in us; it is then
we learn that nothing in this world can give us lasting satisfaction. It is then we begin to see that our desire for abiding happiness and perfection can only be realized in the eternal truth of
God.

This perfection is our divine heritage. In the words of St
Paul: 'The Spirit itself beareth witness with our spirit that
we are the children of God: And if children, then heirs; the
heirs of God and joint-heirs with Christ.' But where are we to
seek perfection? Where is God? Vedanta teaches that there is
a Divine Ground underlying the universe of name and form.
The Hindus call it *Brahman*, Christians call it the Godhead.
Since this Godhead is omnipresent, it must be within every
creature and object in the universe. In its immanent aspect,
Hindus refer to it as *Atman*, the Self within. *Atman* and
Brahman are one. Man must first realize the *Atman* within
himself in order that he may realize *Brahman* everywhere.

Patanjali, the father of Indian psychology, explained the
existence of this Godhead in man by means of an illustration
from agriculture. The farmer who irrigates one of his fields
from a reservoir does not have to fetch the water. The water
is there already. All the farmer has to do is to open a sluice
gate or break down a dam, and the water flows into the field
by the natural force of gravity. The 'water' is the evolutionary
force which, according to Patanjali, each one of us carries
within himself and only waits to be released from the 'reservoir'. By our efforts and through the grace of God, 'the sluice
gates open'; the water runs down into the field; the field bears
its crop and is thereby transformed.

Christ, like other great spiritual teachers, stated quite plainly
that man must seek God within himself. In the Gospel according to St Luke, we read: 'The kingdom of God cometh not
with observation: Neither shall they say, "Lo here!" or "Lo
there!" for behold, the kingdom of God is within you.' Some

theologians have interpreted the word 'within' to mean 'amongst'; that Christ was referring to himself as the Kingdom of God, to mean amongst his disciples. But if we do not accept Christ's statement as referring to the divinity within man, how can we understand his prayer to the Father: 'I in them and thou in me, that they may be made perfect in one . . .'? And the apostle Paul's reminder to the Corinthians: 'Know ye not that ye are the temple of God and that the Spirit of God dwelleth in you?'

What prevents us from realizing the truth that God is always within us? It is our ignorance – the false identification of our true nature, which is Spirit, with body, mind, senses, and intellect. 'The light shineth in darkness, and the darkness comprehended it not.' The light of God is shining, but the veil of our ignorance covers that light. This ignorance is a direct and immediate experience. It can only be removed by another direct and immediate experience – vision of God or union with him. Buddha likened our state of darkness to sleep and God-realization to awakening.

While in ignorance, it is hard for us to believe that God can be realized. Yet in every age, among the followers of all religions, there have been men and women who attained him. Christ, Buddha, Sri Ramakrishna, and others not only realized God but insisted that everyone must do so. A Vedic seer declared: 'I have known that Great Being of effulgent light, beyond all darkness. You also, having known that Truth, go beyond death.' And Jesus said: 'Except a man be born again, he cannot see the kingdom of God.' The German mystic Angelus Silesius explained Jesus's words as follows: 'Christ may be born a thousand times in Bethlehem, but if he be not born anew within your own heart, you remain eternally forlorn.' What does it mean to have Christ born in our hearts? It is to come face to face with God and thereby to attain perfection. That is the one purpose of religion.

Now let us consider, from the psychological standpoint, what this rebirth in spirit, or inner awakening, means. Today a great emphasis is laid on what is known as logical positivism. Only data verifiable through sense-perception and intellectual reasoning are accepted as truth by the logical positivists. On the basis of this logic, scriptural truths and truths taught by illumined souls throughout the ages are not taken seriously because they cannot be verified through the senses or reason. The mistake in the reasoning process of the logical positivists is that they take for granted that truth can be verified only by the senses or the intellect. Sense-experiences and intellectual reasoning are, no doubt, criteria of truth, but they do not include all human experience. Human consciousness extends above as well as below the surface consciousness. Modern psychology has primarily explored the area below. It has shown that there are different states of the human mind – conscious, subconscious, and unconscious – but has ignored one important area – the superconscious. By not taking into consideration the experiences at all levels of the mind, psychology and philosophy are only giving us half-truths.

It is the mystics who have supplied us with the experiences of the superconscious. And their experiences are verifiable. We can test the truth of their experiences for ourselves, if we are willing to follow the methods taught by these great religious teachers.

According to the psychology of the Upanishads, there are three states of consciousness known to all mankind. They are waking, dreaming, and dreamless sleep. But there is a state of consciousness transcending these three, known only to the mystics. It is called the Fourth. It cannot be emphasized too strongly that this state has nothing whatever to do with occultism or psychic hallucinations. It is the state of perfection which Christ and other God-men have asked us to manifest in our lives. When this consciousness becomes unfolded, the kingdom of God is experienced. In Hindu terminology, this Fourth is known as *samadhi*; the Buddhists call it *nirvana*, or the awakened state; and Christ has referred to it as birth in Spirit. The experience of this transcendental consciousness is not contradicted at any time by any other experience (unlike the dream state, for instance, whose fantasies are usually contradicted by our waking state). The Fourth is beyond time, space, and causation. Although it transcends the mind, it does not contradict reason. Moreover, there are tests to determine whether an individual has actually experienced the transcendental state or has become subject to mere hallucinations. The criteria are these: Has it been experienced by men of God?

Are similar experiences recorded in the scriptures? Also, the experience of the Fourth results in a permanent transformation of character for the better. Swami Vivekananda said that if by chance a fool were to go into the transcendental state, he would come back a wise man; but if the experience is not genuine, he will still remain a fool.

In the *Mandukya Upanishad* the transcendental state is described as follows:

'The Fourth, say the wise, is not subjective experience, nor objective experience, nor experience intermediate between these two, nor is it a negative condition which is neither consciousness nor unconsciousness. It is not the knowledge of the senses, nor is it relative knowledge, nor yet inferential knowledge. Beyond the senses, beyond the understanding, beyond all expression, is the Fourth. It is pure unitary consciousness, wherein awareness of the world and of multiplicity is completely obliterated. It is ineffable peace. It is the supreme good. It is One without a second.'

Why do we see so few individuals who have experienced this rebirth in Spirit? It is because few really struggle for perfection. As the *Bhagavad-Gita* says: 'Who cares to seek for that perfect freedom? One man, perhaps, in many thousands.' Of course there are millions of Christians who attend churches regularly and millions of Hindus and Buddhists who worship in temples and pagodas. But of those who do, few make earnest efforts to attain the Reality. Most people are satisfied with living a more or less ethical life on earth, in the hope of being rewarded in an after-life for their good deeds. Christ's ideal of perfection is either generally forgotten or misunderstood. True, many people read the 'Sermon on the Mount' and other scriptures, but these teachings do not penetrate their understanding. Few try to live them. Although theologians may argue today whether or not perfection can be achieved in this life, Christ taught that man can and should be as perfect as God himself – by realizing his oneness with him. 'Blessed are the pure in heart, for they shall see God.' And his disciples, who hungered for the truth of God, knew that their master could teach them how to satisfy that hunger.

Neither Christ nor Buddha nor Krishna taught that God can be known and perfection attained only after the death of the body. If we go to the actual founders of any religion, we find one truth expressed: Realize God here and now! The Upanishads tell us: 'Blessed is he who realizes God in this life. If not, it is his greatest calamity.' And Christ said: 'Seek ye first the kingdom of God. . . .' The great obstacle in the path of God-realization is mankind's laziness and lack of enthusiasm. Buddha called such laziness man's greatest sin. Christ expressed the same idea when he said: 'No man, having put his hand to the plough, and looking back, is fit for the kingdom of God.'

'But what is God? How shall I think of him?' These are the first questions that come into the mind of the spiritual aspirant. He reads in the scriptures that God is indefinable, inexpressible, beyond all thought. Yet the world's great teachers say that God is realizable in this very life. Also God has been defined in many ways, both by theologians as well as by seers of God. Sri Ramakrishna would explain the reason for the many different conceptions of God by saying: 'Bees make a buzzing noise before they settle on a flower; but while sitting on the flower and sipping the nectar, they are silent; and then, having had their fill, they make a sweet humming noise.' Similarly, before we know anything of God we fight and quarrel; we claim that God must be this and cannot be that. When we begin to taste the sweetness of God, we become speechless. And the sages who have been immersed in God-consciousness try to express their experiences in various ways. They point out that God may appear as personal, as impersonal, with or without attributes, with or without form. All contradictions meet in God. To quote Sri Ramakrishna again: 'Infinite is God and infinite are his expressions. He who lives continuously in the consciousness of God, and in this alone, knows him in his true being. He knows his infinite expressions, his various aspects.'

There are many methods by which perfection in God may be reached. Different ways suit different temperaments. In the religious literature of the Hindus, four main paths to the attainment of union with God (known as *yogas*) are generally recognized.

In *karma yoga*, the path of selfless work, every action is

offered to God as a sacrament. By dedicating the fruits of one's work to God, one gradually achieves non-attachment and eventually goes beyond both action and inaction – at the same time remaining active.

Jnana yoga is the path of discrimination. By analysing and then rejecting all transitory phenomena, the Reality or Godhead in its impersonal aspect is finally perceived. It is a difficult path, not suited for the majority of spiritual aspirants.

Bhakti yoga is the path of devotion. By cultivating intense love for God as a personal Being, the worshipper merges his own ego in his Ideal. In this path, God is often worshipped as a divine incarnation – a Christ, or Buddha, or Krishna. Most believers in the world's religions are *bhakti yogis*.

Raja yoga is the path of formal meditation. It is the method of concentrating the mind one-pointedly on the Reality until complete absorption is achieved. This path may be followed exclusively, often by those who lead predominantly contemplative lives. But, in a sense, *raja yoga* may be said to combine the other three paths, since meditation is involved in God-dedicated action, worship, discrimination, and concentration on the chosen ideal of God. Although a balanced spiritual life demands a harmonious combination of all four yogas, one or the other usually predominates, depending on the temperament of the spiritual aspirant. All four paths lead to the same transcendental experience of union with God.

Although in Christ's teachings there are suggestions of all four paths, Jesus emphasized the path of devotion, which is considered the easiest and most natural way to God-realization. Why? Because in every human heart there is the desire to love and be loved. Everyone wants the affection of a father, a mother, a friend, or a sweetheart – not recognizing that it is really a desire for God and nothing else. That is why, ultimately, in our human relationships we feel frustrated and lonely because the love we know and express on the human plane is merely a shadow. We are not aware that it is only a reflection of the infinite God dwelling in each heart, waiting to be manifested. This is the truth we have to recognize. That great love of God attracts us, but we misread it. And to read that love truly, to find fulfilment or the desire for love within each one of us, is to turn that love toward God, who is Love itself.

This does not mean that human love is wrong and must be avoided. On the contrary, it is an experience through which every soul must pass before it can realize God. Through human love, such qualities as kindness and unselfishness are unfolded. But when the soul learns through repeated bitter suffering that the nature of its love is transitory because it is human, it begins to yearn for eternal fulfilment – which is possible only on the spiritual plane. But human affections need not be uprooted; they can be transformed into divine love when their object is adored, not as a human being, but as God himself. After all, the fact is that the universe of many names and forms which we perceive is superimposed by our minds upon the true Self, the all-pervading Spirit.

In the Upanishads we read that the sage Yajnavalkya taught his wife Maitreyi:

'It is not for the sake of the husband that the husband is dear, but for the sake of the Self. It is not for the sake of the wife that the wife is dear, but for the sake of the Self. It is not for the sake of the children that the children are dear, but for the sake of the Self. . . . It is not for the sake of itself that anything whatever is esteemed, but for the sake of the Self.'

We must know that the ideal of the path of devotion is to be united with God in one's consciousness and to see him, the one Self, in every being. But we cannot see God in anyone unless we first learn to find God in our own heart.

The question now arises: How can we love God, whom we have never seen? Both Vedanta and Christianity point out that we must worship a chosen aspect of the Godhead. A Hindu prayer says: 'They call you by so many names; they divide you, as it were, by different names; yet in each one of these you manifest your omnipotence. You are reached through any of them.' Whether we worship the Lord as personal or impersonal, with or without attributes, with or without form, we must acquire single-minded love for the aspect we have chosen. But at the same time we must remember that our own Chosen Ideal is also manifested in every other aspect of God.

If we worship Christ, for instance, we must know that he is the *Atman*, the Self within us, and at the same time the transcendent Godhead. Swami Vivekananda has explained the necessity of accepting a Chosen Ideal as follows:

'God is both the subject and the object. He is the "I" and the "you". How is this? How to know the knower? The knower cannot know himself; I see everything, but cannot see myself. The Self, the knower, the Lord of all, the real Being, is the cause of all the vision that is in the universe, but it is impossible for him to see himself or know himself, excepting through reflection. You cannot see your own face except in a mirror, and so the Atman, the Self, cannot see its own nature until it is reflected, and this whole universe, therefore, is the Self trying to realize itself. This reflection is thrown back first from the protoplasm, then from plants and animals, and so on and on from better reflectors, until the best reflector – the perfect man – is reached. Just as the man who, wanting to see his face, looks first in a little pool of muddy water, and sees just an outline. Then he comes to clear water and sees a better image, and at last to a looking glass, and sees himself reflected as he is. Therefore the perfect man is the highest reflection of that being who is both subject and object. You now find why perfect men are instinctively worshipped as God in every country. They are the most perfect manifestations of the eternal Self. That is why men worship incarnations such as Christ or Buddha.

'It is true that you and I, and the poorest of us, the meanest even, embody that God, even reflect that God. The vibration of light is everywhere, omnipresent; but we have to strike the light of the lamp before we can see the light. The omnipresent God of the universe cannot be seen until he is reflected by these giant lamps of the earth – the prophets, the man-Gods, the Incarnations, the embodiments of God. Our scriptures say, "These great children of Light, who manifest the Light themselves, who are Light themselves, they being worshipped, become, as it were, one with us and we become one with them."'

As I have already mentioned, in the path of devotion the

worshipper frequently chooses a divine incarnation – Christ or Krishna, for instance, as his Ideal. The incarnations, who come to earth for the good of mankind, are like so many doors opening to the divine Beyond. We must remember here that it is the same Spirit which manifests in human form during various ages; it merely chooses a different dress.

The divine incarnations are always aware of their special mission, which is to remind man of the eternal truth he has forgotten and to show him once more how to reach perfection. This is why Christ declares: 'I am the light of the world: he that followeth me shall not walk in darkness, but shall have the light of life.' Similarly, Sri Krishna tells his disciple Arjuna: 'Lay down all duties in me, your refuge. Fear no longer, for I will save you from sin and from bondage.' And Sri Ramakrishna says: 'I am the sanctuary. Give me the power of attorney. I release you from all the bonds of karma.' We must understand that when these great religious teachers say 'I', they do not mean the ego, the individual self. They are referring to the universal 'I', God, because they are united with him in their consciousness.

To come to God, to surrender ourselves to him, is to observe what Christ called the 'first and great commandment': 'Thou shalt love the Lord thy God with all thy heart, and with all thy soul, and with all thy mind.' As he expressed it in the Beatitudes, it is to mourn for God, to hunger and thirst for him. But in order that this hunger may arise, there must be some preparation. We must practice spiritual disciplines in order to achieve the purity of heart that opens up the vision of God.

We read in one of the Hindu scriptures: 'By gathering pure food, the heart is purified.' By 'food' is meant whatever we receive through our senses – the impressions we gather through sight, hearing, touch, and so on. The secret of this spiritual discipline is to cover everything with the presence of God. No matter where the unruly senses go and the mind wanders, we must try to see the Lord.

We are also to practice ethical virtues, such as chastity, non-violence, and compassion, remembering that these are not the end but the means to the attainment of the vision of God.

And we have to pray and meditate regularly. In the words

of the Hindu seer-philosopher Shankara: 'To worship is to hold the Chosen Ideal of Godhead before you as an object of love, and in his living presence to direct your thoughts uninterruptedly toward him, like oil poured from one vessel to another, for a long time.' This is what St Paul called to 'pray without ceasing'.

Through these practices, constant recollectedness of God awakens in the devotee's heart. The thought of the beloved Lord is in his consciousness all the time. Then arises that intense longing for God expressed beautifully in *The Imitation of Christ*: 'O Lord God, when shall I be made one with thee and be molten into thy love, so that I wholly forget myself? Be thou in me, and I in thee; and grant that we may so abide, always together in one.'

Such yearning for God is beyond ordinary comprehension. Most of us do not know what selfless love is. In our human relationships we are used to bargaining: 'I love you, so you must love me. I am giving you this, you must give me something in return.' But the true lover of God loves Him for His own sake, for love's sake only. No matter what the circumstances of his life are, he lives in complete self-surrender to God.

This single-minded devotion to God leads to absorption in him and to his vision. And the experience of joy which accompanies this vision has a lasting effect. Narada, the great Indian teacher of *bhakti yoga*, expressed the nature of this one-pointed devotion as follows: 'Obtaining which, man becomes perfect, immortal, satisfied; he desires nothing, grieves not, hates none, does not delight in sense objects, becomes intoxicated – rejoices – in the bliss of the Atman.' Such a devotee realizes God in all beings and all beings in God. Sri Ramakrishna once remarked: 'When I close my eyes, I see God within; and when I open my eyes, I see him everywhere.'

The ultimate experience in the path of devotion is complete union with God. Love, lover and beloved have become one. This is the state of perfection.

II

GOD IN EVERYTHING

'Through many a long life
His discrimination ripens:
He makes Me his refuge,
Knows that Brahman is all.
How rare are such great ones.'

So says Sri Krishna in the *Bhagavad-Gita*. To know that
'Brahman is all' is the last word of religion. After many
struggles, 'through many a long life', when a man takes his
utter refuge in God, when he is completely free from ego, he
realizes this ultimate truth and sees God in everything.

'His heart is with Brahman,
His eye in all things
Sees only Brahman
Equally present,
Knows his own Atman
In every creature,
And all creation
Within that Atman.'

How does a man become illumined? Where does he realize
God and His presence? First he must learn to look within,
and learn to see the Infinite Presence within his own *Atman*;
for only when he learns to see God and the whole of creation
within himself is he able to see that one Infinite God equally
and infinitely present everywhere in all creatures and in the
whole of creation.

'That Yogi sees me in all things,
And all things within me

Absorbed in Brahman
He overcomes the world even here,
Alive in the world.'

This is the point we should note. An illumined soul who is
absorbed in the consciousness of God and sees His Infinite
Presence in everything 'overcomes the world'. What is our
experience of the world? We experience birth and death,
happiness and misery. We experience the shifting, changing
world. The illumined soul, on the other hand, overcomes the
world of our experience, by realizing behind the appearances
of life and death, of happiness and misery, the one Unchangeable Reality, the Immortal God, the Blissful *Atman*.

'His mind is dead to the touch of the external.' Just as the
dream experience becomes dead to us as we wake up, and no
longer affects us, similarly as we become illumined and see the
Unchangeable Reality behind the appearances, the appearances no longer affect us. We experience the immortal, blissful
consciousness.

'God in everything' is the transcendental experience of an
illumined seer. To say merely, 'God is all', and continue living
in the world attached to the shadows and appearances, remaining subject to birth and death, to happiness and misery, does
not help us to attain God. It is a matter of experience when the
world-appearance no longer has the power to throw a man off
his balance. He becomes established in the consciousness of
God, and finds satisfaction and delight in Him.

And that is the ideal to be realized. In our present state of
so-called normal consciousness, God remains hidden behind
the world-appearance. The basis, the background of this
appearance, however, is God. To quote Shankara: 'No matter
what a deluded man may think he is perceiving, he is really seeing Brahman and nothing else but Brahman. He sees mother-
of-pearl and imagines that it is silver. He sees Brahman and
imagines It is the universe.'

Philosophers and theologians have argued for ages about the
creation of the universe. They have tried to prove the existence of a Creator, an extra-cosmic, intelligent Being who is the
cause of this universe. But before we do this we should first
inquire into the nature of the universe. For example, a man

sees a rope lying on the ground before him, and thinks it is a snake. Furthermore, he even tries to find out who created the snake. Should he not first find out whether it really is a snake and not something else?

In the same way, before we try to find out the cause of this universe of our perception we should first inquire into its nature and our own perception of it. Though in all our practical behaviour we take for granted the empirical reality of the universe, there is, in every intelligent human being, always a sense that things are not what they seem, that there is something more, something deeper, something behind the appearance which our senses cannot grasp.

The scientist who inquires into the nature of this universe does not rely solely upon his observations of sense. He invents instruments, the telescope, microscope, and so forth, in order that he may see behind and beyond the vision of the naked eye. And the seer, who inquires after the Ultimate Reality, sees It behind the appearance of things. To the scientist as well as to the seer the world-appearance becomes unreal in the sense that it is not what it appears to be. Although the scientist realizes that the appearance of matter is not really matter but energy, this energy – call it intelligence – remains largely unknown to him, whereas to the seer the universe of mind and matter becomes dissolved in *Brahman*. To him God becomes a fact, known and knowable, through transcendental experience.

What then is the cause of this world-appearance? What causes a man to see a snake instead of a rope? Faulty vision. This world-appearance is caused by ignorance. Therefore, the questions why and how God created this world, why there is evil in God's creation, cannot arise.

In order that we may arrive at any truth we must base our reasoning upon experience; we must take into account all the facts of our experience. We know that there are many varied experiences with lesser or greater degrees of reality. For instance, I have the dream experience. As long as I am dreaming, I cannot deny the experience as unreal. Yet we cannot base any philosophy or science solely upon the basis of dream-experiences. We have varied experiences in different states of consciousness. As we wake from the dream, the experience which seemed so real, vanishes; the dream-experience no longer touches our life.

The waking consciousness is a greater reality to us. In that state we see and experience this universe. We experience the pairs of opposites – pleasure and pain, birth and death, and so on. If, however, we try to base our philosophy or science solely upon the reality of this experience, we shall never arrive at the whole truth. Beyond all these there is the transcendental experience which contains the greatest reality, inasmuch as it is abiding. It remains forever in our consciousness and when once we are awakened to *the* Reality, all sorrow and misery melt away into the everlasting peace of God.

As in relation to the waking consciousness the dream-experience becomes unreal, so in relation to the transcendental experience of the illumined seers, the experience of our waking consciousness becomes unreal. The seer, the prophet, the incarnate God, tell us to wake up from this long dream of ignorance, and not to remain forever subject to the woes and tribulations of the world. But to most people the call goes unheeded.

In Hindu mythology there is a story of Indra, king of the gods, who once became a pig and lived very happily in his sty with his family. Missing their king, the gods came down from heaven and said: 'O Indra, you are king of all the gods, why do you wallow in this mire?' And Indra replied: 'Leave me alone. I am quite happy here. Why should I care for gods and heaven when I have my family?' Being at their wits' end, the gods finally slew Indra's sow and all the little pigs; seeing them all lying dead, Indra began to wail and mourn. Whereupon the gods ripped open the pig-body of their king and Indra came out, and laughed at the hideous dream he had had. He wondered how he ever could have been happy in such a life, even to the point of wanting the whole world to share in it!

Man in his ignorance clings to his limited consciousness and the surface life of his wakeful state. Yet he is not exactly satisfied, for there is always a sense of lack and of unfulfilled desires as long as he remains within the boundary of his limited consciousness. When his discrimination ripens he begins to realize the vanity and emptiness of this prolonged dream – the so-called normal consciousness – and there arises in him a longing for God for the abiding Reality behind the changing phenomena of life. This longing has to be intensified. Sri Ramakrishna used to give this illustration: a disciple went to a teacher and asked to be taught the knowledge of God. The teacher remained silent. When the disciple had repeated his request many times, the teacher took him to a river, and suddenly taking hold of him, held his head under water for a long time. When he let go he asked the disciple how he had felt while under the water. As soon as the disciple could speak he said, 'O for a breath of air!' Then the teacher said, 'When you can long for God as intensely as you longed for air, you will find Him.'

Intense longing for God is one of the fundamental conditions for the vision of the Reality, and when God becomes revealed, the world-appearance disappears. God alone is. You may dream that a tiger is chasing you, but as soon as the dream breaks, where is the tiger? Both it and your fear have disappeared. To the illumined seer the dream has broken, and with his inner awakening the world also has disappeared. There remains the Blissful Immortal Consciousness. He has overcome the world and its relative existence. He is established in *Brahman*. True, he comes back and again experiences this manifold universe, but his vision has changed, his consciousness has expanded. He never loses sight of the Reality.

Where lies the difference between the lower animals and man? The main difference is in the degree of consciousness. A dog, for instance, lives in the same world, but because of his limited consciousness is cut off from the world of man. A dog cannot enjoy the beauty and fragrance of a flower as a man does, because his consciousness is limited. In man there is an expansion of consciousness, and in an illumined soul the consciousness has expanded to the infinite consciousness of God. He lives in the same world as other beings, but his experience of the world is totally different from others. He sees the manifold universe and at the same time experiences the presence of God in every being and thing in the universe.

There is a saying in India, 'Make the end the means also.' That is to say, learn to see God existing behind the veil of appearances. Even while we are living in ignorance we must learn to see, or at least try to see the Reality. It is like being in a dark room; you know your beloved is there also, but you don't see him. You seem to imagine he is there because you cannot see him, and yet it is more than imagination. In the same way, we are told by the illumined seers who have seen God that He is present everywhere, and then we try to *imagine* His presence, or rather we attempt to imagine His presence. To quote Swami Vivekananda's words: 'Seek not God but see Him.'

Religion is a dehypnotizing process. We are hypnotized into the belief and imagination that this world-appearance is real, that we are limited, finite beings. We have to dehypnotize ourselves, and wake up to the Reality and know that God dwells in the hearts of all beings and things.

The spiritual disciplines for this dehypnotization are to cultivate the thought that God is real, and constantly and consciously to live and move and have our being in Him.

We must try to realize the vanity of this world by shutting ourselves off from all its appearances, and become absorbed in the consciousness of God. In other words, we must first close our eyes and realize God within our own self, then shall we open our eyes and see Him in everything.

12

SAMADHI OR TRANSCENDENTAL CONSCIOUSNESS

The Indian philosophy of religion is based upon the transcendental, supersensuous experience of sages and seers, and Indian sages and philosophers have further insisted that the final goal of life must be the attainment of transcendental consciousness. The different systems of Indian thought, and the various teachings of Indian philosophers, deal with the practical ways and means by which this transcendental realization is made possible. From the seers of the Vedas and the Upanishads down to Sri Ramakrishna in our modern age, the history of Indian philosophy of religion is thus a record of the discovery and rediscovery of the eternal verities of life as they find their consummation in transcendental consciousness.

It should, however, be pointed out in this connection, that India has never claimed that such experience is limited only to the seers of India, for we find, for example, that Yaska, the well-known Vedic commentator, stated the fact that attainment of the highest plane of superconsciousness is not always confined to the votaries of Vedic religion alone, but the same kind of experience is also found among those professing non-Vedic religions.

Sri Ramakrishna again emphatically proved the truth that transcendental experience may be had not only by following the Vedic religion but also by following the gospel of Christ or Mohammed.

What this transcendental consciousness is, we hope to make clearer than ever by a study of the life and teachings of Sri Ramakrishna who for twelve years actually practiced the spiritual disciplines as laid down by various religions and through each of them attained the same illumination in transcendental consciousness.

Before we try to explain the nature of transcendental consciousness, let us try to explain what God is, because it is the truth of God that the seers realize when they enter into transcendental consciousness.

Various are the conceptions which men have held of God. Yet not only Indian seers, but great teachers like Christ or Mohammed or Zoroaster claim that God is not a mere conception of the human mind, but that He *is*, and that He can be realized. Why is it then that these teachers and various systems of thought speak of Him differently? The Rig Veda gives the answer: 'Truth is one, sages name it variously.' Sri Ramakrishna used to say, 'God, Allah, Brahman, Self, Mother and so forth are the various names given to the same reality, as the one and the same substance "water" can be called by various names, such as water, *pani*, *jala*, etc.' Thus, great religious teachers differ in form though not in essence, chiefly because they try to express in human terms their experience of the highest consciousness.

Sri Ramakrishna throws great light on this subject, in harmonizing the various conceptions of God in these words:

'What God is, none can define in words. Everything else has been defiled, as it were, like the leavings of food. The Vedas, the Tantras, the Puranas, the systems of philosophy – all are defiled; they have been studied by men, and they have been uttered by human tongue. In a sense, therefore, they are no longer pure. But there is one truth, one substance, that has never been defiled, and that is the truth of God. None has ever succeeded in describing that in words.

'When one attains samadhi (transcendental consciousness), then only comes to him the knowledge of Brahman. Then only does he attain the vision of God. In that ecstatic realization all thoughts cease. Perfectly silent he becomes. No power of speech is left by which to express Brahman. He comes back from his ecstatic consciousness, and thereafter, it may be, talks; but he talks only that he may teach humanity. The bee buzzes until it lights in the heart of the flower. It becomes quiet as soon as it begins to sip the honey. Then again, after it has its fill, when it is at last drunk with honey, it makes a sweet, murmuring sound.

'Brahman, whom the Vedas proclaim the Impersonal, is also the Divine Mother, the source of all power, the repository of all blessed qualities. The true knower of Brahman knows that He who is impersonal, without attribute, beyond the gunas, is again the personal God, the God of love, the repository of all blessed qualities.

'He who lives continuously in the consciousness of God, and in this alone, knows Him in His true being. He knows His infinite expression, His various aspects. He knows Him as Impersonal no less than as Personal.

'Brahman, absolute existence, knowledge, and bliss, may be compared to an infinite ocean, without beginning or end. As through intense cold some portions of the water of the ocean freeze into ice, and the formless water appears as having form, so through the intense love of the devotee the Formless, Absolute, Infinite Existence manifests Himself before him as having form and personality. But the form melts away again with the rise of the sun of knowledge. Then, also, is the universe no more. Then is there but one infinite Existence.'

In short, Sri Ramakrishna declared, 'There can be no finality to the infinite.' And he taught men how to realize God in one's own soul. To quote his words again:

'Only when his heart becomes purified through the practice of spiritual disciplines does a man attain to wisdom. He then becomes convinced of the existence of God through realizing Him in his own soul. There is, however, something greater than this attainment. To become convinced that fire lies hidden in the wood is one thing but greater is it to light the fire, cook food, and satisfy one's hunger.

'He indeed has attained the supreme illumination who not only realizes the presence of God, but who knows Him as both Personal and Impersonal, who loves Him intensely, talks to Him, partakes of His bliss. Such an illumined soul realizes the bliss of God while he is absorbed in meditation, attaining oneness with the indivisible, impersonal Being; and he realizes the same bliss as he comes to normal consciousness and sees this universe as a manifestation of that being and as a divine play.'

So not only do the seers of the Vedas but also modern prophets claim that God as the ultimate reality can be experienced in one's own soul. This experience, let me repeat, is not the experience of the senses, nor of the emotions, nor of the mind. This experience of God is the experience in *samadhi* or transcendental consciousness, which can be attained only by diligent, earnest, and strenuous practice of spiritual disciplines.

What is *samadhi*? Is it like the visions which an aspirant may occasionally experience? As one practices spiritual disciplines, sometimes wonderful visions of an ethereal light, or various spiritual forms of gods and goddesses, Christ, Krishna, or any one's own *guru* may appear. One may hear or see many truths which are not normally experienced. These are mystic visions and should not be confused with the attainment of *samadhi*. These are real experiences no doubt; that is, they are not to be discarded as dreams or hallucinations. But the great seers who have attained the highest spiritual illumination point out to us that too much importance must not be placed on these visions. They are indications of spiritual progress, or as Swami Vivekananda said, they are 'mile-stones on the way to progress'; but they are not what one experiences in *samadhi*. We must also note that such visions may not come to every spiritual aspirant, yet an aspirant may be progressing toward spiritual illumination. Once a disciple of Sri Ramakrishna appealed to the Master with the request that he might have mystic visions such as many other disciples were having. Ramakrishna said to him: 'Why are you anxious to get visions? Do you think that visions make up the whole substance of spiritual illumination? Try to cultivate devotion to God and learn perfect control of self. These are much greater than visions.'

These mystic visions have value in spiritual life inasmuch as with their appearance, greater self-control and purity of heart are achieved; from them arise greater faith in spiritual attainment and the aspirant finds encouragement to proceed with his spiritual practices.

Samadhi, however, is a much higher stage, beyond the

mystic visions, and that this is so is known by its effects upon the life of the aspirant. When one attains *samadhi*, his whole life becomes completely transformed. As Sri Ramakrishna says, a man then touches God, who is like the philosopher's stone, and is turned into gold. All doubts and ignorance then forever vanish away. In the words of the *Mundaka Upanishad*: 'All the knots of ignorance in the heart are loosened, all doubts cease to exist, all the effects of past deeds become exhausted when one attains illumination.' Swami Vivekananda has humorously declared that even if a fool by any chance were to enter into *samadhi*, he would come back a wise man. Can one then relate what he experiences in *samadhi*?

In this connection let me quote what Father Poulain in interpreting Christian mystic experiences writes:

'Noble scenes, profound ideas are offered to their spirits. But they are unable to explain what they have seen. This results not from any lethargy of their intelligence, but because they have been elevated to the vision of truths that the human spirit cannot attain to, and for which they have no terms. Will you ask a mathematician to express the profundities of the infinitesimal calculus with the vocabulary of a child?'

Professor James B. Pratt thinks 'it is usually lack of memory rather than lack of terms that makes it impossible for the mystic to communicate to others the truths revealed to him in his ravishment'.

Though I am quite sure some of the great Christian mystics have attained the height of realization we call *samadhi*, yet the above description of Father Poulain of the experience of 'noble scenes, profound ideas' is not the description of the experience of *samadhi*. In this connection let me also quote two other descriptions of ecstasy cited by Professor Pratt. One relates the experience of Herman Joseph: 'Suddenly God enlarged the field of his insight; He showed him the firmament and the stars and made him understand their quality and quantity, or to speak more clearly, their beauty and immensity.' Another quotation is from St Francis Xavier: 'This state of intuition lasted about twenty-four hours; then, as if the

veil had fallen again, I found myself as ignorant as before.'
These are certainly not the experiences in *samadhi*; I would
simply interpret them as mystic visions. In *samadhi* the experience is not of many ideas or many truths, but rather the *one*
truth of God. In the lower form of *samadhi*, the idea of ego,
separate from God, is there, but only in relation to and in
connection with God. The universe of many is then obliterated. And after one returns from *samadhi*, he does not find
himself as ignorant as before, but he finds that 'he lives, moves,
and has his being in God'. To quote Sri Ramakrishna:

'When one has attained the supreme illumination, he lives
always in God. With eyes closed, transcending the senses,
absorbed in samadhi, he sees Him; and he sees Him with eyes
open. For he sees Him as becoming all. Sri Chaitanya lived in
three states of consciousness: the inner consciousness, wherein
he would remain absorbed in samadhi, attaining his oneness
with the Supreme Being; the middle consciousness, between
the inner and the outer, wherein he would see the universe as
the playground of Krishna, and Krishna playing in many
forms and ways; and the outer consciousness, wherein he
would sing the praises of God.'

I would say that Father Poulain's explanation of the reason
why these mystic visions cannot be communicated – that
ordinary language lacks sufficient terms for true account –
and Professor Pratt's conclusion that want of memory of the
visions was the cause are probably both correct, as some visions
may have fled from the memory as soon as the subject returned
to normal consciousness, and again he may have been quite
unable to tell what he had seen. The majority of true mystic
visions are, however, remembered, and can be communicated
to others. With regard to the experience of *samadhi*, however,
may I emphatically assert that I have heard it directly from
certain great souls who to my knowledge have attained
samadhi, that there is no lack of memory of one's experience
in that state after one has returned to normal consciousness.
Some part at least of that experience is moreover carried back
into the normal state.

Can the experience of *samadhi* be communicated to others?

Yes and no. The reason why it cannot be expressed by word of mouth is not far to seek. To express is to define and limit. In *samadhi* is experienced the indefinable and unlimited Existence, Knowledge, and Bliss. Let me quote in this connection what the great neo-Platonist Plotinus says:

'How, then, are we to speak of the One? How can we speak of it at all, when we do not grasp it as itself? . . . The answer is that though the One escapes our knowledge, it does not entirely escape *us*. We have possession of it in such a way that we speak of it, but not in such a way that we can express it. . . . We are like men inspired and possessed who know only that they have in themselves something greater than themselves – something they know not what – and who therefore have some perception of that which has moved them, and are driven to speak of it because they are not (wholly) one with that which moves them. So it is with our relation to the Absolute One. When we use pure intelligence we recognize that it is the mind within the mind, the source of being and of all things that are of the same order with itself; but we see at the same time that the One is not identified with any of them but is greater than all we call being, greater and better than reason and intelligence and sense, though it is that which gives them whatsoever reality they have.'

Perhaps in similar words will a Hindu mystic, who has experienced *samadhi*, describe it.

Though, however, the experience in *samadhi* cannot be related by tongue, it can be communicated in silence to others more directly and perhaps more tangibly. In Krishna, Buddha, Christ, and Ramakrishna this power to transmit spiritual experience, even to give *samadhi* to others, was most manifest, and this power has been proved and testified to, as we shall see later, most effectively by Ramakrishna in our modern era. In lesser souls, also, this power to communicate in silence has often been witnessed. This is the reason why scriptures advise living in the society of the holy.

Samadhi is chiefly of two kinds: *savikalpa*, lower *samadhi*, and *nirvikalpa*, the higher kind. In the lower form of *samadhi*, there exists the sense of 'I' as distinct though not separate from

God, wherein is realized the personal aspect of God. God the Creator, God the Father, God the Mother, God the Friend, God the Beloved – any or all of these aspects of God may then be realized in their completeness.

Nirvikalpa is the higher form of *samadhi*, wherein no sense of the separate ego is left, and there is realized the oneness of the self with God, the Impersonal. In that experience, there is neither *I* nor *you*, neither *one* nor *many*. Patanjali defines it as the cessation of all waves of the mind, that is, the complete stoppage of all thoughts and impressions of the mind, conscious and subconscious. Patanjali advises that the means to the attainment of this *samadhi* is the practice of concentration through which may come the cessation of all thought waves. The Christian mystic Meister Eckhart mentions the same method of attainment: 'Memory, understanding, will, all tend toward diversity and multiplicity of thought, therefore you must leave them all aside, as well as perception, ideation, and everything in which you find yourself or seek yourself. Only then can you experience this new birth – otherwise never.'

Sri Ramakrishna points out that in the attainment of *nirvikalpa samadhi* all sense of ego is completely wiped out and though this sense of ego is repossessed by the individual as he returns from *samadhi*, his ego is no longer the same 'unripe' ego as before; it has 'turned into gold by the touch of the philosopher's stone'. It remains as the 'servant of the Lord, as the child of God'.

Nirvikalpa samadhi, however, is not to be confused with unconscious trance. Sri Ramakrishna tells a story to illustrate the difference between *nirvikalpa* and unconscious trance:

'A story is told of a magician who was once showing tricks before a king, and was repeating, "King, give me money, give me food and dress." Suddenly his tongue turned upward and was joined to the throat inside. As a result he attained the state of Kumbhak (suspension of breath). He was silent, and there was apparently no sign of life. So he was buried. After a time when somebody dug into the burial place, the magician was found seated in yoga posture. Thereupon he was brought out of the grave, and people flocked to the place where he was, thinking that he was a holy man. Then he regained his consciousness and once more began to repeat, "King, give me money, give me food, give me dress." '

The crucial test of *nirvikalpa* or of *savikalpa samadhi* is that when a man returns from *samadhi* he is not the same ignorant man as before his experience, for his whole life has become transformed with the attainment of illumination, and he now lives always in God and experiences the joy and freedom of a man in whom the divine side of his nature is expressed. After unconscious trance, on the contrary, or after deep sleep wherein the ego seems to have vanished, when a man returns to normal consciousness, his ego returns and he is the same ignorant individual. In contrast to unconscious trance and sleep, *nirvikalpa samadhi* is full of light. It is consciousness *itself*.

PART III

THE METHODS

13

WHY SPIRITUAL
DISCIPLINES?

The ultimate truth with regard to man and his true nature has
been declared in the Upanishads by such definite statements as
'That art thou,' 'I am Brahman,' 'The Atman is Brahman,'
'That pure Consciousness which exists everywhere and in man
is Brahman.' These great sayings, known as *mahavakyas*, indicate the identity between man and God. In them one finds the
same truth as expressed in the famous declaration of Christ: 'I
and my Father are one.'

The ultimate truth with regard to the universe and its true
nature has also been clearly defined in the Upanishads, and
expressed in two different ways: cosmic and acosmic. The
acosmic statement declares that 'Brahman alone is; nothing
else exists'; while the cosmic statement declares that 'All this is
indeed Brahman.'

These two statements, though seemingly contradictory, are
not really so, for we must bear in mind that the ultimate truths
and teachings we find in the Upanishads and other great scriptures of the world are revelations. They are the direct experiences as revealed to the many seers in their transcendental
consciousness. These same revelations, however, will appear
as nothing more than meaningless gibberish or they will be
completely misunderstood and misapplied, if we try to understand them at their face value by the aid of our mere human
intellect, instead of trying to discover the truth for ourselves.
The revelations recorded in the scriptures are true only
because they can be verified by every individual through
personal experiment and experience.

The aspirant should be warned not to confuse theological
belief and revelation. Theology is man-made, and frequently

creates barriers between one religion and another; whereas revelations are universal truths, and verifiable by all men of God.

While declaring the truths as revealed to them, the Upanishadic seers insist that every individual must experience the revelation for himself. Sri Ramakrishna, in our present age, said: 'It is one thing to hear about milk, another thing to see milk, and still another thing to taste milk.'

This saying reminds me of the story of a man who tried to explain the nature of milk to a blind man.

'You tell me that milk is white,' said the blind man, 'but what is white like?'

'Oh,' replied the other, 'it is white like a crane.'

'But what is a crane like?' persisted the blind man.

Unable to describe a crane by any other means, the informant raised his arm and bent it at the elbow and wrist to resemble the neck of a crane. He carefully guided the hand of the blind man along the length of his upraised arm and bent wrist.

Delightedly the blind man now exclaimed, 'Ah! At last I know what the whiteness of milk is like!'

Similarly the revealed words of the scriptures are misunderstood if we are satisfied to accept them on mere authority rather than to try to discover their truth for ourselves.

Shankara declared: 'In the matter of inquiry into Brahman, the scriptures are not the only authority; one's own personal experience is the final proof.' Christ also insisted upon personal experience when he said: 'Ye shall know the truth and the truth shall make you free.' And the freedom he spoke of was the freedom from all sufferings, bondages, and limitations imposed upon us by our surface life. Only the transcendental knowledge of the truth of God can give us that freedom, and in order to gain that knowledge we have to be born in spirit.

The question may be asked: Is not intellectual knowledge a process? Yes, it undoubtedly is a process, but *only* a process, a means, to attaining revealed knowledge. The Upanishads speak of three steps: hearing, thinking, and meditating. First we must hear about the truth of God. Then we must reason upon it. And herein lies the scope of philosophy and intellectual ratiocination. But that is not enough. We must meditate upon it. And it is this last of the three that opens the door to revelation. We should always bear in mind that revelation transcends intellect, but is not contradictory to it.

In order to follow these three steps leading to illumination, certain disciplines are required of the spiritual aspirant. Preparation is absolutely necessary, and for the aspirant who obeys the following disciplines explicitly there should arise no misunderstanding or misapplication.

Shankara mentions four primary disciplines. 1 Discrimination between the eternal and non-eternal. 2 Renunciation of the fruits of action, here and hereafter. 3 Acquiring the six treasures of virtue; and 4 Longing for liberation.

Discrimination between the eternal and non-eternal is the firm conviction that *Brahman* alone is real, and everything else is passing and transitory. The second discipline, renunciation of the fruits of action, is the giving up of the pleasures of the eyes, ears and other senses unrelated to *Brahman* – in other words, rejection of all transitory objects. The third discipline, to seek the six treasures of virtue, is explained as follows:

Tranquility is detachment of the mind from all objective things by continually seeing their imperfections and directing the mind steadfastly toward *Brahman*, its goal.

Self-control refers to detachment of the sense organs – particularly those of perception and action – from objective things, keeping them within the boundaries of their respective centres.

Mental poise consists in not permitting the mind to react to external stimuli.

Forbearance means to endure every type of affliction without rebellion, complaint or lament.

Faith implies a firm conviction, based upon intellectual understanding, that the teachings of the scriptures and one's own *guru* or spiritual teacher are true. Sages call this the faith that leads to realization of the supreme Reality.

Self-surrender is to keep the intellect fixed upon the pure *Brahman* by repeatedly concentrating upon it.

The final discipline, *longing for liberation,* is the will to be free from the fetters of ignorance through the realization of one's true nature.

Every true Vedantist, without exception, believes in the
necessity of following these disciplines in order to enter the
realm of spiritual life. Once, many years ago, I remarked to a
man of God: 'If one really becomes established in these preliminary disciplines, he must assuredly attain perfection in
God; where then is there any further need to inquire into the
truth of *Brahman?*'

His answer was: 'That is true. But, in order to become
established in these disciplines, you must first make the attempt
to follow them. Then, as you struggle to follow them, you
move toward God, so that when you reach perfection in the
disciplines, your inquiry into *Brahman* becomes immediately
fruitful – that is to say, you realize *Brahman.*'

At one time, while Sri Ramakrishna happened to be talking
of the ideals of renunciation and non-attachment, there came
certain people to visit him. After listening to him for a while,
one of the visitors took exception to the Master's teachings
and cited as an example the life of the ancient King Janaka,
pointing out that the king, although a knower of *Brahman*,
lived in the world surrounded by luxury and comfort. Laugh-
ingly, Sri Ramakrishna made a pun on the word '*janaka*',
which also means 'begetter of children'. He said: 'Oh yes!
Everybody can become a *janaka*, a begetter of children; but
who cares to follow the severe austerities and complete detachment of the sage Janaka, who though living in the world,
remained untouched by it like a lotus leaf untouched by the
water?'

One who does not follow the spiritual disciplines or who
considers them unnecessary will not only misunderstand the
lives and teachings of the great teachers and the revealed scriptures, but misapply the teachings and create confusion in his
own life. Instances are not lacking of this misunderstanding.
When Sri Ramakrishna was living at the temple garden of
Dakshineswar, there came to live nearby a so-called holy man,
whose way of life was anything but holy. After observing him
for some time, Sri Ramakrishna pointed out his faults and suggested he change his way of life. At this the man replied: 'But
why should I? I am *Brahman*; the world is illusory. Therefore
my actions are also illusory. The deeds I do cannot affect me,
who am *Brahman*!' Even though the man was literally quoting

the scriptures, Sri Ramakrishna was appalled at his ignorance and said in disgust, 'If that is your Vedanta, then I spit on it!'

Let us quote another example. Referring to Sri Ramakrishna, a teacher of philosophy was heard to say, 'Sri Ramakrishna enjoyed the bliss of *samadhi* by renouncing "woman and gold". But a new cult has arisen which claims that we must learn to see *Brahman* everywhere, and enjoy the bliss of *samadhi* in the loving embrace of the wife.'

Many such examples can be given to illustrate the diabolical travesty of truth in the name of religion and scriptural truths, not only in our present age, but also in ancient times. Such an example is illustrated in the *Chandogya Upanishad*. It runs as follows:

'It was said of old:

' "The Self, which is free from impurities, from old age and death, from grief, from hunger and thirst, which desires nothing but what it ought to desire, and resolves nothing but what it ought to resolve, is to be sought after, is to be inquired about, is to be realized. He who learns about the Self and realizes it obtains all the worlds and all desires."

'The gods and demons both heard of this truth, and they thought to themselves, "Let us seek after and realize this Self, so that we may obtain all the worlds and all desires."

'Thereupon Indra from the gods and Virochana from the demons, went to Prajapati, the renowned teacher. For thirty-two years they lived with him as pupils. Then Prajapati asked them why they had both lived with him so long.

' "We have heard," they replied, "that one who realizes the Self obtains all the worlds and all desires. We have lived here because we want to learn of this Self."

'Then said Prajapati: "That which is seen in the eye – that is the Self. That is immortal, that is fearless, and that is Brahman."

' "Sir," inquired the disciples, "is that the Self which is seen reflected in the water, or in a mirror?"

' "The Self is indeed seen reflected in these," was the reply. Then Prajapati added, "Look at yourselves in the water, and whatever you do not understand, come and tell me about it."

'Indra and Virochana gazed on their reflections in the water, and returning to the sage, they said: "Sir, we have seen the Self; we have seen even the hair and the nails."

'Then Prajapati bade them don their finest clothes and look again in the water. This they did, and returning to the sage, they said: "We have seen the Self, exactly like ourselves, well adorned and in our finest clothes."

'To which Prajapati rejoined: "The Self is indeed seen in these. The Self is immortal and fearless, and it is Brahman." And the pupils went away well pleased.

'But Prajapati, looking after them, lamented thus: "Both of them departed without analysing or discriminating, and without truly comprehending the Self. Whosoever follows a false doctrine of the Self will perish."

'Now Virochana, satisfied for his part that he had found out the Self, returned to the demons and began to teach them that the body alone is to be worshipped, that the body alone is to be served, and that he who worships the body and serves the body gains both worlds, this and the next. Such doctrine is, in very truth, the doctrine of the demons!'

But Indra could not remain satisfied with his false understanding of the Self and returned to his teacher, analysed, discriminated, and meditated upon the truth of the Self. At last he realized what Prajapati meant when he said:

'This body is mortal, always gripped by death, but within it dwells the immortal Self. This Self, when associated in our consciousness with the body, is subject to pleasure and pain; and so long as this association continues, freedom from pleasure and pain can no man find. But as this association ceases, there cease also the pleasure and the pain.

'Rising above physical consciousness, knowing the Self to be distinct from the senses and the mind – knowing it in its true light – one rejoices and is free.'

In recent times there has arisen a school of thought in the West, influenced no doubt by the teachings of Vedanta and Buddhism, particularly Zen Buddhism, which discredits the need of following any set pattern of spiritual life or the practice of any spiritual disciplines. The propositions put forth by this modern school of thought correctly follow the scriptural truths, which summarily are as follows:

The Self, by its very nature, is free, perfect, immortal. Perfection, or immortal life, is an already accomplished reality – not something to be attained at some future time. The Self, or God, cannot be made an object of knowledge. Illumination, or the knowledge of God, is not the effect of any action or deed, or, to quote the words of a contemporary illumined seer: 'God is not a commodity that can be bought by spiritual practices or by any other means whatsoever.'

From these scriptural propositions, which are revelations, and therefore cannot be contradicted, the natural conclusion arrived at is that spiritual disciplines are not only not necessary, but misleading also. To seek for God implies that God is not present; to long for eternal life obscures the awareness of its presence.

Anyone who, in his present state of ignorance, considers himself illumined will naturally arrive at such conclusions and consider them as following a 'relentless logic'. But – as already stated – the propositions set forth above are revelations, and as such can be properly understood only when one has personally experienced the revelation of those truths.

When a man seeks to find God or longs for eternal life, he is actually striving to remove the ignorance covering the self-luminous *Atman*. To quote the words of the Gospel according to St John: 'The light shineth in darkness and the darkness comprehended it not.' All struggles for the spiritual life, all practices of spiritual disciplines, have but one aim: to remove the darkness that covers the light. The sun is self-luminous, and its luminosity is never affected by the clouds that cover it. But a gust of wind is necessary to remove the clouds that hide its brightness. In the same manner spiritual disciplines, which bring purity of heart, remove the ignorance and reveal the Self – the kingdom of God within.

In the Upanishads it is written: 'This Brahman, this Self, deep hidden in all beings, is not revealed to all, but to the seers, pure in heart, concentrated in mind – to them it is revealed.' And again: 'As one not knowing that a golden treasure lies buried beneath his feet, may walk over it again and again, yet never find it, so all beings live every moment in the city of Brahman, yet never find him, because of the veil of illusion by which he is concealed.'

Shankara tells us:

'A buried treasure is not uncovered by merely uttering the words, "come forth". You must follow the right directions, dig, remove the stones and earth from above it, and then make it your own. In the same way, the pure truth of the Atman, which is buried under maya, and the effects of maya, can be reached by meditation, contemplation, and other spiritual disciplines such as a knower of Brahman may prescribe – but never by subtle arguments.

'There the wise must personally exert all their powers to get liberation from the bondage of the world, just as they would personally take remedies against physical ailments.'

As long as there is ignorance, spiritual practices are necessary. There are two classes to whom such disciplines are unnecessary. To one class belong those whose ignorance is so great that they are not even aware of its existence. Sri Ramakrishna describes that class in the following illustration: 'One experiences no difficulty in driving a nail into a mud wall, but its point will break if one tries to drive it into a stone; even then it will not pierce it. Similarly, there are people whose spiritual consciousness does not awaken even though they hear about God a thousand times. They are like the crocodile on whose hide it is impossible to make any impression, even with a sword.' At the other extreme is another class of people, the illumined souls, the perfected ones. There is a saying which applies to these: 'A fan is needed so long as there is no breeze, but what need is there of a fan when the spring breeze blows?'

Sri Ramakrishna used to tell the story of Sukadeva, the narrator of the *Bhagavatam*, who went to King Janaka to learn of the truth of *Brahman*. Before beginning his instructions Janaka asked Sukadeva for his tuition fee. Surprised at such a strange request, Sukadeva asked the teacher why he wished to be paid in advance. King Janaka replied: 'After I have taught you the truth of *Brahman* you will no longer have the consciousness either of teacher, or disciple, or teaching. Therefore I wish to be paid my fee beforehand.'

But until we attain that illumination for ourselves, we have need of teacher, teachings, and the practice of spiritual disciplines. To say, while still in the state of ignorance, that such aids are unnecessary is ignorance indeed. One in such a density of ignorance would consider the flux of life as life eternal, and, in his ignorance, he would continue to drift on the surface tide of life. The inevitable result of such ignorance is explained in the statement of Christ: 'He that loveth his life shall lose it.'

One extremely pertinent question arises in this connection. Is it ever possible for one to attain illumination without undergoing spiritual disciplines? Sri Ramakrishna's answer to this question is:

'Some souls realize God without practising any spiritual disciplines. They are the ever-free. The ever-free soul is in a class apart. He is born free. He is like *arani* wood – wood used for kindling the sacred fire by friction. A little rubbing produces fire. You may even get fire from it without any rubbing at all. The ever-free soul realizes God after practising slight spiritual disciplines, and sometimes without practising any at all. But, after realizing God, he does practise spiritual disciplines in order to set an example to mankind. Again there are those who attain perfection *suddenly* through divine grace. A room may remain in darkness for a thousand years, but the moment a light is brought into it, its darkness disappears. There is yet another class of devotees who have had the vision of God in a dream.'

No doubt there have been exceptional instances when illumination has come suddenly and has instantly transformed a life. These, however, are the exceptions to the general rule. For the majority, there must arise the longing for liberation and also the struggle to reach the goal of illumination.

All such struggles and disciplines are no doubt within the realm of *maya* or ignorance. To worship God or to meditate on him is also within *maya*. For, after the attainment of the unitive knowledge of Godhead, who is there to worship whom? All that remains in that state is the 'one without a second'. My master, Swami Brahmananda, once said: 'There are times when I am in that state where I see God everywhere, playing and wearing so many masks. How, then, can God teach God? But again, as the mind comes down from that state to a lower level of consciousness, I see differences. I see your mistakes then and I try to correct them.'

All teachings and all spiritual practices are within time, space and relativity. Everything within the limits of time, space and relativity is within *maya*. Good and evil, both are within *maya*. *Maya* has two distinct aspects: *vidya* and *avidya*. *Vidya* is that aspect of *maya* which leads beyond *maya*, and *avidya* is that which creates greater bondage within *maya*.

Although within the domain of *maya*, spiritual disciplines lead the aspirant beyond *maya* – beyond space, time and relativity – the main objective of all spiritual striving is to have our consciousness firmly centred in the *Atman* or God. It is written in the Upanishads: 'The Self-existent made the senses turn outward. Accordingly man looks toward what is without, and he sees not what is within. Rare is he who, longing for immortality, shuts his eyes to what is without and beholds the Self within.'

In the *Gita*, Sri Krishna says:

'How hard to break through
Is this, my maya,
Made of the gunas!
But he who takes refuge
Within me only
Shall pass beyond maya:
He and no other.'

And again:

'Maya makes all things: what moves, what is unmoving.
O Son of Kunti, that is why the world spins,
Turning its wheel through birth
And through destruction.
Fools pass blindly by the place of my dwelling
Here in the human form, and of my majesty
They know nothing at all,
Who am the Lord, their soul.
Vain is their hope, and in vain their labour, their knowledge:

All their understanding is but bewilderment;
Their nature has fallen into the madness
Of the fiends and monsters.
Great in soul are they who become what is godlike:
They alone know me, the origin, the deathless:
They offer me the homage
Of an unwavering mind.
Praising my might with heart and lips forever,
Striving for the virtue that wins me, and steadfast
In all their vows, they worship adoring
One with me always.'

In short, the practice of disciplines is essential in order to
reach that state of unceasing prayer. When the aspirant has
reached the stage of constant remembrance and steady recollectedness of God a new vision opens for him – he attains
samadhi. In that state of transcendental consciousness the ego
disappears, the universe vanishes; *Brahman* is revealed in his
true being. Then is it that he truly knows that 'Brahman alone
is real; there is not this manifold universe.'

Returning from *samadhi* the universe reappears, but now
it is seen with the eye of the spirit. He sees *Brahman* everywhere; he realizes the truth that, 'Verily, all is *Brahman.*' Ex-
plaining this, my master once said: 'Can you tell me where
matter ends and spirit begins?' Indeed, *Brahman* is everywhere, and He is all things.

Said Sri Ramakrishna:

'Why should the universe be unreal. This is merely a specula-
tion of the philosophers. After realizing God, one sees that it
is God himself who has become the universe and all beings.

'The Divine Mother revealed to me in the Kali temple that it
was She who had become everything. She showed me that
everything was full of Consciousness. The image was Consciousness, the altar was Consciousness, the water vessels were
Consciousness, the door-sill was Consciousness, the marble
floor was Consciousness – all was Consciousness.

'I saw everything inside the room steeped, as it were, in Bliss
– the bliss of *Sat-chit-ananda*.

'After realizing God, one sees that it is He who has become

this universe, all living beings, and the twenty-four cosmic principles. But what remains when God completely effaces the ego cannot be described in words. I lose myself in that state now and then.

'A man sees a thing one way through reasoning, and in quite another way when God Himself reveals it to him.'

14

THE WAY TO FIND GOD

Liberation, or the illumined knowledge of God, is attained by man in a number of distinct ways. In fact, the words 'liberation' and 'illumined knowledge' have true meaning only to those men who have attained the vision of God, those who possess the knowledge of God.

Among these knowers of God are those we call 'ever-free souls'. They are literally born 'free'. They are human beings, but they are born with the knowledge of God. They practice spiritual disciplines to help others attain that knowledge. As a general rule, these great ones, these ever-free souls, come with Divine Incarnations (such as Christ, Rama, Krishna, Buddha, or Ramakrishna) and are known in the Hindu philosophy as *Ishvarakotis*, i.e. 'associates of God'. In Buddhism they are known as *Bodhisattvas*. In a sense, they do not want liberation. They attain liberation, but they do not accept it; instead they come back to the world to serve mankind by leading others toward God, toward truth and freedom. They are like great ocean liners in that they carry a large load of passengers across the ocean of worldliness.

There is another class of people, often busy, worldly people, who experience sudden illumination. They are rare cases, but in the history of the world there have been such saints and sages who attained this sudden awakening; and, as a result, their lives were transformed. They were no longer worldly, but from that day forward completely dedicated to God. St Paul was one such example. But, again, these are exceptional souls.

Another class of people attains God-realization in an equally unusual manner. While asleep they experience *samadhi* or superconscious vision in the dream state, and in this way attain illumined knowledge of God. These people are also very rare.

Then there is the more common class of people that have the desire for liberation, that yearn for God, and practice spiritual disciplines as taught by a *guru*. Through their struggles they attain liberation or union with God.

But no matter through which means these saints attained their illumination, or by what manner, they all, as one, attribute it to the 'grace of God'.

Now what is meant by religion? Religion is realization or experience of God. God is; he can be known and experienced, and that is the objective of human life. Today this truth has become large forgotten. Many theologians of the younger generation do not even believe in God! Some say, 'God is dead. Jesus is his only son.' In England, an Anglican bishop has written a book titled, *Honest to God*. His primary thesis is that our image of God must go, that the conventional idea of God in Christianity must be re-evaluated. He has referred to Professor Tillich's idea of God, his 'ground of being'. Tillich, by abandoning orthodox Christianity, has rejected the divinity of Christ. He states Christ was 'born conditioned', meaning he was a finite man; but that he became 'unconditioned', or infinite, when he realized his oneness with God or the 'ground of being'. He has said everyone must become unconditioned; and, of course, this is much the same as the Vedantic idea.

But other theologians are saying that we do not need God, but rather a merging of Christianity with the secular world. To support this, they refer to the Lord's Prayer: 'Thy kingdom come. Thy will be done on earth, as it is in heaven.' A wonderful truth. But what is their idea of 'Thy kingdom come'? Abundance of everything! A millennium on earth! Health and wealth. They do not understand this simple truth: that even if you have everything this world can give you, there is still an emptiness within. Without God, life *is* empty. In him alone there is true joy and freedom. And he is right here, within you and everywhere, if you will only realize his presence. Many Christian theologians have forgotten the main principle of religion, its real meaning. It is realization, it is experiencing God. You can see him, you can talk to him, you can realize your oneness with him. In this alone is freedom, in this alone is peace.

Swami Vivekananda once made this observation. He quoted

The Way to Find God

Christ: 'Blessed are the pure in heart, for they shall see God.'
And he then remarked, 'If all religions die out, if only this one
truth lives, there will still be religion.'

The one ideal of life should be to realize God. Never forget
that goal. It is possible for each and every one to realize God
– through His grace. 'Ye have not chosen me,' Jesus said, 'but I
have chosen you.'

Christ identified himself with God unceasingly. While he
spoke, while he taught, God was speaking, God was teaching.
And his one great lesson was that you also can find God. There
is only one condition: you must yearn for him. Believe that
he can be known and that you can know him. You don't have
to believe in any particular conception of God, any particular
idea of God. Just pray, 'God, are you real? Are you true?' And
hunger for an answer to that.

As we read in the Upanishads: 'The Atman is not known
through the study of the scriptures, nor through subtlety of
intellect, nor through much learning.' And, 'Whom the Atman
chooses, by him is He attained. Verily, unto him does the
Atman reveal his true being.'

Whom does the *Atman* choose?

When a man chooses a wife, or a girl chooses a husband,
why do they choose? Because they love each other. So we
must learn to love God and yearn for Him. There is a beautiful
saying of Sri Ramakrishna that 'the breeze of grace is blowing
all the time, you need only set your sail to catch that breeze'.

Suppose that you are struggling, you are concentrating or
meditating; you are practising all the ethical disciplines, but
seem to get nowhere. Then suddenly you catch that breeze of
grace, and there is a vision. That is how it happens. My master
Swami Brahmananda once said, 'If you move one step towards
God, he moves a hundred steps towards you.' All those who
have attained to that realization, that experience, that ultimate
vision, that Reality, will say it is through divine grace.

Let me explain to you how this divine grace is felt. Of
course it cannot be limited, but I personally know of only
three ways in which to describe it.

You are struggling to concentrate, to meditate, and you
become very restless. A storm is raging inside you. And suddenly you feel a power apart from you, pouring blessings upon

I   129

you; and then your body, nerves, everything becomes soothed. Your whole being becomes quieted. A door opens, and you experience the vision of God. You know that it is grace; your mind says, 'grace, grace, grace'.

There is another way. You are struggling to concentrate, to love God and meditate upon him. You become more concentrated. Then suddenly your mind is under control, and you feel a magnet drawing your mind, and you are in another world.

There is a third way. You are not expecting anything, you are not thinking of God particularly; but you at once feel a power striking you, as if like thunder – you hear a great sound, but which others do not hear. For a moment you are terrified; yet you have no time to live in that fear, for you are in another realm. You become God-intoxicated. You lose all physical consciousness. From inside you hear, 'God, God, God', and you are in the midst of an effulgent light and waves of bliss are striking you. The universe of name and form disappears.

Now you may ask, 'What is God?' He is pure consciousness. You too are a conscious being. Although this consciousness is most highly manifested in the human being, it is present everywhere in the universe; and it has the nature of bliss. Yet, though you have this consciousness within you, you are not conscious of it! I am conscious of myself and you; I am aware, in other words, of the contents of consciousness. But remove the contents, and there is God. And that pure consciousness is blissful. One great teacher said: 'Everybody, in fact, has the feeling – though unconsciously – of the presence of God, because that consciousness is present always. Even when we are unconscious, there is consciousness present.'

It is the light of consciousness that enables us to talk, enables us to think, and act, and live, and breathe; but that consciousness remains unknown. Yet it is there, all the time; it is the *Atman* – God immanent. St Augustine defined God as 'He whose centre is everywhere, but whose circumference is nowhere.'

That centre is everywhere. The *Atman* is in you. Its presence is felt in every human heart. To quote the Upanishads: 'The Self-existent made the senses turn outward; accordingly, man looks toward what is without, and sees not what is within. Rare is he who, longing for immortality, shuts his eyes to what is without and beholds the Atman.'

'But,' you may ask, 'who answers prayers, whose grace reaches us?' As a general rule, the first thing that arises in our minds is that God has to be personal. He must have love in his heart, he must have feeling within him. He must have these qualities in order to respond to our prayers, to our love.

Well, philosophically speaking, *Brahman* (God transcendent), when associated with the universal *maya*, is known as the personal God. 'He who creates, preserves, dissolves, in whom this universe is dissolved, is known as 'personal'. And when we consider *Brahman* as *Brahman*-Itself, then it is 'impersonal'. But these are mere words. 'It is only when we realize, only when we experience God, that we come to know he is personal, he is impersonal, that he is with attributes, he is without attributes, and he is beyond all. His name is Silence. A person who has realized God will never define God as this and not that.

So what is one to do while still in ignorance? How you think of God, how you conceive of God, does not matter. Your conception is true to you; it is the reading of Reality with your limited mind. You are grasping a limited concept, but you are reading the Reality.

Sri Ramakrishna gave a beautiful illustration. Suppose a baby, who cannot utter the word 'father' perfectly, says 'da-da' or just makes a peculiar sound when seeing his father. Does the father wait until the baby learns to speak distinctly the word 'father'? No. He takes the baby in his arms. Similarly, He also knows, when the very thought arises, even before the thought arises. He knows when you are going to think of Him. 'Not a leaf falls from the tree without His knowledge.' That is God.

He is the *Atman*, the Self. He is pure consciousness, pure intelligence. But how can you see him? We have a beautiful saying in the Upanishads: 'A knower of Brahman has become one with Brahman.' See God in the knowers of *Brahman*. Wherever men develop any true religious feeling or urge to understand, they worship a Christ, or a Krishna, or a Ramakrishna. For they are the greatest mirrors, where the *Atman* is reflected perfectly.

Religion in Practice

People who say there is no God are ignorant, foolish, and irrational. They are struggling in vain to find perfect happiness in the world. There is only this difference between the believer and the non-believer: the spiritual aspirant struggles consciously to find God, to unfold that divinity that is within each soul; the non-believer unknowingly, unconsciously struggles to find God; but lacking the will to find God, he fails time and time again. Swami Vivekananda said: 'You, the almighty cause of the universe, are trying to see your reflections in little mud puddles!' The ignorant think, 'If I can achieve this, I'll feel so good and perfect; I'll be so happy!' But disappointment piles upon disappointment, until, at last, they turn their backs on the world and face toward God. Thus, those who deny God are really affirming him, by virtue of their frustrated actions and behaviour. But they also will wake up one day to find that God alone is real, God alone is true, God alone exists everywhere.

15

MIND–ITS POWERS
AND USES

What is the nature of man's mind? How should he use it? These questions are of fundamental importance to the spiritual aspirant. But most people are not interested in such inquiries – except, perhaps, in an academic way. They blindly follow their moods and impulses; like dry leaves caught in the wind, they are tossed about in the current of life. They alternately experience misery and happiness, desperately hoping that they may avoid the former and enjoy the latter. And each time misery faces them, they firmly believe its solution will bring them lasting peace. Only after numerous experiences of suffering and frustration in many lives do they learn the inevitable lesson that sense enjoyment is fleeting; that finite objects cannot give eternal fulfilment.

The world's great scriptures and spiritual teachers have proclaimed a great truth: that life itself teaches us to beware of the transitory nature of worldly objects. But they do not stop there. They also tell us that abiding peace is possible and show us where to find it. In the Upanishads we read: 'There is no happiness in the finite; the Infinite alone is happiness.' Christ taught in the Gospel according to St John: 'These things I have spoken unto you, that in me ye might have peace. In the world ye shall have tribulation: but be of good cheer; I have overcome the world.' Buddha based his whole philosophy on the fact that there is suffering in the world. He pointed out that no one can avoid the three woes of mankind – old age, disease, and death. And then, like Christ, he taught that suffering and misery can be overcome, and unalloyed peace attained in *nirvana*.

It is only when the life experience has taught us the inevita-

133

bility of suffering in the world that the words of the scriptures
and illumined souls really move our hearts. Then we become
inclined to seek consciously for the Eternal among the noneternals of life. We try to overcome the world.

What is this world we have to overcome? And where is it?
More than twelve hundred years ago the Indian seer-
philosopher Shankara wrote:

'The mind of the experiencer creates all the objects which he
experiences, while in the waking or the dreaming state. The
mind deludes him. It binds him with the bonds of the body,
the sense-organs, and the life-breath. . . . It makes him wander
endlessly among the fruits of actions it has caused.'

The problem of overcoming this world seems overwhelming to us because we are not aware that we create this world of
ours in our own minds. Someone hurts us, someone else gives us
pleasure – and we react. Where is the hurt, where is the pleasure? In our own mind.

Voicing the position of modern science, Professor White-
head, the great scientist-philosopher, points out:

'Nature gets credit which should in truth be reserved to ourselves – the rose for its scent, the nightingale for its song, the
sun for its radiance. The poets are entirely mistaken; they
should address their lyrics to themselves and should turn them
into odes of self-congratulation on the excellency of the human
mind. Nature is a dull affair, soundless, scentless, colourless,
merely the hurrying of materials endlessly, meaninglessly.'

How differently, in truth, each of us sees this universe! A
Christ, a Buddha, and a spiritually ignorant man – all live in the
same world; all are subject to hunger, disease, pain and physical
death. Yet what a vastly different world meets the eye of a
Christ from that of the ignorant. A Vedic seer expressed his
experience of the world as follows: 'From joy springs this
universe; in joy exists this universe; unto joy goes back this
universe.' Whereas the spiritually ignorant suffer, the illumined
souls continually feel the bliss of God. They live, move and
have their being in him.

Are we really apart from God? No, God is the *Atman,* the indwelling spirit, the essence of our being. What obstructs our knowledge and experience of this truth? The impurities, desires, and restlessness of our mind. In the words of the *Bhagavad-Gita*:

> 'The uncontrolled mind
> Does not guess that the Atman is present:
> How can it meditate?
> Without meditation, where is peace?
> Without peace, where is happiness?'

We may read in the scriptures that the kingdom of God is within us, that the *Atman* is our true Self, but that does not help us as long as our understanding of this truth is merely intellectual. Ignorance is a direct and immediate experience, which is wiped out only by the direct and immediate experience of God. As long as we do not have this realization and our mind is uncontrolled, we each suffer in our own world of tribulation. We feel separate from God and from one another. We are not aware that perfect knowledge, infinite wisdom, and infinite love are within us. Sri Ramakrishna once said: 'If I hold this cloth before me you cannot see me any more, though I am still as near to you as ever. So also, though God is nearer to you than anything else, because of the screen of egotism you cannot see him.' This egotism is our sense of 'me' and 'mine'; it expresses itself in our cravings for sense-objects.

How can we get rid of this egotism? Shankara said: 'Seek earnestly for liberation, and your lust for sense-objects will be rooted out.' Liberation in its negative aspect means complete cessation of suffering and misery; in its positive aspect, it is the peace of God. The more we long for the vision of God, the more our worldly desires fall away from us. Eventually we will feel that God-realization is such a great treasure that we do not care for anything else. This is the meaning of Christ's parable: '. . . the kingdom of heaven is like unto treasure hid in a field; the which when a man hath found, he hideth, and for joy thereof goeth and selleth all that he hath, and buyeth that field.' Then we feel the tangible presence of God, and we realize that we think and act and breathe because of that presence within us and everywhere.

But intense longing for that treasure does not manifest itself all at once. We must develop it slowly and patiently. And in order to do so we have to practice spiritual disciplines. In Shankara's words: 'Therefore, the seeker after liberation must work carefully to purify the mind. When the mind has been made pure, liberation is as easy to grasp as the fruit which lies in the palm of your hand.' Christ expressed the same idea in his beatitude: 'Blessed are the pure in heart, for they shall see God.' This purity does not arise without self-effort. Sri Ramakrishna has given an example of the effort needed:

'Through the practice of spiritual disciplines one attains perfection, by the grace of God. But one must also labour a little. Then one sees God and enjoys bliss. If a man hears that a jar filled with gold is buried at a certain place, he rushes there and begins to dig. He perspires as he goes on digging. After much work he feels the spade strike something. Then he throws the spade away and looks for the jar. At the sight of the jar he dances for joy. Then he takes up the jar and pours out the gold coins.'

Now what is the main principle of our spiritual disciplines? Psychologically speaking, it is the control of the waves of the mind. Once a holy man was asked: 'Who has overcome the world?' His answer was: 'He who has controlled his own mind.'

The mind is like a lake of dirty water, lashed into waves. The reflection of the sun in that lake is not clear. The sun, the light of the *Atman*, shines on the lake of the mind within each one of us, but because of the impurities of the mind the light is imperfectly reflected. The thought waves must be calmed so that the divinity within us will be reflected perfectly.

This is not so easy. Control of the thought waves does not mean merely control of the conscious thoughts of the mind; it also refers to those thoughts which exist below the threshold of consciousness. St Paul said: 'Be ye transformed by the renewing of your mind.' A complete renewal, a complete transformation of the mind – of its conscious, subconscious, and unconscious areas – is taught in the psychology of religion.

Our conscious thoughts and acts are not lost. They create impressions, and these are stored in the mind's subconscious and unconscious regions. Memory is possible because of these stored impressions. The total of all the impressions form what we call character. And our character, in turn, controls our conscious mind to a great degree; it causes us to repeat the same thoughts and acts, good or bad, in the future. Our character, our entire past – not only of this life but also of previous lives – must be renewed. Perfect control or renewal of the mind means discharging it of all contents of consciousness.

This point of controlling or emptying the mind has been greatly misunderstood in the West. Many people think that they should make their minds blank in meditation, that they should become unconscious. But every day we become unconscious in deep sleep, yet we do not realize the *Atman*. We must free the mind from all contents of consciousness *without becoming unconscious*. Then we become aware of that contentless Pure Consciousness, which is the same as the *Atman*, or God.

How is this to be done? How is the mind to be controlled? Every spiritual aspirant faces this problem. Those who have made some attempt to still the thought waves will sympathize with Arjuna's complaint to his teacher, Sri Krishna, in the *Gita*:

> 'Restless man's mind is,
> So strongly shaken
> In the grip of the senses:
> Gross and grown hard
> With stubborn desire
> For what is worldly.
> How shall he tame it?
> Truly, I think
> The wind is no wilder.'

Sri Krishna answers his disciple: 'Yes, Arjuna, the mind is restless, no doubt, and hard to subdue. But it can be brought under control by constant practice, and by the exercise of dispassion.'

What is this constant practice? It is the practice of meditation, of turning the mind toward God and not letting it drift according to its desires and tendencies. The objective world is a great attraction, and the mind runs easily toward it. A young man can meditate perfectly on the face of a beautiful girl. But once he learns to free his mind from distractions and to fix it on God, he will find in him a far greater attraction, since all expressions of beauty and happiness in the external world are only dim reflections of Him who is the source of beauty and happiness. And when that divine attraction is felt, meditation becomes easy.

People tend to consider 'control of the mind', 'spiritual discipline' and 'exercise of dispassion' as austere and forbidding. They do not realize what a joy and freedom there is in spiritual life. If we even make but a small attempt to keep our minds in God, we will get a taste of his blissful presence.

We have just referred to dispassion. What do we mean by this term? In its negative aspect, dispassion means denying the little self, renouncing the sense of 'me' and 'mine'. In its positive aspect, it means the practice of certain disciplines. These disciplines include the practice of non-injury (not hurting anyone in thought, word or deed), truthfulness, non-covetousness, and chastity. These are universal principles, positive aids to the purification of the mind. Although we may fail many times, nothing must deter us. Struggle! My master, Swami Brahmananda, told me at one time: 'Have you ever watched a newly-born calf? It tries to stand up again and again, but no matter how many times it falls it does not give up the attempt. Then, finally, it not only stands, but begins to run.' In the same way, we must persevere in our spiritual struggle; if we do, we will attain our goal.

We must form certain habits. For what is character? As we have already seen, it is a bundle of habits, the sum of our past thoughts and actions. How can we change this character? By creating new habits. Of course, the mind is subject to those characteristics and tendencies created by us earlier. This is a matter of experience. Often we know perfectly well what is right, but we are unable to do it; we would like to change, but find ourselves helpless slaves to our subconscious mind. Yet in each of us there is an area of free will; that is the freedom of the

Atman, of the indwelling spirit. If it were not for that freedom, there would be no hope for any individual. Life would not be worth living. But a spark of this free will exists in each of us, and continues to exist regardless of how weak or ignorant we may become. Strengthening of our will through the practice of spiritual disciplines and the formation of new habits will lead us to salvation.

The first habit we must form is physical and mental cleanliness. Although avoiding egotism, we should try to feel that our mind is already pure. After all, it is true. God dwells within everyone; how can there be any impurity? My master once said: 'Sin? Sin exists only in man's eyes. People suffer from the consequences of their evil actions, but if one gracious glance of God falls on them their sins are burnt like heaps of cotton.' What we think we become. If we think that we are pure, we will be pure.

Additionally, we must practice the habit of contentment, no matter what circumstances we are placed in. We must also establish a routine of study. 'Study' includes prayer (chanting the name of the Lord) and reading of the scriptures. And every day we should offer the fruits of our actions to God. Monk or householder – each must do his duty; if he surrenders the results of his work to God, his work becomes worship. It no longer binds him, but leads him to freedom.

As we have already indicated, a regular habit of meditation on one's ideal of God must be acquired. Psychologically speaking, the process of trying to meditate may be compared to the problem of emptying an ink bottle that is fastened to a table. You cannot take the bottle and empty the ink out. Instead, you must pour water into the bottle to force out the ink. At long last the bottle will be filled with perfectly clear water. In the same way, the mind cannot be emptied by throwing out the contents of consciousness. But by pouring the clear water of the thought of God into the mind, the dirt will spill out. Eventually, the thought of God completely fills the mind.

When the spiritual aspirant first begins to meditate, he often feels that he is getting worse rather than better. For a while it seems that his mind is more distracted and impure than before. This happens because the mind has been stirred. Unconscious and subconscious impressions are beginning to rise to the conscious level. In other words, the ink has started to overflow. Let it. Through persistent practice of meditation, the mind will clear itself naturally and gradually.

This gradual emptying of the mind is the great advantage of integrating the personality through religious psychology. The spiritual aspirant is no longer pledged to analysing his complexes, blaming his parents for them, or discussing his troubles with everybody, thus becoming more self-centred. Instead, he is meditating on his Chosen Ideal. As he moves toward that Light, darkness leaves him. He becomes increasingly attached to the thought of God. As he thinks of Him more and more, constant recollectedness arises. When he reaches this state he feels the presence of God continually. Then the door to the illumined knowledge of God opens, and he attains abiding peace and bliss.

16

CONTROL OF THE SUBCONSCIOUS MIND

What is the subconscious mind? We all know something about the nature of the conscious mind. We think, we feel, we act, and we are conscious of our thoughts, feelings and actions. And whatever we think and feel and do, in short, all our experiences, are stored in the subconscious mind. You can remember certain things you did. Why can you remember? Because what you did remained imbedded in the mind. Every thought, every feeling, every action leaves its impression on the mind. Nothing is lost. The sum total of those impressions is what we may call the *character* of an individual. You are the result of what you have thought, felt and done. In turn, your accumulated tendencies determine and control your conscious thoughts, feelings and actions. Your reactions to this objective universe are governed by your individual character, which is the deposit of your past reactions. That is why individuals vary in their reactions to experience. To take a crude illustration: nowadays the papers carry headlines reporting many thousands of people killed. To some minds, these headlines bring a reaction of joy; to other minds, a reaction of pain and suffering. The reactions vary according to the character of the individual, which has been formed by past thoughts, feelings and actions, which remain imbedded in the mind.

But what about free-will? Can we not choose the way we will react to given conditions and circumstances? Yes, we can choose; but the will is not absolutely *free* will. The will, by which I make choices, behaves in accordance with my character, that sum total of all my past deeds, thoughts and feelings. And not only of this present life. The subconscious mind carries the record of many, many past lives.

So then, we are what we have made ourselves, not in this one life, but in many, many past lives. We have this subconscious mind, carrying our whole record, past and present, defining the character and the tendencies we are born with, which in turn determine the way we react to present conditions. The subconscious, that part of the mind below the level of the conscious or surface mind, is a very influential factor in our present life.

We all realize the power of the influence exerted by the subconscious mind. Through experience, a certain growth takes place in the ideas held by the conscious mind. You grow a sense of good and evil. Certain new ideals and principles come into your conscious mind. You realize that you must live according to these new ideals and principles. In other words, you begin to know a better way of life. But you find yourself helpless to live in that better way. This is an experience every one of us has had. We know, but we cannot do. A thief, for example, wants to reform himself; he does not wish to steal any more. Then he goes to a place where he sees that it would be very easy to steal without being caught. He knows better, but he steals. So with any other bad habit. We have become slaves to our own subconscious minds, to our own characters.

Is there no way out of this? Yes, there is. I have already pointed out that the so-called free-will is also controlled by your character, so that the term 'free-will' is really a misnomer. There is, however, a certain freedom, which is not of the will or of the mind or of the intellect, but it is a *freedom of the spirit* within us which says, 'I cannot will, yet I must will.' Although our mind says, and our character says, 'I cannot do it,' the spirit says, 'You must do it.' That is the freedom left in every one of us, and through that freedom of the Spirit each one of us may find salvation.

We recognize that there is something greater, something higher we have to achieve. Because of our habits and tendencies created by past actions, we find our struggle difficult — but not completely impossible. If it were completely impossible, then life would not be worth living for any of us. But, because of that freedom of the Spirit, though we may fail many times, still we struggle, and this struggle is life. And, whether we know it or not, the real struggle is to overcome the subconscious mind, to be free again.

Now, how are we to achieve that? The psychology of religion goes to the root of this. In my opinion, the only way to overcome the subconscious mind is to obey the psychology of religion. Merely to analyse yourself and to recognize this slavery does not help you. You have to root out completely your impressions and your character – and that is the psychology of religion. What does St Paul say? 'Be ye transformed by the renewing of your mind.' This complete transformation, this complete renewal of the mind, is what is taught in the psychology of religion. The very first aphorism in Patanjali's *Yoga* is: *Yogaschitta-vritti nirodha*. This defines *yoga* as complete control of the modifications of the mind. The word 'modifications' means the thoughts and contents of the mind. A complete renewal and emptying of the mind of all its contents – that is *yoga*!

Now, before we can learn the methods and means of doing this, this question must be answered: 'What do we achieve by this complete emptying and renewal of the mind?' Patanjali says that by this renewal of the mind you realize your true being, you live in that kingdom which is God. In the words of the Christian Bible, you realize the Kingdom of God within.

Simply to try to overcome your past and be good in the future does not work. It cannot work because, however you may try, your tendencies are left. The only way is to change your whole mind completely – wipe out the whole past, the whole content of consciousness. That is the only way. And what is the effect when you do that? What happens then? In the words of Vedanta philosophy, you realize the Kingdom of Self. In the words of the Christian Bible, you realize the Kingdom of Heaven which is within you. Now, what is this true nature that we realize? What is this Kingdom of God? It is said to be perfection. Christ says: 'Be ye perfect, even as the Father in heaven is perfect.' This perfection is to be achieved. And it is not a relative perfection. The theologians interpret this perfection which Christ speaks of as a relative perfection toward which we grow eternally, but never fully achieve. Christ did not mean that. He said definitely, 'Be ye perfect.' Not relatively perfect. Relative perfection is imperfection.

Perfection, to be perfection, must be an absolute perfection, nothing less. And we can achieve this perfection by emptying from our minds all the contents of consciousness, which contain our imperfections. We can compare the conscious and subconscious mind to a jar filled with all sorts of useless articles. In order to fill the jar with pure air, we must first empty it of these things. Similarly, in order to permit the Divine Self access to our mind, we must dissolve the imperfections of the mind. The light of God will then be clearly reflected within us.

What are those imperfections? They are the *samskaras*, or the impressions that we have created which, in turn, create thoughts in us that lash the mind into waves, so that the sun within us, the light of God, cannot be properly reflected, and we are not even conscious of that sun within. But the moment you free yourself you purify yourself of all those tendencies you have carried over from the past. The moment you attain to that tranquility of mind that Christ calls purity of heart, God can be seen. 'Blessed are the pure in heart, for they shall see God.' And not until we have seen God, not until we have realized pure consciousness, can we say that the subconscious mind has been overcome.

Now, what is really meant by those phrases, 'making the mind tranquil' and 'freeing the mind of all its contents of thought and consciousness'? *Brahman* – or God – is said to be eternally existent. He *is*. Then He is *chit*: consciousness itself; and He is *ananda*: happiness, or love, itself. That *Brahman*, that God, is in some way reflected in our minds. You are always carrying God with you and within you, every moment of your life. This *sat*, this *am*, or existence, is reflected in every one of us by the knowledge: *I am, I exist*. We are all conscious of that existence; none of us can imagine non-existence. We must exist even to try to think of ourselves as not existing. We exist then, and we have knowledge of that existence; but this knowledge embraces only the contents of our minds, not of Reality – that which *is*. There is only a partial reflection. Only when we can free ourselves from this content of consciousness can we become aware of pure consciousness, that is, God, the Infinite Consciousness, and of Absolute Existence – the life eternal.

Also, we all feel. What is it we wish to feel? We wish to feel love, we wish to feel happiness. These are the two strong desires that exist in us, the desire for love and happiness. And that also is a reflection; but, when we free ourselves from the waves that arise in the mind and go to the source of it, to that pure consciousness, then we realize the *fulfilment* of the desire for love and happiness, which is infinite love and infinite happiness!

It seems so easy to say, 'Free yourself from the contents of consciousness and be pure in heart, and you will reach God.' But, owing to our different states of consciousness, we find that it is quite impossible to reach freedom, to reach God. In our waking state of consciousness, with our physical senses, with our human minds which can only become conscious of objects and things, we cannot reach that pure consciousness, however we may try. Then we go to sleep, we dream. There again, in the sleep of dreams, we cannot realize that pure consciousness. Then we go into deep sleep, we become unconscious; but, although we seem to be freed of the content of consciousness, there is still a veil of darkness covering our consciousness. We do not realize pure consciousness. So long as we live and move within these three states of consciousness, it is not possible to reach the realization of pure consciousness. We cannot see God, cannot realize God, within the province of these three states of consciousness that are known to us.

In order to free ourselves from the contents of consciousness we must reach a state beyond these three states of consciousness. This state is called in the Upanishads *Turiya*, the Fourth. And it is possible to reach that Fourth while still living on earth. In the experience of pure consciousness you lose the contents of consciousness, ignorance is removed, all doubts cease to exist; you are freed from the effects of all your past deeds and you become one with the infinite and pure consciousness—one with *Brahman*. That is what is meant in the psychology of religion when we are taught to become pure in heart that we may see God, to empty ourselves of all our past impressions and live in the Kingdom of the *Atman*.

But how is that to be achieved? As the goal is made very plain, so also the means to attain it are made very clear and simple. It is done by uniting our minds with pure consciousness by the practice of *dhyana* or constant meditation, a flow of meditation, when in the mind there is nothing but God. That is the method, and it develops with practice. It takes practice to grow into that stage where there is a constant flow of thought towards pure consciousness.

Through ignorance many teachers have taught that the mind must be made blank in meditation. They think that, since the mind must be made empty of all objects of consciousness, if they can become unconscious and thus make the mind a blank, they will attain *samadhi* or transcendental consciousness. They do not stop to consider that, when we go into deep sleep, we are unconscious and there is no content of consciousness in the mind, and yet we do not attain *samadhi*. What is the nature of *samadhi*, and what is the difference between it and deep sleep or becoming unconscious? A fool goes to sleep and he comes out still a fool; but, if even a fool should go into *samadhi*, he would come out a wise man, an illumined soul. That is the difference.

Likewise, in your meditation, if you try to make the mind blank, try not to think of anything at all, what happens? A fool you went in, or tried to get in; the same fool you come out —even a worse fool, for you become lazy, what we call *tamasic*. This laziness is not meditation. Meditation requires a great, strenuous effort to concentrate the mind definitely upon pure consciousness, upon God. It does not matter just what the conception, the ideal of the Godhead, may be. But there must be a positive something to concentrate upon. We have to raise one strong wave of thought to the exclusion of the rest. That is the right practice. Never try to make your mind blank—which is, in fact, impossible. But think of God, concentrate upon some conception of God, and you will become God!

That is what the Hindu means by meditation, a constant flow of thought toward that one ideal. In other words, you walk with God, you sleep with God, you eat with God, you live with God. Struggle to maintain that constant flow of the mind toward God. When the mind is constantly united with God, when it is established in the constant remembrance of God, you have achieved that stage of meditation called *dhruva smriti*, or constant recollectedness. To reach that stage you must acquire a certain purity of the mind by the control of the outgoing senses. You have to practice bringing the senses back from sense objects, so that your attention may be fastened upon God.

It is not possible to empty the mind by throwing out the contents of consciousness and making the mind blank; but what you *can* do is to keep on pouring the clear water of the thought of God into your mind until the dirt spills out. That is the experience of everyone in the beginning. At first you find yourself worse in character than you ever thought you were. Such horrible thoughts and distractions arise when you try to meditate, that you say, 'Surely I was not as wicked as that before. Why should such wicked thoughts come into my mind just now when I try to meditate?' That is a universal experience. In the beginning, it seems as if greater passions arise, because, as you pour in the clear water, the dirty ink flows out. Thoughts buried in the subconscious are released. Just as in a lake with a layer of mud at the bottom, if you stir up that mud, the whole lake becomes muddy for some time. We all pass through that stage of muddy water, muddy character. It quite often happens that, when a person starts to lead a spiritual life, his character apparently grows worse instead of better. All the worst things come to the surface. That is inevitable. Let them come up, and you get rid of them naturally. With patience and perseverance we have to go on pouring in that clear water of God. Distractions – evil thoughts, wicked desires – will arise in your mind. Struggle! Struggle to bring back the thought of God into the mind again and again; *dhruva smriti*: practice constant recollectedness.

When Arjuna learned of this ideal, he said to his teacher, Sri Krishna, 'Yes, what you say seems all right, but I consider this control of the mind more difficult than the control of the elements.' Then Sri Krishna replies, 'Yes, I know it is difficult, but it is not impossible; through practice and struggle it becomes easy.' You do not achieve it in a moment or in a day. Nevertheless, keep your ideal high. Although you fail innumerable times, get up and keep getting up. Struggle, struggle, struggle, my Master would tell me. If there is no struggle in life you are either a saint or completely bound to the world. But you are neither. You are a spiritual aspirant. Struggle you must. Do or die! Let that be your motto in life – and you will surely reach the supreme goal.

17

OVERCOMING OBSTACLES IN SPIRITUAL LIFE

Man has two selves, as it were, the apparent self and the real Self. The apparent self is the phenomenal or empirical self, which is subject to feelings of pleasure and pain, subject to birth and death, the experiencer and the enjoyer of this objective universe. The real Self is known in Sanskrit as the *Atman*. *Atman* is ever pure, free, divine, unborn and undying, immortal, changeless – one with *Brahman*. *Atman* is described in the Upanishads as *Sat-chit-ananda* – Existence-Knowledge-Bliss Absolute. Not that *Atman* exists, but it is existence itself; not that it knows, but it is knowledge itself; not that it is blissful, but it is bliss itself.

We read in the *Mundaka Upanishad*:

'Like two birds of golden plumage, inseparable companions, the individual self and the immortal Self are perched on the branches of the self-same tree. The former tastes of the sweet and bitter fruits of the tree; the latter, tasting of neither, calmly observes.

'The individual self, deluded by forgetfulness of his identity with the divine Self, bewildered by his ego, grieves and is sad. But when he recognizes the worshipful Lord as his own true Self, and beholds his glory, he grieves no more.

'When the seer beholds the Effulgent One, the Lord, the Supreme Being, then transcending both good and evil, and freed from impurities, he unites himself with him.'

We too must 'behold the Effulgent One', unite ourselves with Him, realize our true being, our divine nature. This must be a direct, immediate experience. Ignorance, which keeps us forgetful of our divine nature and causes us to taste the sweet and bitter fruits of the tree of life, is direct and immediate. Only a direct experience of the real Self, attained in *samadhi*, removes this ignorance. Such is the goal of all that live and breathe.

The *Atman* remains forever pure and unsoiled. Although a gem may remain buried beneath mud for centuries, its luster is never lost. No matter what you are, or what you may be doing, or how you are living – as a saint or a sinner – your true nature, the indwelling God in you, remains God forever. A saint is one in whom God has become unfolded or manifest; a sinner is one in whom God remains hidden and has yet to be unfolded. There is that well-known saying of Oscar Wilde: 'The only difference between the saint and the sinner is that every saint has a past, and every sinner has a future.'

Through the process of evolution each one of us will one day be immersed in the ocean of immortal bliss by manifesting that Godhead which is our very birthright. Patanjali, the Hindu psychologist, explains the Indian theory of evolution by using the illustration of a farmer who needs only open a sluice gate to a reservoir in order to irrigate his fields. He does not have to fetch his water. It is there already and flows into the fields by the natural force of gravity.

To quote Vivekananda in this connection, 'Perfection is every man's nature, only it is barred in and prevented from taking its proper course. If anyone can take the bar off, in rushes nature.' Thus, perfection has been barred by certain obstacles. When knowledge breaks these bars, then God becomes manifest.

The word 'obstacle' is worth our careful consideration because it introduces an important difference between Hindu and Christian thought. What the Hindus call an obstacle, Christians refer to as a 'sin'. By sin a Christian generally means a positive act of disobedience or ingratitude toward God. By God he means God the Father, the Reality as it appears within time and space in the aspect of parent and Creator of the universe. Hindus would call this *Ishwara*. When Patanjali speaks of an obstacle, he refers to the negative effect which follows such an act – the dust cloud of ignorance which arises and obscures the light of the *Atman* within us. That is to say,

Christian thought emphasizes the offence against *Ishwara*, who is other than ourselves; while Hindu thought emphasizes the offence against our own true nature, which is the *Atman*.

The difference is not fundamental, but it is important. The value of the Christian approach is that it heightens our sense of the significance and enormity of sin by relating it to a Being whom we have every reason to love and obey, our Creator and Father. The value of the Hindu approach is that it presents the consequences of sin in their ultimate aspect, which is simply alienation from the Reality within us.

Let us now consider what these obstacles are. 'These obstacles – the causes of man's sufferings – are ignorance, egotism, attachment, aversion, and the desire to cling to life,' Patanjali states. 'To regard the non-eternal as eternal, the impure as pure, the painful as pleasant, and the non-*Atman* as the *Atman* – this is ignorance.'

This ignorance, which hides the true nature of the *Atman*, is universal. One may be intellectual, or he may have an encyclopedic knowledge, yet he remains ignorant until he realizes the *Atman*; that is to say, until he becomes a knower of *Brahman*.

Ignorance creates the other obstacles. The central act of ignorance is the identification of the *Atman*, which is consciousness itself, with the mind-body – 'that which merely reflects consciousness'. Thus arises egoism or the sense of the phenomenal, empirical self.

'At whose behest does the mind think?' is asked in the *Kena Upanishad*. 'Who bids the body live? Who makes the tongue speak? Who is that effulgent Being that directs the eye to form and colour and the ear to sound? The Atman is the ear of the ear, mind of the mind, speech of the speech. He is also breath of the breath and eye of the eye. Having given up the false identification of the Atman with the senses and the mind, and knowing the Atman to be Brahman, the wise become immortal.'

Western philosophy produced two schools of thought with regard to the problem of consciousness – the materialist and the idealist. Consciousness, according to the materialist, is a product in the process, and is not the property of any single substance. Consciousness arises when certain conditions are fulfilled, and is lost when these conditions do not exist. Today, materialists are a rarity.

The idealist believes that consciousness is the property of the mind. But if we accept this proposition as true, how is it that the mind can ever be unconscious? The property of fire is heat. If the heat is extinguished there is no longer fire. So we must therefore conclude that if the mind ceases to be conscious it must therefore cease to exist. Hence, consciousness cannot be the property of the mind.

Modern scientists seem inclined to reject both these hypotheses, and accept the fact that consciousness is present throughout the universe, even though its presence may escape detection by scientific methods. In this, they approach the viewpoint of Vedanta. Vedanta contends that the *Atman* is pure consciousness itself, one with *Brahman*. As already mentioned, identification of the *Atman* with the mind-body – 'that which reflects consciousness' – gives rise to the sense of ego or an individual self, which is a major act of ignorance.

We must relinquish this false identification of the *Atman*, and realize that the *Atman* is *Brahman*. This is the supreme goal.

Although it is certainly necessary for us to transcend ego-consciousness in order to attain union with *Brahman*, such is often misunderstood. It is not so easy to rid ourselves of the sense of ego. Only when one attains direct, immediate experience of *Atman* as *Brahman* in *samadhi* does the ego drop away. Then, when one comes back from *samadhi* to normal consciousness the sense of ego again arises, but it is only an appearance, like a burnt rope that cannot bind.

However, we need the sense of ego to transcend it. Were it not there, who is there to struggle to attain union with *Brahman*? Sri Ramakrishna used to say that there are two kinds of ego – the ripe ego and the unripe ego; one is the ego of knowledge, the ego that considers itself a child of God, a devotee of God, the spiritual aspirant that struggles for the union. The unripe ego is that of the egoist, the vain, the selfish, which leads one to greater ignorance and greater bondage. It is this ego from which we must be freed. This unripe ego is also the cause of other obstacles: attachment, aversion, and the desire to cling to life.

The spiritual aspirant must not love the things of this world or remain attached to them. Sri Ramakrishna used to say that people are busy with God's creation, but how few seek to know the Creator. To quote St John of the Cross in this connection: 'The more the soul cleaves to created things relying on its own strength, by habit and inclination, the less is it disposed for this union, because it does not completely resign itself into the hands of God, that he may transform it supernaturally.' And the German mystic Jacob Boehme writes: 'Nothing truly but thine own willing, hearing, and seeing do keep thee back from it, and do hinder thee from coming to this super-sensual state. And it is because thou strivest so against that, out of which thou thyself are descended and derived, that thou breakest thyself off with thine own willing from God's willing, and with thine own seeing from God's seeing.'

The desire to cling to life is the most subtle of the obstacles, and it is felt by all spiritual aspirants. It is instinctive and universal; it is the 'fear of death' itself.

Those who are spiritual aspirants and have been practising meditation for some time eventually reach a point where the mind is about to become absorbed and seem to lose consciousness. But frequently they become afraid, and hesitate to plunge into deep meditation. However, through the grace of God their minds are helplessly drawn by the Divine Magnet, and they are blessed with His vision. God's grace sometimes falls upon the aspirant like thunder, and he feels a terror akin to dying; but within moments this fear leaves him, and he is in ecstasy.

Although all of the enlightened God-men and sages of the world have unequivocally proclaimed the necessity of disassociating ourselves from this surface life, and that a deeper life is to be found in all of us, Vedanta and most other Oriental religions have long been accused by Christian spokesmen as 'life-negating'. In turn, they consider their own religion as 'life-affirming'. But they have forgotten the teaching of their own master. Did he not say: 'He who loves his life shall lose it'? Or, again, 'If any man love the world, the love of the Father is not in him'?

The problem before us is: how do we overcome these obstacles? The way in which this is to be accomplished has been likened to the washing of a piece of dirty cloth; first the dirt must be loosened with soap, then washed away with clean water. The mind is like this dirty cloth, stained with the impressions of deeds and thoughts of the past. We must apply soap; that is to say, we must practice certain disciplines to loosen the 'dirt' of the mind; and then wash it away with clear water – the thought of God – through the practice of meditation.

'Blessed are the pure in heart for they shall see God.' This is the whole substance of religion. The main objective of all spiritual disciplines, including the practice of meditation, is to make the mind pure so that God may be revealed in the shrine of the heart.

Now what are these disciplines? According to Patanjali, 'Austerity, study, and the dedication of the fruits of one's work to God: these are the preliminary steps to yoga.'

The English word 'austerity' has a forbidding sound. It is generally understood or misunderstood to mean mortification of the flesh, which eventually degenerates into a perverse cult of self-torture. There is also the mistaken idea amongst some groups of people that mystic visions may arise from excessive fasting or mortification. In a body and mind weakened by such practices, visions may occur; but they are only hallucinations and illusions as experienced in delirious states. A healthy mind in a healthy body is required to attain God-vision. To quote the Upanishads, 'This Atman is not to be known by the weak, nor by the thoughtless, nor by those who do not rightly meditate. But by the rightly meditative, the thoughtful and the strong, he is fully known.' Sri Krishna in the *Bhagavad-Gita* also counsels moderation: 'Yoga is not for the man who over-eats, or for him who sleeps too much, or for the keeper of exaggerated vigils. Let a man be moderate in his eating and his recreation, moderately active, moderate in sleep and wakefulness.'

A Sanskrit word closely allied to the English word 'austerity' is *tapas*. *Tapas* means, in its primary sense, that which generates heat or energy. *Tapas* is the practice of conserving energy and directing it toward the goal of union with *Brahman*. Obviously, in order to do this, we must exercise self-discipline; we must control our physical appetites and passions.

In the *Gita*, Sri Krishna has described *tapas* as of three kinds:

'Reverence for the holy spirits, the seers, the teachers and the sages; straightforwardness, harmlessness, physical cleanliness, and sexual purity – these are the virtues whose practice is called austerity of the body.

'To speak without ever causing pain to another, to be truthful, to say always what is kind and beneficial, and to study the scriptures regularly – this practice is called austerity of speech.

'The practice of serenity, sympathy, meditation upon the Atman, withdrawal of the mind from sense objects and integrity of motive, is called austerity of mind.'

Study here means a regular reading of the scriptures and other books which concern spiritual life. It also means regular practice of *japa*, the repetition of the holy name of God, or repetition of a prayer.

In the Hindu scriptures we find the phrase, 'to take refuge in his name'. In the Book of Proverbs (xviii, 10) we read: 'The name of the Lord is a strong tower: the righteous runneth into it and is safe.' Repetition of God's name should be accompanied by meditation on its meaning. The one process naturally follows upon the other. If we persevere in our repetition, it will inevitably lead us into meditation.

Lastly, dedication of the fruits of one's work to God. This is known as *karma yoga*; the way to union with God through the performance of God-dedicated action. The aspirant's whole life must become one unending ritual, since every action is performed as an offering to God. To quote the *Bhagavad-Gita*:

> 'Whatever your action,
> Food or worship;
> Whatever you vow
> To the work of the Spirit,
> O Son of Kunti,
> Lay these also
> As offerings before me.'

155

The way to God is not by way of subtle metaphysics or complicated theology. It is by sheer self-giving – dedicating ourselves to God in every way.

As you practice the disciplines, you must also practice meditation regularly. Before we explain what meditation is, let us point out how a spiritual aspirant passes through different stages of unfoldment.

First, he becomes an inquirer. As he grows interested in discovering God, as there arises the desire for liberation, he approaches a *guru* or a teacher who himself is a knower of God and can show the disciple the way to find Him. He then begins to follow the disciplines as taught by the *guru*. He is now a spiritual aspirant.

As the aspirant struggles to follow the disciplines, various obstacles will arise. According to Patanjali these are often 'sickness, laziness, doubt, lack of enthusiasm, sloth, craving for sense pleasure, false perception, despair caused by failure to concentrate, and unsteadiness in concentration'.

These distractions occur because the body and mind naturally resist all unaccustomed disciplines. There are, as it were, two currents flowing in every one of us. There is the surface current flowing towards enjoyment, towards sense pleasure; what the modern psychologist might call the 'will to live'. And there is another current beneath flowing the opposite way, the desire for inner control, the desire for liberation, in short, the yearning for God; what might be called the 'will to die'.

Though both these currents are in every individual, only spiritual aspirants are aware of the current beneath. They aspire to the Infinite, knowing fully there can be no real happiness in the finite. However, old habits are not easily dismissed. There will therefore be relapses; periods of struggle, dryness and doubt. But these ought not to unduly trouble an aspirant. Conscious or surface feelings, however exalted, are not the only indications of spiritual progress. We may be growing most strongly at a time when our minds seem 'dark and dull'. Whenever we would complain that we were not growing spiritually, my master would urge us to practice and practice and not yield to sloth. There can be no failure in spiritual life if we continue to struggle.

Struggle and practice the disciplines, and the heart will be purified. The main objective of all spiritual disciplines and struggles, as we have already mentioned, is to achieve purity of heart. We read in the *Katha Upanishad*: 'By learning a man cannot know him, if he does not desist from evil, if he control not his senses, if he quiet not his mind, and practice not meditation. By the purified mind alone Brahman is to be attained.' And in the *Mundaka Upanishad*: 'By the pure in heart is he known. The Self exists in man, within the lotus of the heart, and is the master of his life and of his body. With mind illumined by the power of meditation, the wise know him, the blissful, the immortal.'

I would define purity of heart as the spontaneous tendency of the mind to flow towards God. However, in order for this spontaneity to arise, we need to practice recollectedness of God as often as we can. My Master used to call this practice *sahaja yoga*, i.e. the 'easy' way of union with *Brahman*. The most effective way to keep recollectedness of God is to constantly repeat the *mantra*, the holy name of God which one receives from the *guru*.

Through such practice, the aspirant begins to feel the living presence of God. He becomes convinced that God *is*. Although he has no vision of Him as yet, he has no longer any doubt of His existence, and he feels His living presence within the shrine of his own heart. And with this feeling of the living presence, there is felt a sweetness, a joy in His thought. He then truly arrives at the stage of meditation, which leads to illumined knowledge of Brahman. This state of meditation is described in the *Bhagavad-Gita*:

'The light of a lamp does not flicker in a windless place: that is the simile which describes a yogi of one-pointed mind, who meditates upon the Atman. When through the practice of yoga, the mind ceases its restless movements, and becomes still, he realizes the Atman. It satisfies him entirely. Then he knows that infinite happiness which can be realized by the purified heart but is beyond the grasp of the senses.'

Let us conclude with a quotation from the *Katha Upanishad*:

'There are two selves, the apparent self and the real Self. Of these it is the real Self, and he alone, who must be felt as existing. To the man who has felt him as truly existing he reveals his innermost nature.'

18

WORSHIP AND MEDITATION

Worship and meditation form the inner core of every true religion, for it is through loving worship of God and continuous, unbroken communion with Him, that the inner vision of Reality opens. When we experience God, our life becomes transformed, our consciousness illumined.

Religion, to be practical and effective, must transform our life and consciousness. Life as we know it is full of discord, disharmony, and suffering. It seems to have no purpose, no meaning.

True, there is no denying the facts of experience, of happiness, of the possibilities of great successes in our life in the world. But what do they amount to after all? There is no ultimate satisfaction in them. They are always mixed up with pain and suffering, with failure and frustration. Happiness and misery, health and disease, birth and death – these are called the pairs of opposites. They are like the two pages of the same leaf. Take the one and you have the other also.

It is for this reason that Buddha was so emphatic in saying that the spiritual aspirant, who seeks an illumined consciousness, must learn first the noble truth that life is full of suffering. Christ echoed the same truth when he declared: 'He who loveth his life shall lose it,' or when he said: 'In the world ye shall have tribulation; but be of good cheer; I have overcome the world.'

We all see suffering in the world. We do not need a Buddha or a Christ to tell us about it. And yet, while we all have the experience of evil and suffering, we do nothing to change our state; even though a Christ or a Buddha shows the way to overcome all misery, and to reach the bliss of liberation in life.

The illumined seers who have attained that supreme goal tell us unequivocally that behind this surface life there is a deeper life which knows no death; behind the play of happiness and misery there is the infinite happiness; beneath the limited, obstructed and distorted consciousness there is the pure, infinite consciousness. In short, there is *Brahman*, God – behind the world-appearance. It is only when we realize God that we overcome evil and suffering, and experience unalloyed bliss; and this we can experience while living in the world.

Know God. Realize Him. That is the one chord running through the varied notes that make up the many religious teachings of the world. That is the one chord which Sri Ramakrishna, in these modern times, touched upon again and again. His central theme has been: see God, realize Him, and thus make your life blessed. At one time some people complained to Sri Ramakrishna that he was leading the young men gathered around him away from the world and their worldly duties, by teaching them the ideals of renunciation and the knowledge of God. To this complaint Sri Ramakrishna replied that he was not asking the young men to neglect their worldly duties, but merely teaching them how to know God, so that, by the light of that knowledge, their hearts would be illumined, and worldliness would not touch them.

In order to know God, an inner vision needs to be awakened. The power of inner vision, the transcendental consciousness, is in every one of us. Only it lies dormant. It needs to be awakened. This awakening comes through loving worship of God and an unbroken communion with Him.

God *is*. The proof of this fact lies in that He can be known. This knowledge is neither inferential nor is it derived from sense perception. It is a direct, immediate experience. To clearly distinguish between this God-knowledge and our ordinary knowledge, let me state that in all our inferential or so-called direct experience, there is always the division of the subject, the knower, and the object of knowledge. In the immediate experience of God, this division does not exist. If God were known in the same way as an object is known or perceived, He would still remain unknown, inasmuch as the true nature of objects, which Kant calls the thing-in-itself, remains unknown. What we know of an object is only an idea, a sensation, interpreted by our own minds, suggested, of course, by the given object. The Hindu philosophers point out that there is an inherent division between *thought* and *being*. To quote Shankara: 'The slightest interval between subject and object is detrimental to truth. In the idea or knowledge of an object there is something given with a touch of foreignness.' To know God, the thing-in-itself, God must be realized not as separate from the subject, which *has* the idea, nor as separate from the object, which *suggests* the idea, but as the resolution of both subject and object into absolute unity. This resolution is transcendental consciousness.

The experience of pure, transcendental consciousness is, however, not communicable through words; but communicable, perhaps, in the sense that a Christ or a Ramakrishna could awaken this consciousness in his disciples through a touch. We learn how all the disciples of Sri Ramakrishna received this immediate knowledge of God by a touch from the Master. The effect of this knowledge is described in the Upanishads as follows: 'When one knows Him, who is the Supreme, the bondages and the attachments of the heart are loosened, all doubts cease, the effects of evil karmas are burnt up.'

God is indefinable and inexpressible. Sri Ramakrishna used to say, 'Everything has been defiled through the lips of man. (That is, uttered and expressed by man.) The scriptures have come out through the lips of man, but the truth of God remains unexpressed.' Scriptures only indicate, they simply attempt to express the inexpressible. To further quote Sri Ramakrishna: 'True it is that the Vedas and other scriptures speak of Him. But do you know what their speaking is like? When a man returns from seeing the ocean for the first time and is asked to describe it, he exclaims in amazement, "Oh, what a vast expanse! What huge waves! What a thundering roar!" Like unto this is the talk about God.'

Now the question is, how is it possible to worship God, to meditate on Him 'whom words cannot express, and from whom the mind comes away baffled, unable to reach?' No, it is not possible to contemplate or worship the absolute Reality. 'There, who sees whom? Who worships whom? Who talks to whom? Who hears whom? Where one sees another, where one talks to another, where one hears another, that is little, that is finite. Where none sees none, where none speaks to none, that is the highest, that is the infinite, that is the Brahman.'

This is the state to be attained. In this state of attainment there is neither creation, nor created, nor creator; there is neither known, nor knowable, nor knowledge. There is neither *I* nor *you*, nor *he*; there is neither subject, nor object, nor a relation between them. Those who have attained to this state have reached that absolute, infinite Reality which the Upanishads describe as *neti, neti*, 'not this, not this'. But to those who have not reached this state, this ultimate Reality, the undifferentiated *Brahman*, the Ground, appears as nature, soul, and the interpenetrating sustainer of both – God, 'from whom all these things are born, by whom all that are born live, into whom they, departing, return'.

In the *Srimad Bhagavatam* we read how, when Prahlada was absorbed completely in the consciousness of Brahman, he found neither the universe nor its cause; all was to him one infinite, undifferentiated by name and form. But as soon as he regained the sense of individuality, there was the universe before him, and with it the Lord of the universe – 'the repository of an infinite number of blessed qualities'. So it was with the shepherdesses of Brindavan. As soon as they lost themselves in their absorbing love for Krishna, they realized their union with him and became Krishnas. But when they knew they were shepherdesses, they looked upon Krishna as one to be worshipped, and immediately 'unto them appeared Krishna with a smile on his lotus face, clad in yellow robes, and adorned with garlands, the embodied God of love'. In the life of Sri Ramakrishna we find how, many times during the day he would become absorbed in God, where he would realize the unitary consciousness; and then again, as he would come back to the normal consciousness, he would speak of God, the blissful Mother. In that state, where the universe disappeared, and the sense of ego was lost, there would remain the one undifferentiated *Brahman*; again, as he remembered himself in normal consciousness, he would have the vision of the benign form of the blissful Divine Mother.

The scriptures, as already stated, *indicate* the one truth, the infinite existence, the infinite wisdom, the infinite love. But as the *Rig Veda* declares: 'Truth is one, sages call it by various names.' The seers, drunk with the intoxicating bliss of that one existence, express that variously. It is from these seers that we learn of God, as it were, in His various aspects. To quote Sri Ramakrishna:

'Infinite is God and infinite are His expressions. He who lives continuously in the consciousness of God, and in this alone, knows Him in His true being. He knows His infinite expressions, His various aspects. He knows Him as impersonal no less than as personal. Kabir used to say, "God the impersonal is my father, and God the personal is my mother." Brahman, absolute existence, knowledge and bliss, may be compared to an infinite ocean, without beginning or end. As through intense cold some portions of the ocean freeze into ice, and the formless water assumes form, so, through intense love of the devotee, the formless, absolute, infinite existence manifests itself before him as having form and personality. But the form melts away again with the rise of the sun of knowledge. Then also is the universe no more. Then is there but one infinite existence.'

Then again, there are the *avataras*, the incarnations of God. In the Upanishads it is declared: 'A knower of Brahman becomes Brahman.' To quote Swami Vivekananda:

'God is both the subject and the object, He is the "I" and the "you". How is this? How to know the knower? The knower cannot know himself; I see everything, but cannot see myself. The Atman, the knower, the Lord of all, the real being, is the cause of all the vision that is in the universe, but it is impossible for him to see himself or know himself, excepting through reflection. You cannot see your own face except in a mirror, and so the Atman, the Self, cannot see its own nature until it is reflected, and this whole universe, therefore, is the Self trying to realize itself. This reflection is thrown back first from the protoplasm, then from plants and animals, and so on and on from better reflectors, until the best reflector – the perfect man – is reached. Just as a man who, wanting to see his face, looks first in a little pool of muddy water, and sees just an outline. Then he comes to clear water and sees a better image, and at last to a looking-glass, and sees himself reflected as he is. Therefore the perfect man (the avatara) is the highest reflection of that being who is both subject and object. You now find why *perfect* men are instinctively worshipped as God in every country. They are the most perfect manifestations of the eternal Self. That is why men worship incarnations such as Christ or Buddha.'

Truth cannot be limited or restricted. There exist an infinite number of facets, as it were, to the infinite God. He can be loved and worshipped and meditated upon through any of these facets. Some worship Him as the inner light – the sorrowless light within the shrine of the heart. Others worship Him as a personal being, 'the repository of the infinite blessed qualities'. Others worship him as 'God the father' or 'God the mother'. Others again worship Him in His incarnations as Krishna, Christ, Buddha, or Ramakrishna. He is with form and without form; He is personal and impersonal, and beyond; He is absolute existence, absolute knowledge, and absolute bliss; and He is the indefinable, inexpressible Reality.

Sri Ramakrishna gave the illustration of the water in the ocean. It is formless. But when vessels of many shapes and sizes are dipped into the water, the water assumes the forms of the vessels. What is contained in them is the formless water. Similarly, though God is indefinable, inexpressible, predicateless, the various ideas of God, are, as it were, the forms and expressions assumed – and they contain nothing but the inexpressible, indefinable truth.

There is a Hindu prayer which says: 'They call you by so many names; they divide you, as it were, by different names, yet in each one of these is to be found your omnipotence. You are reached through any of these.' Religion becomes narrow, the spiritual aspirant becomes dogmatic and fanatical, when there is an insistence upon one ideal of God, or just one door as an approach to truth. The religion of Vedanta gives freedom to choose any ideal of God, to follow the path of God through any door. To quote Swami Vivekananda:

'The eternal Vedantic religion opens to mankind an infinite number of doors for ingress to the inner shrine of Divinity, and places before humanity an almost inexhaustible array of ideals, there being in each of them a manifestation of the Eternal One. With the kindest solicitude, the Vedanta points out to aspiring men and women the numerous roads, hewn out of the solid rock of the realities of human life, by the glorious sons, or human manifestations of God, in the past and in the present, and stands with outstretched arms to welcome all – to welcome even those that are yet to be – to that Home of Truth, and that Ocean of Bliss, wherein the human soul, liberated from the net of Maya, may transport itself with perfect freedom and with eternal joy.'

But this liberalism or universality does not mean that today you worship God in one way and tomorrow in another; it does not mean that you can worship God as Christ one day and as Krishna or Divine Mother or the inner light another day. It is amazing to see how many different subjects the so-called liberal teachers of religion give their students to meditate upon. The tender plant must be hedged around until it has grown into a tree. The tender plant of spirituality will die if exposed too early to a constant change of ideas and ideals. Vedanta, which is founded upon the ideals of liberalism and universality, insists that there must be one chosen ideal, one chosen deity to love, worship, and meditate upon. To quote Sri Ramakrishna:

'You must be like the fabled pearl oyster. It leaves its bed at the bottom of the ocean, and comes up to the surface to catch the rainwater when the star Swati is in the ascendant. It floats about on the surface of the water with its shell wide open, until it has succeeded in catching a drop of the rainwater, and then it dives deep down to the bottom of the ocean, and there rests until it has fashioned a beautiful pearl out of the raindrop.'

Have one chosen ideal or chosen aspect of the deity, which in Sanskrit is called *ishtam*, and worship that ideal with single-minded devotion; yet know at the same time that He who is your own ideal is worshipped in all ideals by all sects, under all names, and through all forms. Suppose your ideal is Christ or any avatar; as you worship him, know that it is that same Christ who is worshipped in other names and other forms, and who is also one with the formless, undifferentiated *Brahman*. That Christ is your own *Atman*, the Self within, and you must learn to see him as the *Atman* of all beings.

Now to come to the practice of religion. All religions unanimously declare that the aspirant must have *faith*. The Sanskrit word for faith is *shraddha*. This word has a deeper meaning than is ordinarily understood. In the first place, faith indicates faith in the words of the scriptures and of illumined seers. What do they teach? Simply this: God *is*. Others have attained Him and you also can know Him. Thus faith indicates *self-reliance* and the understanding that it is possible for *me* and for *you*, and *you*, to know God, to realize Him. This faith, again, must be such that it will pleasantly incline our hearts to the realization of this ideal. That is what is meant by living faith. To feel and know that He is our treasure, spiritual discrimination needs to be awakened. We must discriminate between the real and the unreal. We must know that God alone is the abiding Reality, and that everything else is *an appearance*. Give your heart to Him and to Him alone, knowing that He is the end of the path, the witness, the Lord, the sustainer. He is the abode, the friend and the refuge'.

However, *faith* alone is not enough; you must also earnestly desire to know Him, and with enthusiasm make the earnest effort to reach Him. Buddha called lethargy the greatest sin. Lethargy, lack of enthusiasm, and want of spiritual fervour arise from the impurities of the mind, the passionate desires for feeding the senses. The Hindu scriptures say: 'When the food is pure, the heart becomes purified. In a pure heart meditation becomes unwavering.' The word 'food', according to Shankara, is 'that which is gathered in'. Commenting on the above scriptural passage, Shankara says:

'The knowledge of the sensations such as sound, etc., is gathered in for the enjoyment of the enjoyer (ego); the purification of the knowledge which gathers in the perception of the senses is the purifying of the food. The phrase "purification of food" means the acquiring of the knowledge of sensations untouched by the defects of attachment, aversion, and delusion; such is the meaning. Therefore, such knowledge or "food" being purified, the *sattwa* material of the possessor of it – the internal organ – will become purified, and the sattwa being purified, an unbroken memory of the Infinite One who has been known in His real nature from scriptures, will result.'

This 'unbroken memory of the Infinite One' is meditation. To quote Shankara again:

'Meditation is a constant remembrance of the Infinite One, flowing like an unbroken stream of oil poured from one vessel to another. When this kind of remembrance has been attained, all bondages break. Thus constant recollection is spoken of in the scriptures as a means to liberation. This recollection again is of the same nature as sight: "When he who is far and near is seen, the bonds of the heart are broken, all doubts vanish, and all effects of work disappear." He who is near can be seen, but he who is far can only be remembered. Nevertheless the scripture says that we have to *see* him who is near as well as him who is far, thereby indicating to us that the above kind of *remembering* is as good as *seeing*. This remembrance when exalted assumes the same form as seeing. Worship is constant remembering, as may be seen from the essential texts of scriptures. Knowing, which is the same as repeated worship, has been described as constant remembering. Thus meditation, which has attained to the height of direct perception, is spoken of in the scripture as a means of liberation. "This Atman is not to be reached through various sciences, nor by intellect, nor by much study of the Vedas. Whomsoever this Atman desires, by him is the Atman attained." The extremely beloved is desired: by whomsoever this Atman is extremely beloved, he becomes the most beloved of the Atman. So that this beloved may attain the Atman, the Lord himself helps: "Those who are constantly attached to me and worship me with love – I give that direction to their will by which they come to me." Therefore it is said that to whomsoever this remembering, which is of the same form as direct perception, is very dear, because it is dear to the object of such memory-perception, he is desired by the Atman, by him the Atman is attained.'

Religion in Practice

In order that we may have an unbroken memory of God, we need to practice concentration with regularity, patience, and perseverance. Meditation, that is, an unceasing flow of thought toward God, when we constantly 'live, move, and have our being in Him', is a stage in spiritual growth to be attained by the practice of concentration. To practice concentration, we need to sit quietly and properly. This is known in *yoga* philosophy as *asanā* or posture. After assuming the proper posture, shut the doors to your senses. The idea is that you have to concentrate upon God within the temple of the body; you have to learn to worship God within yourself. Whatever may be your chosen ideal or chosen deity, you must learn to see Him as your *Atman,* dwelling within you. You do not have to pray to God to come to you from afar, but know that He is already dwelling within. Enter within the chamber of your own heart and see the effulgent Lord. The pearl lies at the bottom of the sea; dive deep, and you are sure to find it. God is beneath your outer consciousness, shining within the lotus of your heart. *See* Him. Feel His presence, *seem* to *see* Him. Practice this again and again. My Master used to say: 'His grace is upon you. Feel His grace. Pray that you may feel His grace.'

Leave the world with all its distractions at the outer gate, as it were. Enter alone into the chamber of your heart. Shut the doors and be alone with God. He is, and you are. Should you pray? Yes, pray, but 'pray not for the meat which perisheth'; pray for devotion to the Lord, pray that you may know His grace, and that your heart may be illumined by His knowledge. Yes, pray also for others; pray for all mankind, that He may become manifested in them, and that His grace may be realized by all. Chant the name of the Lord in His presence. If you have been given a *mantram* – the name of God – repeat it before Him. Practice this concentration every day regularly during the early hours of the morning and evening, at noon and at night. Keep up a regularity. That is very important. Form the *habit* of concentration.

That is not enough. At all times during your waking hours form the habit of thinking of God, or practising His presence. To form such a habit, learn to work as a form of worshipping God. As an initial step toward it, try to surrender yourself to

168

God before you undertake any kind of work, and again to surrender yourself and the fruits of your actions when your work is finished. Also, instead of worrying and fretting over your problems, repeat your *mantram*, chant His name and His praises.

As you continue in your practice of habitual thinking of God, your mind will be purified, joy and sweetness will overflow in your heart. Absorption in Him will follow in due course. You will become drunk with the intoxicating love of God, and your heart will be illumined by His knowledge. 'From joy springs this universe, in joy lives this universe, and unto that joy this universe goes back.'

19

SELF-SURRENDER

I will begin by quoting two famous passages from the *Mundaka Upanishad*:

'Like two birds of beautiful golden plumage – inseparable companions – the individual self and the immortal Atman are perched on the branches of the self-same tree. The former tastes the sweet and bitter fruits of the tree. The latter remains motionless, calmly watching.

'The individual self, deluded by forgetfulness of its identity with the Divine Atman, grieves, bewildered by its own helplessness. When it recognizes the Lord – who alone is worthy of our worship – as its own Atman, and beholds its own glory, it becomes free from all grief.'

These are revealed truths. They have been directly and immediately experienced by the seers and sages, within the depths of their own souls. Such truths are, of course, universal; and can be realized by every one of us who is ready to make the effort to do so.

The fable of the two birds is intended to teach us the truth about man's real and apparent nature. It teaches that man suffers only because he is ignorant of his true Being. God *is*. He is the absolute Reality, 'ever-present in the hearts of all'. He is the blissful *Atman* which sits, calmly watching the restlessness of its companion. And the fable goes on to tell us that, at last, the two birds merge into one. The *Atman*, at one with *Brahman*, is all that exists.

Therefore, our suffering has no real cause, no necessity. This external life, this tasting of the sweet and bitter fruits of the tree of experience, is a dream, from which, at any moment, we may awake. Sometimes our dream is pleasant, sometimes unpleasant. There are philosophers who tell us that the unpleasant and evil things of life are an illusion, and that only the pleasant and good things are real. But this cannot be true. Pleasure and pain, good and evil, belong inseparably together – they are what Vedanta calls 'the pairs of opposites'. They are like the two sides of a coin. Their nature cannot differ. Either both are real or both are unreal.

Theologians have argued for centuries over the problem of evil. Why does this ignorance exist? Why is man unaware of his Divine Nature? But this question can only be answered by those who have transcended our human consciousness, with its belief in good and evil. Why do we dream? We can only find the answer to that problem after we have awakened. The seers who have attained transcendental consciousness tell us that the so-called problem of evil is no problem at all, because evil does not exist and has never existed. But for us who still live in the consciousness of the relative world, the problem of how our ignorance arose is merely academic. We need only to ask how we shall remove our ignorance.

What is the nature of this ignorance? It resides in our sense of ego, our belief that we are individual beings. The ego veils our eyes, as it were, and causes us to dwell in ignorance. Man is the *Atman*, the Spirit. He has a mind, senses and a body. When he forgets that he is the *Atman*, and identifies himself with body, mind and senses, then the sense of ego originates. With the birth of this ego-sense, the transcendental nature is forgotten. Man lives on the sense-plane and becomes subject to the law of *Karma* and rebirth.

In our ignorance, we are no longer aware of the Lord within us, and yet, nevertheless, because our true nature is divine, we feel a lack, an emptiness. We want to find something, although we do not know exactly what it is. We want some kind of happiness which will be lasting. And so desire rises in us, a craving for everything which seems to promise happiness and seems pleasant; a shrinking back from everything which seems unpleasant. Behind all our desires – even the very lowest and basest – there is the urge to find real, unalloyed happiness and freedom, to find immortality. This strong craving, which does not know what is its real object, involves us in all sorts of action. We try everything, in order to find what it is that we are seeking. And our actions, in their turn, involve us in the limitations and bondages of *karma*: as we sow, we reap. We begin to taste the fruits of the tree of experience. We wish to taste only the sweet fruit; but this is impossible, for the bitter fruit grows on the same tree, and we cannot have the one without the other.

Out of this attachment to what is pleasant and this aversion to what is unpleasant there grows a clinging to life. The ego clings to its ego-life, its sense of individuality: it does not want to die. Yet this 'life' which the ego clings to is really death, because it is separation from our true nature, from God. That is why Jesus said: 'He who loves his life shall lose it.'

To find real life, the life of our true nature, we must transcend the ego. We shall never know happiness until we realize *Brahman*, the ground, in which we are rooted. The ego is the only barrier to this knowledge. Sri Ramakrishna used to say that when the ego dies all troubles cease. And Jesus tells us: 'Except a man be born again, he cannot enter the Kingdom of God.' This rebirth, this birth in spirit, is the death of the ego. The Hindus have a saying: 'Die while living.' Die the death of the ego and be reborn spiritually, even in this life.

So the problem of all spiritual life, no matter whether you are a Christian, a Buddhist or a Hindu, simply amounts to this: How can I kill the ego? And the answer given by every one of these religions is the same: Surrender yourself. Give yourself up to God, completely and wholeheartedly. Love God with all your heart, all your soul and all your mind. Become absorbed, and forget yourself in the consciousness of God. The ego is the only obstacle to God-consciousness. The great yogi, Patanjali, compares it to the bank of a reservoir. You want to irrigate your fields. In the reservoir there is plenty of water – the living water of the *Atman*. All you have to do is to break down the bank, and the water will flow over the fields. Each one of us has that reservoir inside him, ready to flood his life with joy, wisdom and immortality, if only he will break down the ego, the barrier.

It sounds so simple: to love God, to surrender ourselves to Him, to kill this ego. But it is the hardest thing one can possibly do. It involves great spiritual disciplines; and the practice of these disciplines with the utmost patience and perseverance.

The mind is always straining to go outward, toward everything that seems pleasant in the external world. And the ego reasserts itself perpetually. However we may try to banish it, it keeps reappearing, as it were, in different disguises. So we have to keep on trying.

What are these disciplines we have to practice? They are discrimination and dispassion. We have to discriminate, perpetually, between what is real and what is unreal. God, the infinite, the unchanging, is the only reality. Everything else, all these appearances and forms of the external world, are unreal. As you practice this discrimination, you become convinced that God is, that He really exists. And, further, you begin to realize that, if there is a God, He must be attainable. Most people think that they believe in God, and there it ends. They imagine that mere belief in God is enough. It is sufficient to be what they call 'a God-fearing man'. But the great spiritual teachers have told us that religion means something far more than mere faith, a mere opinion that God exists. You have to believe that God is actually attainable. Otherwise, the practice of dispassion and discrimination does not mean anything at all. Simply by saying that we believe in God we cannot free ourselves from these experiences of life and death, pleasure and pain. These are the direct, immediate experiences of the dream which we call life. We have to wake from this dream, and know the Reality, which is also a direct, immediate experience. We have to break this dream while living on earth. We have to die while living, in order to enter the Kingdom of God. The proof of God's existence is not to be found in theological arguments, or even in the revealed scriptures. Yes, Jesus saw God; Ramakrishna saw God; but that is no proof for us. We must see God for ourselves: that is the only real proof.

Again, the practice of dispassion and discrimination does not mean that we are to give up the activities of life. It does not mean running away from the world. It is the mind which has to be trained. We have to cultivate yearning for God. We have to train our minds in such a way that we are surrendering our ego to God, every moment of our life.

How shall we cultivate this yearning, this love for God? It cannot be done simply by sitting down, closing our eyes and fixing our hearts on God. That is only possible at a very advanced stage. What shall be our method of training? The *Gita* teaches *Karma Yoga*. In *Karma Yoga* we learn to surrender ourselves to God through our actions, through every breath we breathe. There are different ways of doing this. For instance, you can regard yourself simply as a machine. Who is the operator? The *Atman* within you. You have to try to forget the ego: for a machine has no will of its own. Or you can think of the fable of the two birds. You are the *Atman*, motionless, actionless, calmly observing. The senses move amongst the sense-objects, but you remain free from all action. You are actionless in the midst of action. Or again, you can make every action into a sort of ritual, an offering to God. As Sri Krishna says to Arjuna, in the *Gita*:

'Whatever your action,
Food or worship;
Whatever the gift
That you give to another;
Whatever you vow
To the work of the Spirit;
O son of Kunti,
Lay these also
As offerings before me.'

And he continues: 'Thus you will free yourself from both the good and the evil effects of your actions. Offer up everything to me. If your heart is united with me, you will be set free from Karma even in this life, and come to me at the last.'

When you fall in love with someone, your mind dwells on that person, no matter what you may be doing, all day long. That is how we should love God. Every day, we must fall in love with Him afresh. Mere human love wears out and ceases; but love of God grows. You do not get tired of it. It is always a new thing. It gains in intensity. To cultivate this love, we must try to be conscious of God continually; and this is only possible if we practice regular meditation. Without meditation, *Karma Yoga* is impracticable. Just by being a good person, by living an ethical life, by trying to be selfless in your service, you cannot reach the transcendental Reality. By meditation, you have to awake the power that is within you.

Then you begin to see the play of God in the outside world. Ethical life and service are an aid, but they are not an end in themselves. The end is to be one with God. Set aside some time each day to devote yourself completely and whole-heartedly to the contemplation of God. Think of nothing else but Him, and so the practice will become easy.

Where should we think of God? We are not to pray to some external Being, who hangs in the sky. God is omni-present. He is nearer than anything we know. He is within us. We have to feel that living Presence within the chamber of our own hearts. Go into your own heart and surrender your-self, there, to the Ruler of the universe, without whom you could not breathe or act, without whom there is no conscious-ness, no reality. Surrender yourself completely and whole-heartedly to Him.

20

RENUNCIATION AND AUSTERITY

Question: Should not a spiritual teacher manifestly demonstrate that he has, for the love of God, given up everything – should he not live with only the barest necessities?

Answer: You would then identify the life of renunciation with a life of poverty and discomfort, and you would say that if a spiritual teacher lives in comfort and in a plentiful household he is evidently not living the consecrated life. Your view has no doubt a surface plausibility, but it is too simple. A man of true renunciation concerns himself neither with poverty nor with riches. One person may live in dire poverty, and another may live in luxury, and yet both be steeped in spiritual ignorance and confirmed in worldliness. What *is* renunciation? Renunciation is *the giving up of everything.* The rich must give up his riches, and the poor must give up his poverty. If the poor man hugs his few trivial possessions and clings greedily to his meagre earnings, he is as much attached, and is as much a worldly man, as the rich man with his limousines and his princely income. Only the poor man is the worse off – because of his envy! To be a man of renunciation one must completely give up everything, without thought of keeping for himself even the barest necessities of life. He must possess nothing but God. How can one really achieve such a state? Only by fully realizing that the ideal is to renounce, utterly, *me* and *mine.* Attachment – whether to a rag and a hut or to silk robes and palaces – does not come from a quality in objects, but from a possessive taint in the soul. Everything belongs either to nature or to God. The moment you label anything as *yours,* you begin to suffer from attachment. The ideal monk, therefore, subdues all *craving* for possessions, renounces the ego-sense, and becomes content to live either in the midst of poverty or in the midst of plenty.

'He who is everywhere unattached,' says the *Gita*, 'not pleased at receiving good, not vexed at evil – his wisdom is fixed.'

The vow of a monk is not a vow of poverty – as the expression would be generally understood in the West: it is a vow to cease craving for things.

'That man who lives devoid of longing' – if we may return to the *Gita* – 'abandoning all craving, without the sense of "I" and "mine" – he attains to peace.'

Remember: the ideal of renunciation is nothing that can be vulgarly demonstrated. It is the inner life, hidden from the eyes of all; for renunciation is in the mind and not in the object. A spiritual man is never eager to convince people of his spirituality. It is only the false and hypocritical who try to show their renunciation and their austerity by practising mortifications of the flesh, and this they do either to gratify some selfish desire or to gain recognition for themselves.

Thus, again, the *Gita*:

'The austerity which is practised with the object of gaining notoriety, honour, and worship, and with ostentation, is said to be *rajasika*, unstable and transitory.

'That austerity which is practised for some foolish purpose, for self-torture or for the purpose of harming another, is declared to be *tamasika*.'

A man who seeks the spiritual ideal always seeks to please God and never seeks to please man.

Question: What is austerity then? Should we not practise austerity?

Answer: In Sanskrit it is called *tapas*, which literally means that which generates *heat* or energy. In other words, it is the practice of conserving energy and directing it towards a single goal – illumination in one's own soul. It is not by observing an externally austere life, in the Western sense of living in discomfort and poverty, or by torturing the flesh, that one can achieve this goal. Mere outward austerity is a degenerate form of ritualism, and is condemned by illumined souls. As to external observances, both Krishna and Buddha teach moderation.

Again I quote the *Gita*:

'Success in Yoga is not for him who eats too much or too little – nor, O Arjuna, for him who sleeps too much or too little.

'To him who is temperate in eating and recreation, in his activity, and in sleep and wakefulness, Yoga becomes the destroyer of misery.'

If by observing certain forms of living, or by undergoing some physical discomfort, one could gain self-control, religious life would be very easy. Degeneration in organized monasticism began only after the introduction of that kind of ritualism. Instances are not wanting of monks who to all appearance lived an austere life yet who, having learned no self-control, even in the loneliness of their cells, were guilty of abominations. The ideal, the spirit, is forgotten: the form is all.

Thus speaks the *Gita*:

'Worship of the higher powers, service to the teacher and to the wise, cleanliness, external and internal, straightforward-ness, continence, and care not to injure any being – these things are known as the austerity of the body.

'Speech which causes no vexation, and is true, and also agree-able and beneficial, and regular study of the Scriptures – these are said to constitute the austerity of speech.

'Serenity of mind, kindliness, silence, self-control, honesty of motive – this is called the austerity of the mind.'

In short: passionless peace can be had only by control of the passions and by devotion, in meditation, to God.

One point in this connection needs to be emphasized: we should never forget that the ideal of life is neither austerity nor renunciation, nor even meditation, but to know God, to be illumined within one's own soul. The means must never be confused with the end.

Question: Should not the life of a spiritual man be confined to communion with God and instruction of seekers, so that the most casual worldling can have no doubt of his sincerity? Should not his only comfort be unmistakably in one thing – exclusive communion with God?

Answer: Yes, truly, the life of such a man must be a continuous communion with God. He must live, move and have his being in Him. Without devotion, in meditation, to God, no illumination is possible. With closed eyes must he meditate, and with open eyes also he must commune with God. In work, in leisure, even while asleep, he must learn to live in God.

But, again, his communion with God must be such that not even his friend would know that he is communing with God – to say nothing of a casual worldling.

'And when thou prayest, thou shalt not be as the hypocrites are: for they love to pray standing in the synagogues and in the corners of the streets, that they may be seen of men. Verily I say unto you, they have their reward.

'But thou, when thou prayest, enter into thy closet, and when thou hast shut thy door, pray to thy father which is in secret.'

No, a spiritual soul never makes any demonstration either of his renunciation or of his communion with God. He even sometimes raises external barriers to shield himself from the eyes of the curious. He does not desire to attract the attention of the frivolous. In the long, long line of illumined souls and teachers, nowhere do we find any that were recognized as such by worldlings. Buddha was denounced as an atheist; Christ was crucified as an impostor; Ramakrishna was shunned as a madman.

21

GRACE AND
SELF-EFFORT

The most important thing necessary to a spiritual aspirant is
the longing for God and the desire to seek and find Him. There
are many religions in the world, innumerable sects with their
varied theories, beliefs and doctrines, but these are helpful to
us only in so far as they help to create in us the desire to
realize God and show us the means and ways to reach Him.
They are of no avail if we simply believe in them and give an
intellectual assent to their philosophical or theological doctrines. Creeds and theories and beliefs alone do not and cannot
transform the character; hence they cannot give us the stability
of inner peace.

Sri Ramakrishna tells the following parable: A pundit hired
a ferryboat to take him across the river. He was the only passenger, so he began to talk to the ferryman. 'Do you know the
Samkhya or Patanjali philosophy?' he asked the man. 'No, sir,
I don't,' he replied. 'Do you know Nyaya, Vaiseshika, or
Vedanta, or any of the systems of thought?' 'No, sir, I don't. I
am just a poor man who earns his living by ferrying this boat.
I know nothing of all these things of which you speak.' The
pundit felt sorry for the man's ignorance, and in a somewhat
superior manner he began to teach him some of the various
doctrines. He was very proud of his learning, and was glad
of the opportunity to air it. Suddenly, however, a storm arose,
and the small boat became unmanageable; the waters became
more and more turbulent, until finally the boatman asked his
passenger: 'Sir, can you swim?' 'No, I cannot,' the pundit said
in alarm. 'Well then, goodbye, sir! I am afraid your learning
and knowledge of the scriptures will avail you little now in
your hour of need if you cannot swim!'

In the same way, when we are battered by the storm and stress of life, our learning and knowledge of theoretical doctrines are of no avail if we have not fortified ourselves by learning how to swim across the ocean of worldliness and to enter the kingdom of heaven, the haven of peace where God dwells. According to the *Chandogya Upanishad*:

'The Self within the heart is like a boundary which divides the world from That. Day and night cross not that boundary, nor old age, nor death; neither grief nor pleasure, neither good nor evil deeds. All evil shuns That. For That is free from impurity: by impurity can it never be touched. Wherefore he who has crossed that boundary, and has realized the Self, if he is blind, ceases to be blind; if he is wounded, ceases to be wounded; if he is afflicted, ceases to be afflicted. When that boundary is crossed, night becomes day; for the world of Brahman is light itself.'

Therefore, the only struggle must be to reach the light, the world of *Brahman*. Our sufferings and tribulations are direct and immediate experience, and it is only the direct and immediate experience of the Kingdom of God that can overcome the tribulations of the world.

'Erudition, well-articulated speech, and wealth of words, and skill in expounding the scriptures – these things give pleasure to the learned, but they do not bring liberation,' says Shankara. 'A buried treasure is not uncovered by merely uttering the words "come forth". You must follow the right directions. You must dig and work hard to remove the stones and earth covering it, then only can you make it your own. In the same way, the pure truth of the Atman, buried under maya and the effects of maya, can be reached by meditation, contemplation and other spiritual disciplines such as a knower of Brahman may prescribe – but never by subtle arguments.'

Longing for God, longing for liberation from the tribulations of life, is the important thing for the spiritual aspirant. Of course, everyone wants to be free from suffering and misery; but, like some lower animals, our vision does not range beyond a few feet, so that we see only our immediate troubles and sufferings, and struggle to free ourselves from them only. Our vision is limited so that we do not try to get at the root, the source, of all our tribulations. The root cause of all suffering is ignorance, and to free ourselves completely from all suffering is knowledge – knowledge of God, the one Reality.

Sri Krishna says in the *Bhagavad-Gita*:

'Among those who are purified by their good deeds, there are four kinds of men who worship me: the world-weary, the seeker for knowledge, the seeker for happiness, and the man of spiritual discrimination. The man of discrimination is the highest of these. He devotes himself to me always, and to no other. For I am very dear to that man, and he is dear to me.'

It does not matter how the longing for God first arises, for Sri Krishna also says, 'Certainly all these are noble.' The important thing is that, with whatever motive you begin your spiritual life, or for whatever reason you seek God, if your only purpose and goal is God, if you devote yourself solely to God, you will find that all other thirsts and cravings leave you, and gradually, as your heart becomes purified, intense longing arises; that one desire, the desire for God, becomes the one paramount thing in your life. That is the one and perhaps the only condition needed to become a true spiritual aspirant.

Now the problem is: How is our longing satisfied? How do we find God?

Those who have realized Him declare in no uncertain terms that it is only by His grace that God becomes known. I have known a few such blessed souls, the illumined ones, and they all unequivocally have asserted that it is through His grace and His grace alone that they realized God. Christ also tells us: 'Ye have not chosen me but I have chosen you'; and the Upanishads say: 'Whom the Self chooses, by him is he attained.'

Yet again, these very great souls urge us to exert ourselves. They do not teach us to sit quietly and wait for grace. They insist that we ourselves strive strenuously to find God. Sri Krishna says, 'What is man's will, and how shall he use it? Let him put forth its power to uncover the Atman, not hide the Atman: man's will is the only friend of the Atman: his will is also the Atman's enemy.'

This seeming contradiction is resolved in one of the sayings of Sri Ramakrishna: 'The breeze of God's grace is always blowing; set your sails to catch this breeze.' This is further explained by the following saying: 'A man may have the grace of his guru, he may have the grace of God and his devotees, but if he has not the grace of his own mind the others avail him nothing.' The grace of your own mind is needed to set the sail to catch the breeze of grace. God is not partial; neither is His grace conditional. He is like the magnet which draws the needle: when the needle is covered with dirt, it does not feel the attraction of the magnet. But wash away the dirt, and at once the needle feels the drawing power and becomes united with the magnet. One of the names of God in Sanskrit is Hari, which means 'one who steals the heart'. God is the one attraction in the universe, but in our ignorance, and because of the impurities of our heart, we do not feel this attraction. Sri Ramakrishna used to say: 'Weep! Weep for the Lord and let your tears wash away the impurities in your heart.'

But again, this yearning of the heart for God, this longing for Him, does not come suddenly; that is why we need to practice spiritual disciplines and exert ourselves. Those who practice spiritual disciplines and regularly pray and meditate will come directly to the experience of divine grace. It is a psychological experience, almost exactly like the magnet drawing the needle. For example, you are trying to concentrate your mind on God with great regularity, yet the mind still remains restless. Through regular practice there grows yearning in your heart to see Him, yet still you seem to be striking your mind against a stone wall. You see nothing but darkness. Then suddenly from somewhere within, or from somewhere without – you are not sure whence – you feel another power drawing your mind inward, and you find yourself diving deeper and deeper within, in spite of yourself. You seem to be in another domain, the world of light, where no darkness enters. Following this, many spiritual visions come; ecstasies are experienced; you come face to face with God. But whenever these experiences come, whenever you are lifted up into this higher consciousness, it is your experience that it is God Himself who, by His grace, is lifting you up, attracting you unto Himself and giving you the ineffable joy and vision.

This, then, is a direct experience of God's grace, which

comes only when your heart has become purified through the practice of spiritual disciplines.

Vyasa, the commentator on *Yoga* aphorisms, compared the mind to a river flowing in opposite directions. One current of the mind flows toward the world, and the other flows toward God, toward the attainment of liberation from the bondages of the world. First there must arise a struggle in man's life, through the awakening of spiritual discrimination, to dam the flow of the downward current, the current that flows toward the world and worldly enjoyments. It is when one has been victorious in this struggle that he gets completely drawn into the Godward current, and experiences the grace of God. And when he at last realizes this grace, he enters forever into that kingdom which no storm or strife can ever reach.

PART IV

THE EXEMPLARS

22

BUDDHA AND BUDDHISM

In the *Bhagavad-Gita* we read:

> 'When goodness grows weak,
> When evil increases,
> I make myself a body.
> In every age I come back
> To deliver the holy,
> To destroy the sin of the sinner,
> To establish righteousness.'

As if to fulfil this promise of Sri Krishna, Buddha appeared. At the time of his birth, spiritual culture in India was at a low ebb. What was then universally recognized as religion consisted wholly in the observance of rituals and sacrifices, for the people had forgotten the simple fact that religion is primarily a matter of experience and realization. When the externals of religion usurp its inner truth, there ceases to be any struggle towards purification of the soul, or any positive effort to know the *Brahman* within. It was to the end of relighting the flame of religion in the hearts of individual men that Buddha dedicated his life. His protest against the hardening of the outer forms of religion at the expense of its inner light may be compared with the mission of Christ, who sought to purify and revivify the religion of the Jews.

How very much the spirit of religion was misinterpreted at the time of Buddha's ministry may be learned from his own words as recorded in one of the ancient Buddhistic scriptures, the *Tevigga Sutta*. In it we are told of a young man, Vasettha by name, who approached Buddha to learn of the path to union with *Brahman*. However, before the master was able to tell him of this path, he was obliged to remove his ignorance concerning the way of spirit:

'Then you say, too, Vasettha, that the *brahmins* bear anger and malice in their hearts, and are sinful and uncontrolled, whilst Brahman is free from anger and malice, and sinless, and has self-mastery. Now can there then be concord and likeness between the brahmins and Brahman?

'That these brahmins versed in the Vedas and yet bearing anger and malice in their hearts, sinful, and uncontrolled, should after death, when the body is dissolved become united to Brahman, who is free from anger and malice, sinless, and has self-mastery – such a condition of things has no existence.

'So then, Vasettha, the brahmins, versed though they be in the three Vedas, while they sit down [in confidence], are sinking down [in the mire]; and so sinking they arrive only at despair, thinking the while that they are crossing over into some happier land. Therefore is it that the threefold wisdom of the brahmins, wise in their three Vedas, is called a waterless desert, their threefold wisdom is called a pathless jungle, their threefold wisdom is called destruction!'

Thus did Buddha utter the truth to be found in the Upanishads – that *Brahman* is to be realized, not by much learning, but by purity of heart and rightness of conduct. It is easy to interpret him as denouncing the Vedic religion; whereas in fact he only brought to light the truth that religion does not lie in mastering the Vedas or other sacred books, but in realizing the spiritual life in one's own soul. This truth is made manifest in the Vedas themselves – that spiritual life cannot be attained by mere study of the Vedas but only by following their teachings; that is, by living righteously, and by becoming aware of the light within one's own heart. This the *brahmins* had forgotten, and Buddha came into the world to reveal once more the true spirit of the *sanatana dharma* – the Eternal Religion. Buddha taught no new religion; rather he restated and reinterpreted the ancient and genuine Vedic faith, infusing new spirit – the eternally new and eternally old spirit – into a religion that existed before man lived upon this earth, and will exist when man is forgotten.

Buddha and Buddhism

Prince Gautama, the name of Buddha before he attained his illumination, was born in 560 B.C. at Kapilavastu in northern India. At his birth, wise men prophesied that either he would become the greatest monarch on earth or, roused by the sorrows of mankind, would renounce the world and become a great religious leader. King Shuddhodana, his father, meditated within himself: 'Stung by the woes of men, he will renounce the world. My son shall never know the woes of men.' The king was determined that his son should be the greatest ruler in the world, and that there should exist no possibility of his becoming a religious mendicant.

So, legend says, the king built a palace, and laid out a garden opening on a park that stretched for many miles in every direction. There the young prince grew to manhood amid beautiful surroundings and in association with youthful, happy companions. He was bright and cheerful, clever at books and games, and always exhibited a loving disposition. From his earliest years he was kind and affectionate towards all living beings, including all dumb creatures. So true was this that even when he was a little boy his friends called him 'the compassionate one'.

When he had grown to be a young man, he married the beautiful Yasodhara. A son was born to him, whom he named Rahula. Prince Gautama was then about thirty years old.

One day he bade his charioteer drive him through the city that lay beyond the park surrounding the palace. He desired to view the city of Kapilavastu and know life as it was lived by the people. As he rode through the streets of the city, he saw many things, among them children playing and men and women carrying on their work. At all this he was pleased, and he cried to his charioteer, 'I see here labour, and poverty, and hunger; yet so much beauty, love, and joy are mingled with them — surely life, after all, is very sweet.'

No sooner had he uttered these words than there came into view the three woes of men — weariness, disease, and death. This was the turning point of his life.

First came weariness. Before him appeared an old, old man tottering on his crutches, which he held with trembling hands. The charioteer explained: 'All men are subject to old age, and old age, if it lasts long enough, will always end thus.'

Then a man drew near to him, ghastly to look upon, suffering from the deadly poison of leprosy. Prince Gautama ran straight to him, and embracing him cried, 'My brother!' Again did the charioteer explain what the prince saw. He said that the man was suffering from a disease and that, like him, every man is subject to disease in many forms. 'And this is the life,' mused Gautama, 'that I thought was so sweet!' For some time he was silent. Then he asked, 'How can one escape from life? What friend has he to release him?' 'Death,' replied the charioteer. 'Look! There come some bearers of the dead, carrying someone to the riverside to burn. But indeed,' continued the charioteer, 'men do not wish to die. Death, they think, is their worst enemy. Him they hate and try to escape, though there is no escape.'

'Take me home,' Prince Gautama now commanded his driver. He had been 'stung by the three woes of men'. Thenceforth, he sought a way to escape misery; not for himself only, but for humanity. His heart melted in sympathy and compassion for all beings.

The life he was living no longer offered him joy or sweetness. Restlessness came upon him. As he lay on his couch, he heard a voice calling to him, a cry of agony, as it were, from all humanity: 'Awake! Thou the awakened! Arise, and help the world! Sleep no more!' He knew he must seek a way of salvation.

Thereupon he arose and stole to the bedside of his sleeping wife and bade her goodbye by gently kissing her feet. For he knew that she would bear half the sacrifice he was about to make; that hers would be half the wisdom he sought, and half the glory. Thus Prince Gautama renounced the world, the world that was his – a kingdom, a beautiful wife, a loving son – in order to heed the call of suffering humanity.

For six or seven years he wandered through the land, spending his time in prayer and meditation. Though he visited many sages and masters, he never found a reply to his obstinate questioning. At last he seated himself under the now famous Bo-tree in Gaya, and firmly resolved to realize the truth, fell into deep meditation. After prolonged wrestling with his spirit, he discovered the true secret of life and death and the knowledge that can be found only within oneself. Thenceforth he became the Buddha – the 'Awakened One', the 'Blessed One'.

After Gautama had attained illumination, he went straight to Benares, for he was not content to gain eternal peace for himself alone. There, at Sarnath, he preached his first sermon. There also for the first time he called freedom and eternal peace *nirvana*, and the life of struggle in search of it the Way of Peace.

He did not forget Yasodhara, his beloved wife. In the palace she was living the life of a nun, struggling to share her husband's life. On one occasion, as Buddha, in company with his disciple Ananda, entered the palace to meet Yasodhara, Rahula approached his father and asked for his inheritance. Ananda, with the permission of Buddha, gave the boy the yellow cloth, the emblem of renunciation, and admitted him to the Way of Peace.

Then they saw the mother, behind her son, evidently longing to enter the Order. Thereupon Ananda asked, 'Master, may a woman not enter the Order? May she not be one of us?'

And Buddha replied: 'Do not the three woes come to women as well as to men? Why should their feet also not tread the Way of Peace? My Truth and my Order are for all. Yet this request, Ananda, was for you to make.'

For more than forty years the 'Awakened One' preached his truth. At the age of eighty he passed from the earth. After the death of Buddha, his disciples held their first council, at Rajagriha, near Magadha, and organized the remembered teachings of the master. These were transmitted orally until 80 B.C., when they were finally reduced to writing. The original Buddhistic teachings, preserved in three collections called the *Tripitaka* – literally, 'the three baskets' – form the Pali canon. The three collections are named, individually, the *Vinayapitaka*, which prescribes rules, in the greatest detail, for the conduct of the monks of the Order; the *Sutta* ('tales') containing conversations of Buddha which reveal practical methods of spiritual attainment; and the *Abhidhamma* ('doctrines') which deals with Buddha's psychology and ethics.

There exists an ancient charge that Buddha was an atheist, that he disbelieved in the soul and in God, that he denied the existence of anything abiding, permanent or unchangeable. This charge is without foundation. If it had foundation, the whole teaching of *nirvana* – the ideal of Buddhahood – would fall to pieces. Buddha expresses himself very clearly on this point in the *Udana* (viii, 3), where he says: 'There is an unborn, an unoriginated, an unmade, an uncompounded; were there not, O mendicants, there would be no escape from the world of the born, the originated, the made, and the compounded.'

But Buddha steadfastly refused to define the nature of this unchangeable, uncompounded Reality, and he emphatically declared it to be beyond the experience of our senses or our minds. Similarly, the Upanishads declare that *Brahman*, which is identical with the *Atman*, is 'beyond speech, and the mind comes away baffled, unable to reach him'. Sri Ramakrishna, to whom *turiya*, the transcendental consciousness, was as natural as is relative consciousness to us, remarked concerning this ultimate Reality:

'What Brahman is, none can define in words. Everything has been defiled, as it were, like the leavings of food. The Vedas, the Tantras, the Puranas, the systems of philosophy, all are defiled; they have been studied and they have been uttered by human tongues. But there is one truth, one substance, that has never been defiled, and that is Brahman. None has ever succeeded in describing Brahman in words.

'True it is that the Vedas and the other scriptures speak of him, but do you know what it is like? When a man returns from seeing the ocean and is asked to describe it, he exclaims in amazement, "Oh, what a vast expanse! How huge the waves are!" Like unto this is the talk of Brahman.

'When one attains samadhi, then alone comes the knowledge of Brahman. One realizes him. In that realization, all thoughts cease; one becomes perfectly silent. There is no power of speech left by which to express Brahman.'

So Buddha held his peace on this subject. He simply stated the fact that within the range of our normal experience there exist only compound and changeable objects – objects pertaining therefore only to the non-Self. To Buddha, as well as to the seers of the Upanishads, the mind or ego, is as clearly non-Self as is the body. This is the view, confirmed though it is by the entire Hindu religious tradition, that has been misinterpreted by Western scholars into a denial of the true Self, or God. The misinterpretation is highly significant. It indicates a fundamental divergence between Eastern and Western thought, for it is the tendency of the West to identify thought with being, a tendency that reaches as far back as Parmenides; whereas the East, as represented by both Buddha and the Upanishads, declares that the mind or the ego, that which thinks, is as much an object of cognition as the external objects of knowledge; hence, is not being, the knower, the Self.

One important difference, however, between the teachings of Buddha and those of the Upanishads lies in the distribution of emphasis. Buddha stresses the impermanence of the flux, the impermanence of everything within the limits of our sense experience. The Upanishads lay their chief emphasis upon the abiding; the permanent and unchangeable Reality behind the flux, beyond the limits of our sense experience.

Buddha did not deny this permanent Reality, but he did argue against the need to postulate a Reality while we dwell within the limitations of sense experience. Why? Because he felt that the element within man which is commonly known as the self, but which is really the ego dependent on the flux for its character and existence, would be mistaken for the true, unchangeable Self.

We read in one of the Buddhistic scriptures how, when a monk asked Buddha if there is a Self, the master maintained silence. Then, when his disciple Ananda asked why he maintained silence, he explained that if he had declared that there is a Self the monk might have regarded the impermanent element as permanent; and if he had replied in the negative, the monk might have thought that 'belief in annihilation' had been confirmed.

The Upanishads declare again and again that the true Self must not be identified with the body, the senses, or the cognitive mind. To think that they are the same is possible only through ignorance. And this identification, according to the same authority, gives rise to the concept of the individual soul, or *jiva*. Buddha, as a great psychologist, recognizes the falseness of assuming the compound and changeable elements of man to be the permanent Self. He first invokes the fact of ordinary experience, and then he points out that *nirvana* does exist – the way to peace and knowledge – beyond the range of this ordinary experience; that just as soon as the veil of our ignorance is removed, the truth is revealed.

There is no problem in Buddhism as to the relation of the soul to God. Buddha firmly holds to the reality of the final experience, the *turiya* of the Upanishads, and upon the reality of his own personal experience of *nirvana*. In these things he clearly finds a non-duality. What is there to relate to whom, when there is but One?

Buddha based his whole philosophy upon the universal experience from which no one escapes – that there is no unalloyed happiness in this world, that there is suffering. Buddha did not deny that there are joys to be experienced on this earth, but he pointed out that as long as a man takes delight in them, he also has to accept suffering. Pleasure and pain are like the two sides of the same coin. It is only when a man renounces sense pleasures, knowing them to be impermanent in their very nature, knowing that they will end in frustration and misery, that he gains the longing for liberation which will guide him along the road to *nirvana*.

This discrimination, which rejects the ephemeral in favour of eternal happiness, is the beginning of spiritual life. Religion is not an academic study; it is a life-giving truth which can make a mortal man divine and immortal. In order to understand the Buddha's teachings it must be borne in mind that to him religion meant realization. Like the Upanishadic seers he insisted that one should experience the truth for oneself. His attitude toward religion was entirely practical. If anyone came to him in order to satisfy idle curiosity about any problem of the soul and universe or to discuss theories of enlightenment, the inquirer went away disappointed. Buddha's famous answer to one such inquirer was that if a person has been wounded by a poisoned arrow, would he refuse to accept the help of a physician until he had found out the nature of the man who had shot the arrow, his caste, his stature, and his motive for the deed?

Buddha's doctrine concerning suffering has been called pessimistic. But it is no more pessimistic than the message of the other great religious leaders. Christ said: 'In the world ye shall have tribulation . . .' And 'For whosoever will save his life shall lose it . . .' The teachings of these great souls are not ones of despair. They tell us that eternal peace is experienced by those who will rise above the world of the senses. And we see that Buddha, having stated the fact that the world is full of misery, went on to point out the causes for this suffering and the way to overcome it.

He saw that men are ushered into this earthly existence; that they mature, decay, die, and are born again. And he saw that none knew the way of escape. As he meditated upon this hapless lot of human kind, he learned the root cause of suffering, decay and death; and discovered the means to find peace. We read in *Mahavagga*, an early Buddhistic scripture, as follows:

'Then the Blessed One, during the first watch of the night, fixed his mind upon the chain of causation, in direct and reverse order:

'From ignorance springs attachment to the impressions of deeds of the past lives; from this arises ego-sense or self-consciousness; from ego-sense springs the false identity with mind and body; from such identification spring the senses, the fields of contact; from the fields of contact arises sense-contact; from sense-contact arises feeling or sensation; from sensation springs thirst or desire; from desire comes attachment; from attachment spring the deeds which cause rebirth; from such deeds arises birth; from birth spring old age and death.'

In this 'wheel of existence', the first in the series is ignorance – the root cause of all suffering. This ignorance is universal, and how it came into the world is a mystery which neither Buddha nor any other seer or philosopher attempts to explain. For the nature of this ignorance is that it is neither real nor unreal; it is, and it is not. 'It is,' so long as we remain in ignorance; 'it is not' when we attain *nirvana* – illumination.

Buddha, like all other Indian seers and philosophers, accepts the law of *karma* and reincarnation. According to the Upanishads, *karma* attaches itself to one who, because of ignorance, identifies his true Self with the non-self. And, according to Buddha, we are tied by the chain of birth and death and bound to the 'wheel of existence' with its direct consequence of suffering, only so long as we attach ourselves to the flux of life and ignorantly consider our egos as permanent.

The doctrine of the 'wheel of existence' is known also as the 'doctrine of dependent origination', and leads us directly to a central doctrine of Buddhism – that to exist in ignorance is to suffer, and to cling to a false individuality – or, as we should term it, the ego – as something real and permanent, is the root of this ignorance. This doctrine has often been misunderstood by Western scholars. Schopenhauer, for instance, declared that the greatest sin of man is to have been born; that life itself is painful, and that the goal of living is the absence of pain. But Buddha declares that only life as we know it, and as we live it – in ignorance – is painful. Such a life is compared by Buddha to sleep, to forgetfulness; but once we awake from this sleep we attain *nirvana* in this very life.

The possibility of achieving spiritual rebirth is also central in the gospel of Christ:

'Except a man be born again, he cannot see the kingdom of God. Nicodemus saith unto him, How can a man be born when he is old? Can he enter the second time into his mother's womb, and be born? Jesus answered, Verily, verily, I say unto thee, except a man be born of water and of the spirit, he cannot enter into the kingdom of God. That which is born of the flesh is flesh; and that which is born of the Spirit is spirit' (John, iii, 3-6).

And is not this birth in the Spirit the same as awakening from the sleep of ignorance? That which distinguishes Buddha from Christ in this regard is that Buddha couched his doctrine in different terms, declaring that by the death of the ego, one attains *nirvana*. By *nirvana* is meant, not a denial of pain and suffering, but, in Buddha's own words, 'the highest wisdom, the full enlightenment and peace'.

The approaches to the attainment of Christian salvation and Buddhist *nirvana* are different. Christ said, 'Thy will be done.' And Dante reiterated the central Christian doctrine in these words: 'In His will is our peace.' Buddha, on the other hand, taught exercise of our higher will. He said: 'Self is the lord of self.' Christ taught us to efface our ordinary will and ego by submitting ourselves to the will of God. Buddha taught elimination of the false ego, which wills us to desire, through exercise of our will to restrain and control ourselves. As we gain control over our will to desire, the false self is eliminated and *nirvana* is attained. Whichever means may be adopted, the effect is the same – namely, death of the ego and birth in Spirit. Buddha and Christ established the same goal. Their paths only were different.

We read in the *Maha-parinibbana Sutta*, one of the earliest Buddhistic scriptures, these words:

'There the Blessed One addressed the brethren, and said: "It is through not understanding and grasping four truths, O brethren, that we have had to run so long, to wander so long in this weary path of transmigration – both you and I! And what are these four? The noble conduct of life, the noble earnestness in meditation, the noble kind of wisdom, and the noble salvation of freedom. But when noble conduct is realized and known, when noble meditation is realized and known, when noble wisdom is realized and known, when noble freedom is realized and known – then is the craving for existence rooted out, that which leads to renewed existence is destroyed, and there is no more birth." '

The goal is the noble way of freedom – *nirvana* – wherein there is no more birth, suffering, old age, or death. And *nirvana*, let us emphasize, may be attained in this very life. 'Be earnest in effort, and you too shall soon be free from the great evils . . .' This state of attainment, described in negative terms, is a state in which one is 'delivered from time'. It is paralleled by the 'eternal life' of Christian teachings. In general, there exists in the Western world the misconception that eternal life, or immortality, is a continuation of life in time. What, then, is the explanation of Christ's entreaty to his followers to come unto him that in him they might find eternal life? The very fact that a being exists implies a continuity of existence, though this existence may occur in different forms and under different conditions. Modern science has conclusively proved the impossibility of total annihilation. The repeated assurance of immortality by Christ as well as the other great spiritual teachers of the world, cannot, therefore, mean simply a continuity of life after death. Rather, and primarily, it is a life of realization and perfection while still living in this world. To one who achieves this realization, there can be no more birth nor death. The Upanishads regard the true Self as unborn and undying, the unchangeable Reality within us. As we realize that true Self, they say, we realize it as one with *Brahman*; then and then only, by rising above and beyond time, we attain to immortality. It is then that the experience of the Self as living in time, with a past, a present, and a future, passes away like a dream, and the Self is realized as immortal. So Buddha points to this same goal of immortality beyond time that is to be reached by realizing the 'unborn, undying, and changeless'.

The *nirvana* of Buddha is therefore not a state of annihilation, but the attainment of the unchangeable Reality, which can be positively described as eternal peace. But words fail at its description; definitions are only symbols and offer but vague suggestions of the truth. Buddha, instead, employs negative terms for its description – such as freedom from misery and death, freedom from 'sensuality, from the ego, from delusion, from ignorance'. This state of freedom is attainable by the 'noble kind of wisdom' – a phrase already quoted from the Buddhist scripture and signifying what Vedanta calls 'transcendental knowledge'. The wisdom meant is not a wisdom of the intellect, which implies a knower and an object of knowledge, but rather a state, *shunyata*, in which no subject-object relation exists, and in which one transcends both intellect and mind. These two words represent, in Hindu psychology, separate entities. Christ directly refers to this transcendental wisdom when he says, 'Ye shall know the truth and the truth shall make you free.' It is identical with perfection, the same perfection that Christ has in mind when he says, 'Be ye therefore perfect even as your Father which is in heaven is perfect.' It is, in brief, the direct, immediate knowledge of that which is timeless – the unconditional Being. The 'noble kind of wisdom' is attainable by 'noble conduct of life' and 'noble earnestness of meditation'.

This 'wisdom' exists in every being; covered, in the Vedantic phrase, by layers of ignorance, and according to Buddha, by *avijja*, ignorance. Remove this *avijja*, and wisdom shines, *nirvana* is attained. Christ would seem to have referred to the same truth when he said, 'The kingdom of heaven is at hand.' This wisdom, then, this kingdom of heaven, is for Christ, like the self-luminous sun, already 'at hand'; only, if we would find it, we must 'watch and pray'. And Christ's 'watch and pray' is Buddha's 'right conduct of life and meditation'.

Practising 'right conduct of life' is likened by Sri Ramakrishna to 'using soap to clean a dirty cloth' and the act of 'meditation' to 'washing the cloth clean'. 'Both are essential,' he says, 'and not until through these means the evils of ignorance and misconception are washed away can spiritual peace be attained.' Ethical conduct is the foundation of all spiritual life, but it does not represent the whole of religion. It has often been said that Buddha's teachings are merely ethical in their import. Similarly, Christianity has been mistakenly defined – by Matthew Arnold – as only morality touched by emotion. But real Christianity and real Buddhism reach far beyond such a tepid doctrine; for the peace of heaven and of *nirvana* transcends morality and emotion.

Moral conduct, in Buddha's view, has its genesis in psychology. Right conduct is called right because it is a prerequisite to knowledge of the secret of life, the road to illumination. Morality, as well as meditation, is only a means to *nirvana*. All conduct is moral which has that goal in view. As Swami Vivekananda has declared: 'That which leads to illumination is good; that which makes for greater ignorance and greater bondage is evil.'

In order to follow the paths of right conduct and right meditation, we must be earnest and intent upon exercising the will to action – meaning by 'action' the inner control of the mind, the highest form of activity. Mere acceptance of religious doctrine is not sufficient for salvation; it must be reinforced by strenuous spiritual strivings. He who merely acquiesces is compared by Buddha to a 'cowherd who is merely counting others' kine'. On one occasion Buddha begged a rich farmer for alms, but in return was reproached for being an idler. Buddha replied: 'Faith is the seed, penance the rain, understanding my yoke and plough, modesty the pole of the plough, mind the tie, thoughtfulness my ploughshare and goad, exertion my beast of burden. And the harvest of this husbandry is the attainment of immortality.'

To be engaged in husbandry of the spirit is to exert one's will. Moral laziness or failure to be diligent in self-control is the greatest sin or *pamada*. Its opposite is *appamada*. And, according to Buddha, 'not to be morally lazy, but to be strenuous in exerting one's will, is the greatest virtue'. The entire responsibility for either bondage or freedom is placed directly upon one's self. 'Therefore, O Ananda,' says Buddha, 'be ye lamps unto yourselves. Be ye a refuge to yourselves.'

Buddha thus lays extraordinary emphasis upon the psychological importance of the will. The will to satisfy thirst, for instance, which is formed by previous habits of indulgence, leads us to gratification of the senses; the flux within ourselves seeks to remain within the limitations of the flux of the objective world. But another will also exists, within our deepest selves; a higher will, which, though it may be very weak in most of us, seeks to cut loose to freedom from the limitations of the flux and to attain to the permanent, abiding Reality. This is the inner check, the will to attain the supreme goal.

Buddha indeed insists upon the continual strengthening of this higher will in order that we may rise above all the flux of life. He does not say, however, that the will is ultimate and permanent, as does Schopenhauer in his interpretation of Buddhistic philosophy. Will serves a temporary purpose for the spiritual aspirant; to the perfected man, it ceases to have value, and dissolves itself in the flux. For the will is as much a compound substance as any other object.

The teachings of Vedanta bring out this truth with great clearness by declaring that all scriptural instruction and all spiritual struggles are within the limitations of *maya*, or, as Buddha would have said, the flux. They are, however, a necessary part of our effort to attain ultimate liberation. The truth is, in reality, self-luminous; it is only through ignorance that it is ever veiled from the eyes of men. But the veil does exist. To remove it, instruction and struggles are needed. The will to control must be exercised. When it has done the work of removing ignorance, it becomes superfluous. Sri Ramakrishna was in the habit of illustrating this great truth by the simile of using one thorn to remove another thorn from the body.

When the task is done, both thorns may be thrown away. Similarly, we read in the *Gita*: 'When the whole country is flooded, the reservoir becomes superfluous. So, to the illumined seer, the Vedas are all superfluous.'

But so long as the spiritual aspirant is still struggling to attain illumination, the higher will is paramount. 'Let small and great exert themselves,' taught the great Buddhist emperor, Asoka. And this exertion must be directed towards right conduct (*sila*) and right contemplation (*samadhi*).

We read in the *Maha-parinibbana Sutta*:

'Great is the fruit, great the advantage of earnest contemplation, when set round with upright conduct. Great is the fruit, great the advantage of intellect, when set round with earnest contemplation. The mind set round with intelligence is freed from the great evils, that is to say, from sensuality, from egoism, from delusion, and from ignorance.

'Right conduct and right meditation have been further analysed and their parts set forth in what is known as the Eightfold Path, which is also referred to by Buddha as the Middle Path or the Golden Mean. It has been explained by Buddha in "The Foundations of the Kingdom of Righteousness" as follows:

'There are two extremes, O bhikkhus, which the man who has given up the world ought not to follow – the habitual practice, on the one hand, of those things whose attraction depends upon the passions, and especially of sensuality – a low and pagan way of seeking satisfaction, unworthy, unprofitable and fit only for the worldly-minded – and the habitual practice, on the other hand, of asceticism or self-mortification, which is painful, unworthy, and unprofitable. There is a middle path, O bhikkhus, avoiding these two extremes, discovered by the Tathagata – a path which opens the eyes and bestows understanding, which leads to peace of mind, to the higher wisdom, to full enlightenment, to nirvana.

'What is that middle path, O bhikkhus, avoiding these two extremes, discovered by the Tathagata – that path which opens the eyes and bestows understanding, which leads to peace of mind, to the higher wisdom, to full enlightenment, to nirvana? Verily, it is this noble eightfold path; that is to say: right views, right aspirations, right speech, right conduct, right livelihood, right effort, right mindfulness, and right contemplation.'

The first step in the path toward infinite peace is right views, or right faith. There is a saying in Sanskrit that a man is as his faith is, that our actions are guided by our faith. Right faith, according to Buddha, is the faith that *nirvana*, the eternal peace, can be attained in this life if we cease to cling to the false individual self. Wrong faith is faith that results in clinging to the non-self as Self, and must be replaced by right faith, or right views.

Right aspiration arises from right faith. It is the aspiration to renounce the false self, to shun all selfishness, and 'to live in love and harmony with all'. Buddha's own aspiration was not merely to attain *nirvana* for himself, but to show the way to it to all mankind. Such also was to be the aspiration of his followers: to live for their fellow men, renouncing all regard for self.

But to aspire is not enough. We must act to fulfil our aspiration, and our actions must necessarily find expression through our speech, our conduct, and our daily work. Right speech, right conduct, and right work are, in effect, the practice of such virtues as truthfulness, non-injury, non-covetousness, and chastity. In the words of the *Tevigga Sutta*:

'Putting away the murder of that which lives, (the aspirant) abstains from destroying life. He is compassionate and kind to all creatures that have life.

'Putting away the theft of that which is not his, he abstains from taking anything not given. He takes only what is given; therewith is he content, and he passes his life in honesty and in purity of heart.

'Putting away unchastity, he lives a life of chastity and purity, averse to the low habits of sexual intercourse.

'Putting away lying, he abstains from speaking falsehood. He speaks truth, from the truth he never swerves; faithful and trustworthy, he injures not his fellow men by deceit.

'Putting away slander, he abstains from calumny. What he hears here he repeats not elsewhere to raise a quarrel against the people here; what he hears elsewhere he repeats not here to raise a quarrel against the people there. Thus he lives as a binder together of those who are divided, an encourager of those who are friends, a peacemaker, a lover of peace, impassioned for peace, a speaker of words that make for peace.

'Putting away bitterness of speech, he abstains from harsh language. Whatever word is humane, pleasant to the ear, lovely, reaching to the heart, urbane, pleasing to the people, beloved of the people – such are the words he speaks.

'Putting away foolish talk, he abstains from vain conversation. In season he speaks; he speaks that which is, he speaks fact, he speaks, and at the right time, that which redounds to profit, is well grounded, is well defined, and is full of wisdom.'

The practice of these virtues involves a double process, one step of which we may term negative and the other positive: first a vice must be abstained from, and then the opposite virtue must be acquired.

Right livelihood means earning one's living by acceptable means. Such means do not include the occupations, for example, of slave dealer, butcher, publican, or trafficker in poisons.

After proper external conduct, inner purification must be achieved. So right effort is practice with the purpose of controlling the mind, not allowing it to remain a slave to the passions of lust, anger, greed, envy, and pride, and freeing it from the two extremes of self-indulgence and self-mortification.

This practice of right effort, or self-control, is not possible without right mindfulness and right meditation. It is possible to refrain from passion and the life of the senses only when the mind is engaged in something higher or greater.

Right mindfulness is thinking thoughts concerning the evil effects of clinging to the objects within the flux.

The last stage, right meditation, is keeping the mind occupied in spiritual contemplation, in order ultimately to free it from all thought, and, transcending all thought, to attain *nirvana*.

Right faith, right aspiration, right speech, right conduct, right livelihood, right effort, right mindfulness, and right meditation – these form the Eightfold Path of Buddhism, and lead one to the highest goal – nirvana – supreme enlightenment and peace.

Before we discuss the development of Buddhism after the death of its founder, we shall do well to point out once more its relation to the Vedic religion. Swami Vivekananda has expressed this relationship in the following words:

'The relation between Hinduism (by Hinduism, I mean the religion of the Vedas) and what is called Buddhism at the present day is nearly the same as between Judaism and Christianity. Jesus Christ was a Jew, and Shakya Muni was a Hindu. The Jews rejected Jesus Christ, nay crucified him, and the Hindus have accepted Shakya Muni as God and worship him. But the real difference that we Hindus want to show between modern Buddhism and what we should understand as the teachings of Lord Buddha, lies principally in this: Shakya Muni came to preach nothing new. He also, like Jesus, came to fulfil and not to destroy. Only, in the case of Jesus, it was the old people, the Jews, who did not understand him, while in the case of Buddha, it was his own followers who did not realize the import of his teachings. As the Jews did not understand the fulfilment of the Old Testament, so the Buddhists did not understand the fulfilment of the truths of the Hindu religion. Again, I repeat, Shakya Muni came not to destroy, but he was the fulfilment, the logical conclusion, the logical development of the religion of the Hindus.'

In just the same way that Christ abhorred crystallized Jewish dogma and Jewish ritual, Buddha abhorred all ceremonials and the ritualistic portion of the Vedas. Even this was nothing new. The Upanishads, which comprise the later Vedas, insisted that true religion consists not in rites and ceremonies but in realization of the Self; so also did the *Bhagavad-Gita*. Once more was the spirit of religion brought to the fore when Buddha preached his gospel of renewed spiritual life. Nowhere does he actually contradict the teachings of the Upanishads. He does emphasize, however, two elements – *Brahman* as Being (opposed to Becoming) and monastic discipline. The Hindus therefore readily accepted

Buddha as one within their own fold. Later Buddhist followers, however, falsely judged the opposition of Buddha to the ceremonial portions of the Vedas – the Brahmanas – to be his general attitude towards the Vedic faith, and cut themselves off from the main body of the mother religion. For a few centuries Buddhism flourished in India, then died a natural death; though Buddha himself survives as a living, spiritual force. Truly has it been said by Dr Radhakrishnan in his *Indian Philosophy* :

'Buddha today lives in the lives of those Indians who have not given up their past traditions. His presence is felt in all around. Throughout worshipped as a god, he has a place in the mythology which is still alive, and so long as the old faith remains without crumbling down before the corrosive influence of a new spirit, Buddha will have a place among the gods of India. His life and teaching will compel the reverence of mankind, give ease to many troubled minds, gladden many simple hearts, and answer to many innocent prayers.'

After the passing of Buddha, his disciples, who came to be known as the Elders, met together at Rajagriha to compile the three Pitakas, the original teachings of Buddha. About a hundred years later a second council met at Vaisali, where a schism occurred among the delegates. One group, which we might call the 'progressive party', desired some relaxation in the rigorousness of the monastic vows; but the orthodox group clung to the laws and regulations laid down by the Elders, and won the debate. The progressives, however, earned a large following and proceeded to hold a council of their own, which they called the Great Council, and broke with the main body of Buddhists. According to Dr Radhakrishnan, this schism was an early effect of that movement which was to find its full expression in Mahayana Buddhism, which emerged in the first century A.D.

About three centuries after the death of its founder, Buddhism, which had been only a sect within the fold of Hinduism, began to assume a wider aspect after the conversion of the great Indian emperor Asoka (274-232 B.C.). Asoka became actively engaged in spreading his adopted religion through his country and actually succeeded in extending it throughout many other parts of the world. His own transformation from an ambitious and cruel tyrant into a loving, kind, and compassionate ruler provided a great example. He dispatched missionaries to Syria, Egypt, Macedonia, and Epirus, and converted the rulers of these countries to the new religion. Within India itself, Buddhism became, more than ever before, a part of the life of the people. It inspired, for example, the splendid Mauryan stone sculpture, distinguished by its expressive symbolism and technical excellence. In temples and with statues the story of the Buddha was repeated, and these monuments still bear witness to one of the happiest periods in the history of India. Thus, in the third century before Christ, Buddhism reached its greatest power and made its influence mostly widely felt.

Asoka particularly stressed the ethical teachings of the Master – self-control and loving service to all living beings. These he popularized throughout the vast empire of India by engraving them on stone pillars and exemplifying them by his own conduct.

Hinduism, however, did not die out. Asoka, though a Buddhist ruler, showed the same spirit of toleration and the same sympathy toward Hinduism that the Hindus had shown toward Buddhism. Hinduism regained its vigour during the rule of the Guptas, who came into power in the first century A.D.

Coinciding with this revival of Hinduism were the decline of early Buddhism and the rise of Mahayana. Elements of the Mahayana, or the Great Way, had been present in Buddhistic thought and practice almost from the beginning; in fact, had co-existed with original Buddhism, or Hinayana (the 'Narrow Way', as it came to be called) until this time; but now Mahayana achieved a definitive form. It engendered an extensive literature of its own in Sanskrit – not in Pali, the language of the canon of the Elders. Generally speaking, the tendency of the Mahayana was to popularize the original teachings of the Buddha, giving a mystical and devotional turn to his doctrine. Thus it preached that higher than Arhathood (or personal sanctity, which was the ideal of the Hinayana), was Buddhahood, the state of supreme perfection which Gautama reached, a state which was accessible to all. Instead of the asceticism and monastic seclusion of the Hinayana, it visualized the attainment of perfection in the midst of the tumult of the world. Instead of the unaided spiritual effort of the Hinayana, it urged dependence on and worship of Buddha as an incarnation of God. Furthermore, it was responsible for the exalted conception of the *Bodhisattva*, the compassionate being, who vows from the beginning of his spiritual life to postpone his own salvation until all have attained that cherished goal. This was a marked contrast to the objective of exclusive, personal salvation which is generally attributed to the Hinayanists.

As we have noted, the Hinayana, under Asoka's patronage, spread far beyond the boundaries of India, and it remains to this day a dominant religious and cultural influence in countries to the south and east, such as Ceylon, Burma, and Siam. The Mahayana spread to the north, where it still flourishes in Tibet, Mongolia, China, Korea, and Japan. In Tibet alone, a mysterious land long closed to travellers from the outside world, it has not only been made into a national religion but has become the ruling power of the state. (Since its occupation of Tibet, Communist China has succeeded in destroying very nearly the last remnant of Buddhism.) The lamas, many of them holy men, are the priests of a theistic religion, for whose God, Buddha, temples have been built and an elaborate ritual created. In China, Mahayana has exerted a profound influence. There also Buddha has been worshipped, and other Buddhas and *Bodhisattvas* – or heavenly helpers of the aspirant – have found favour. In the year A.D. 648 there were approximately 4,000 Buddhist monasteries in the country. Zen Buddhism, a peculiar blending of Mahayana Buddhism with the native Taoism, by enhancing the tendency to meditation spread throughout China, and was carried to Japan, where it established itself as one of the chief religions of the land. In both China and Japan, Buddhism was the inspiration of their greatest artistic creations.

23

WHAT CHRIST MEANS TO ME

In the Vedas, the earliest scriptures of India, we find this statement: 'Truth is one, though sages call it by various names.'
Later in the *Bhagavatam*, we come across a similar statement:
'As different streams coming from various sources ultimately
flow into one ocean, so do the many religions of the world,
emerging from innumerable sources, at long last mingle in the
great ocean of love.' In this present age, we have again been
taught: As many religions, so many paths – all reach one and
the same goal. Thus, from the earliest Vedic times up to our
modern age this ideal of harmony and universality has been
taught to every Hindu.

A Hindu learns to respect every faith and every prophet; but
it is impossible for him to understand any religion that claims
to be unique. This does not mean that Hindus are actively
interested in other religions. Rather, it means that they respect
them. They respect the beliefs of others and accept their saints
and prophets, though they may not obey their dogmas. For in
India, each individual has, as it were, his own path to follow.
Strange as it may seem to an Occidental, parents and children
may live together collectively, yet individually worship God
in different ways. The husband may be ignorant of how the
wife worships, and the wife totally unaware of her husband's
beliefs. Every member of the family is given a freedom to
approach God in a manner which each finds most suitable to
his or her temperament or inclination. It is this sort of freedom
that has inspired the Hindu's respect for Christ. Now let me
tell you how I personally became attracted to Christ and
Christianity and the teachings of the Bible.

When I was sixteen years old, I left the small town where I
had lived and gone to school, and went to nearby Calcutta
to enter the university. At that time, I received a present from

the YMCA – a New Testament. I tried to read it, but, having the impatience of a typical teenager, I never seemed able to get beyond the 'begats!' So I did not look at the Bible again for a long time. Then, several years later, when I joined the Ramakrishna Order, I had an interesting experience. A few days after my admission we held a Christmas celebration at our monastery. Christmas is celebrated at all the monasteries of the Order (though not in Hindu homes). In one of the large halls the monks had built an altar, upon which was a picture of the Madonna and Child. Seated near the altar were many of the direct disciples of Sri Ramakrishna. Imagine, if you will, the physical presence of Peter, James, John, Matthew, and so on. This is how we felt, as though the counterparts of Christ's disciples were present before us.

A disciple of Swami Vivekananda, who had dressed himself up as a Christian padre, performed the worship. He offered candles, flowers, and, strange as it may seem, a fruitcake – the kind you buy in a Western market. It was unusual because I don't believe fruitcake existed when Christ was alive! Also we offered a cigar to him. You see, this again was our idea how Westerners worship Christ. As the worship proceeded, all of us remained silent. Then my master, Swami Brahmananda, told us: 'Meditate on the Christ within and feel his living presence.' We all felt – suddenly – that a spiritual atmosphere had been created.

Later, after the worship, my master made us all laugh with his jesting and playful humour. This is one of the characteristics, I am told, he shared with Sri Ramakrishna – this ability to make others literally roll on the ground with laughter. Yes, he would make such witty remarks, and then the next moment create an atmosphere of serenity and holiness. It was in that atmosphere that everyone of us felt that Christ was as much our own as Krishna or Ramakrishna.

There is also another reason why Christ is offered worship at our monasteries. As you may know, Sri Ramakrishna was interested in every religion, *actively* interested; for he followed their particular paths to discover the truth of them. And he found that all of them, like streams, mingled in the great ocean of love. A disciple of his would occasionally read the Bible to him, and then explain it in Bengali. In this way

Ramakrishna came to know something of Christianity. One day, while visiting a devotee, he chanced to see a picture of the Madonna and Child. As he was looking at the picture, it suddenly became living to him. His heart was filled with love for Christ. For a period of three days and three nights he stayed in his room, filled with the presence of Jesus. He even refused to go to the Hindu temple or worship any of the Hindu gods or goddesses. And anxious to know how the followers of Christ worshipped their Lord, he saw in a vision devotees kneeling before Jesus and praying to him. On the third day, as he was seated outside his room, Ramakrishna noticed a luminous figure approaching him. At once he knew that this was Christ the Saviour. The figure approached and embraced him and entered into his body. And so Ramakrishna came to understand that Jesus was an avatar, a divine incarnation.

Christ has another significance for the Ramakrishna Order. After Ramakrishna passed away in 1886, his disciples took their final vows of *sannyasa* on Christmas Eve. So you can understand why Christmas Eve is particularly sacred to us, for the disciples of Sri Ramakrishna were formally ordained as monks on that day. But now let me try to explain the significance of Christ and his teachings.

It is not possible to have an intellectual understanding of anything unless we relate it back to some other thing. In other words, it is impossible to understand a religion or a prophet of a religion without comparing them to some other teaching or teacher. If something is unique or has no parallel in history, it cannot be understood on an intellectual level. Therefore, I must try to explain Jesus in relation to other great teachers.

Anyone who has sincerely made a comparative study of the world's great teachers will find that they speak the same truth, though they may not express themselves alike. In this country it is a bit different. Here religions are often studied with the idea that, 'Well, my religion is best, but let us see what the others have to say.' This is not the way to examine comparative religion. First of all we must go to the source. For instance, if I were to consider Christianity on the evidence presented to me by the theologians, I think I might be quite confused! We must consult the scriptures to appreciate and understand any religion. Read the 'Sermon on the Mount' or the *Bhagavad-*

Gita or the teachings of Buddha, not the interpretations of a Buddhist monk or Hindu priest. If you go to the source, you will find that the same truth lies beneath all religions.

Who was Christ? The Gospel according to St John gives us some indication of his role as an avatar. It begins: 'In the beginning was the word and the word was with God and the word was God. . . . And the word became flesh and dwelt among us and we beheld his glory, the glory of the only begotten of the Father, full of grace and truth.' Without involving ourselves in a lengthy discussion of *Logos* – the Word – we should mention that there is a parallelism in the Vedic scriptures. As you know, it is the *Logos* that is considered the only begotten of God, and it is the *Logos* which is at one with God and became flesh in Jesus. Now in the Vedas, we find this statement: 'In the beginning was God; with him was the Word, and this word is Brahman.' Of course, I am not of the opinion that John translated from the Vedas! But it indicates the universality of truth. This truth is in the very atmosphere; it exists eternally, in every human heart. It only waits to be unfolded. For instance, let us consider the discovery of a scientific truth. How did Isaac Newton arrive at his theory of gravity? He saw an apple fall to the ground. This thought came to him: 'I am seeing a law of nature in operation.' He realized its existence. It is the same way with spiritual truths; they too exist as eternal verities of life. When we read the 'Sermon on the Mount' or the *Bhagavad-Gita* are we not simply seeing the same truth dressed in different ways?

How often we find a truth directly before us, yet even then refuse to accept it. Such has been the case with the greatest of men. Sri Ramakrishna, for instance, was regarded while living as an avatar by many of his disciples and devotees, but Swami Vivekananda steadfastly refused to accept this. He refused to accept the concept of divine incarnation. Of course, he accepted the presence of God in all men (and in that sense we are all incarnations of God), but he did not believe in any special manifestation of God in man.

When Sri Ramakrishna lay on his death-bed, Vivekananda was seated next to him. He knew that his teacher would not last much longer. 'If now you say you are God incarnate,' Vivekananda thought to himself, 'I'll believe you.'

Suddenly Ramakrishna looked at him and spoke in a clear voice, 'I see you still do not believe. He who was Rama and he who was Krishna is born again as Ramakrishna – but not in your Vedantic sense.' By the phrase 'not in your Vedantic sense' he meant not in the sense that the *Atman* or Self of all men is identical with *Brahman* or the all-pervading God. What he conveyed to his disciple was that he was God himself, descended as man.

What is so special, so extraordinary about a divine incarnation? About his own birth, Jesus said: 'Ye are from beneath, I am from above. Ye are of this world, I am not of this world.' This Jesus told his disciples, and it is a peculiar feature of incarnations to reveal their unique status first to their intimate disciples.

Sri Krishna, speaking in the *Bhagavad-Gita*, replies to his disciple Arjuna: 'I am the birthless, the deathless, Lord of all that breathes. I seem to be born: but it is only seeming, only my *maya*. I am still master of my *maya*, the power that makes me.' This statement of Krishna's adds support to Christ's declaration: 'I am not of this world.' We must understand that man is born in ignorance, as a result of his past *karmas*. We are bound to the world by these *karmas;* indeed, we are of this world. But God comes through his own choice. He chooses to be born within *maya*, the world of relativity. However, he is master of this *maya*, and we are slaves to it. That is the difference.

Why does he come? Because of his grace and in the cause of truth. We also read in the *Gita* why God comes down as man: 'When goodness grows weak, when evil increases, I make myself a body. In every age I come back to deliver the holy, to destroy the sin of the sinner and to establish righteousness.'

A study of world history reveals a most interesting fact— that every culture develops and degenerates in accordance with laws of cyclic change. Like ocean waves, the cultures of the world rise and fall. Once so grand, where is the Roman Empire today? And the British Empire? Religion, as well, is subject to these same oscillating patterns. Great religious movements spring up and inspire millions; saints are born and carry the banner of truth. Then all becomes forgotten. Certainly we still have the Bible, the scriptures; and we still know the names of Jesus and Buddha. Yet where are the exemplars, the saints? Sadducees and Pharisees abound who can quote the scriptures to us; but how many are there who can live them?

It is during such a time that an avatar is born. And how beautifully is expressed in the *Gita* that by worshipping the avatar, truth is easily reached. Arjuna asks Sri Krishna: 'Some worship you with steadfast love, others worship God the un-manifest and changeless. What kind of devotee has the greater understanding of yoga?'

Krishna answers, 'Those whose minds are fixed on me in steadfast love, worshipping me with absolute faith, I consider them to have the greater understanding of yoga.

'As for those others, the devotees of God the unmanifest, indefinable and changeless, they worship that which is omni-present, constant, eternal, beyond thought's compass, never to be moved. They hold all the senses in check. They are tranquil-minded, and devoted to the welfare of humanity. They see the Atman in every creature. They also will certainly come to me.

'But the devotees of the unmanifest have a harder task, because the unmanifest is very difficult for embodied souls to realize.'

How have the other avatars expressed their love for man and their assurance that they are the way and the truth? Christ said: 'I am the light of the world. He that followeth me shall not walk in darkness, but shall have the light of life.' And again, 'Come unto me all ye that labour and are heavy laden and I shall give you rest.'

Sri Krishna promised: 'He who knows the nature of my task and my holy birth is not reborn when he leaves the body. He comes to me. Flying from fear, from lust and anger, he hides in me, his refuge and his safety. Burnt clean in the blaze of my being, in me many find rest.' And again, 'Lay down all duties in me, your refuge. Fear no longer. I will save you from sin and bondage.'

From Sri Ramakrishna we hear: 'Take refuge in me. I am the sanctuary.'

As we read these passages, it appears as though one is quot-ing the truth of the other, so close are they in spirit. But is there any reason why we should doubt this? For is it not the same God, the same spirit speaking, only appearing in different forms and in different ages to suit the needs of the times?

Let us now try to understand what Krishna meant when he said, 'Come unto me . . .' or Ramakrishna's statement, 'Take refuge in me.' First, we must understand that the essence of the religious struggle is to be absorbed in the consciousness of God. When Christ wants us to 'abide in me, and I in you', he is asking us to feel that constant presence of God, through constant recollectedness. Sri Krishna also says:

'Be absorbed in me
Lodge your mind in me.
Thus you shall dwell in me.
Do not doubt it,
Here and hereafter.'

But absorption in God is only possible when we have that complete and total love for him. In this same connection, let me quote a Christian mystic, Angelus Silesius: 'Christ may be born a thousand times at Bethlehem, but if he is not born anew within your own heart you will remain eternally forlorn.' That is what it means, expressed in a negative way, to take refuge in Christ or Krishna or Ramakrishna – to see him in the shrine of your own heart. You must talk with him. You must be completely united with him. For he is your *Atman*, the Self within.

Once a disciple of Sri Ramakrishna, Swami Turiyananda, was approached by a lady in this country, who told him: 'Swami, I wish I could read your thoughts.'

The Swami smiled and said, 'Well, on the surface you will find many of them; but go deeper and there is nothing but Ramakrishna.' In other words, our entire lives must be moulded into His life, the life of Christ, Krishna, or Ramakrishna.

Sri Ramakrishna used to say there are three classes of devotees. The lowest class conceives of God in heaven; the second class of devotee sees God within; and the highest class sees God both within himself and outside himself. He sees nothing *but* God. My master, Swami Brahmananda, taught me this truth: that as long as you think the Lord is somewhere outside of yourself, you will be restless. 'But when you feel he is here, he added, pointing to his own heart, 'then only will you find God everywhere.'

As we pray, as we meditate, as we learn to live our lives in God, sweetness will come to us. My master would often say that if you take only one step toward God he will come a hundred steps toward you. Only a little struggle, a little striving – strengthened by his grace – will lead you to the realization that, truly, He *is*. The Upanishads tell us that first one must realize his presence within. Then when you go to pray or to meditate you feel his presence, very near to you, nearer than your hands or your feet; for he is the mind of the mind, the eye of the eye, and the ear of the ear. You feel that – tangibly. And then he becomes manifest, and it is then you give your whole heart to him, and you know him to be pure consciousness itself and infinite love.

That eternal Christ is not to be found in churches, nor in temples; not in books, nor in scriptures – but within your own heart. Find him there.

24

VIVEKANANDA AND HIS MESSAGE

Before we can understand the message of Swami Vivekananda
– or of any other great spiritual leader or prophet – we must
understand the true spirit of religion. And by religion I do not
mean any particular faith, such as Hinduism, or Christianity,
or Mohammedanism, or Buddhism, but what in India we call
Sanatana dharma – the eternal religion. In this eternal religion there is no dogma, no creed, no doctrine, no theology.
Three truths are preserved at the core of the eternal religion,
and these may be very simply expressed.

The first of these truths states that *God is*. This proposition
has been proclaimed by God-men in every age, and in every
age people have asked for proofs that it is true. Many plausible
arguments have been devised by philosophers and theologians
to establish the existence of God. But every single argument
substantiating his actuality on the basis of logic and reason may
be contradicted by equally plausible arguments of opposing
philosophers. All attempts to prove the existence of God
through logic and reason are essentially futile. What, after all,
can the philosophers and theologians establish? Only their particular *idea* of an absolute Reality, not the Reality itself. And
what guarantee is there that their idea of God and the reality of
God are one and the same?

The only proof of the existence of God is to be found in the
second proposition: *God can be realized*. You can know him,
you can see him, you can talk to him, and you can experience
your oneness with him – in the transcendental state of consciousness.

And the third proposition is that *God-realization is the
supreme goal of human existence*. We ask ourselves, 'Why am

I here? What am I to achieve?' The answer to these questions is to find the abiding Reality in the midst of the transitoriness of life. Everything is ephemeral, everything passes away; everything – except the truth of God, which is eternal.

When we come to the conclusion that these three propositions are true, then we begin to understand that every being in the universe is divine. Divinity is our birthright. In the words of Vivekananda: 'Each soul is potentially divine. The goal is to manifest this divinity within . . .' Behind the sinner's sins, behind the saint's saintliness, behind all activities and desires in this world is that one goal – though it may be an unconscious one – to unfold the indwelling Godhead. Every human being wants to rid himself of his bondages and frailties and overcome death. And after experiencing pleasure and pain, good and evil in many lives, a man finally learns that abiding peace and freedom can be found only in God-realization. And who realizes the eternal truth of God? He who consciously directs his mind and life toward this attainment.

Once we understand this message of *Sanatana dharma*, we can understand any great prophet or divine incarnation. And we can test whether a spiritual teacher is genuine or not. The criterion is: Does he give the message of eternal religion? Does he teach that God is, that he can be known, and that the purpose of life is to know him?

If a man becomes convinced that he should devote himself to the attainment of God-realization, naturally he will ask: 'Are there any exemplars of divine knowledge in this present age who can say: "I have known the truth of God. I have reached immortal life. I have overcome the fear of death"?'

This question arose in the heart of young Naren, the future Swami Vivekananda. Naren was born with the ability to discriminate between the eternal and the non-eternal. Sense pleasures and enjoyments did not attract him. He knew them to be ephemeral. Philosophy and books failed to satisfy him. He wanted to find the abiding Reality behind the fleeting things of life. He wanted to meet a man of enlightenment, a living example of religious truth. And so he went to various priests and preachers, asking each one, 'Sir, have you seen God?' Not one of them could answer that he had.

At last Naren went to Sri Ramakrishna, who was serving as

priest in the Kali temple at Dakshineswar. This meeting between Naren and Sri Ramakrishna has a great significance. The Master was living in the Dakshineswar temple garden – isolated – far away from the noise of the world. He barely knew how to read and write. He had no idea of Western culture, education or politics. Naren, on the other hand, was steeped in Western science and philosophy. And he approached religion with a Western viewpoint – at once rational and sceptical. As he had asked the others, so he asked Sri Ramakrishna: 'Have you seen God, sir?' And the answer was: 'Yes, I have seen him, just as I see you here – only much more intensely.'

From the very first, Sri Ramakrishna behaved with Naren as if he had always known him. He said: 'You have come so late! Why did you keep me waiting so long?' Then, with folded hands, the Master addressed the young man: 'You are the ancient sage Nara, a part of Narayana (the Lord), born on earth to remove the sufferings of mankind.'

Naren thought to himself, 'Who is this man to whom I have come? He must be mad!' Yet the Master's behaviour with others seemed perfectly normal, and Naren could not help being impressed by his evident renunciation and saintliness.

After returning to Calcutta, Naren could not get Sri Ramakrishna out of his mind. He began to visit the Master often, feeling the attraction of his magnetic personality. Sri Ramakrishna, on his part, recognized Naren as his apostle at their first meeting. Furthermore, he knew his future disciple to be a *nityamukta*, an ever-free soul. An associate of God, the *nityamukta* incarnates on earth for the good of mankind. Sri Ramakrishna regarded six of his disciples as belonging to this category of perfect souls; and among these was Naren.

The Master was very careful to train each of his disciples according to his own particular temperament and capacity. He considered Naren ready to follow the path of Advaita Vedanta, or non-dualism, from the very beginning. In this path, the aspirant rejects all transitory phenomena, asserting that *Brahman* – the impersonal Existence behind name and form – alone is real.

In this connection, the following reminiscences, which I heard directly from Swami Turiyananda, may be of interest.

This brother monk of Swamiji (Vivekananda's familiar name in later years) told me: 'At one time I was very interested in Advaita Vedanta. I spent much time reading Shankara and studying the scriptures, and therefore did not visit Sri Ramakrishna often. Later, one day, the Master said to me: "Why did you not come to see me?" I explained to him that I had been studying Advaita Vedanta. So he asked me: "Well, what is the truth of Vedanta? Isn't it that Brahman alone is real and that the world is unreal?" The Master added: "You may say that the world is unreal, but if you put your hand on a thorn, the thorn will prick your hand. But there is one – Naren. If he says there is no thorn, there will be no thorn." '

Then Swami Turiyananda told a story which proved how rightly Sri Ramakrishna had estimated Vivekananda's capacity to follow the path of non-dualism. Turiyananda said that years later, while Swamiji was in America, some Texas cowboys heard him speak on Vedanta. They decided to test his assertion that a knower of *Brahman* is unperturbed in any situation. They asked Swamiji to lecture out-of-doors, standing on a wooden platform. While he was speaking, they suddenly began to fire shots on either side of him. But Swamiji continued his lecture unshaken, saying: 'I am divine; you are divine.' When he had finished, the cowboys, won over by his fearlessness, lifted him on their shoulders, exclaiming: 'This is our man!'

When Naren first came to Sri Ramakrishna, he was imbued with the religious ideal of the Brahmo Samaj, a theistic movement whose members worshipped God as a Personal Being with attributes, but formless. Naren, in those days, therefore thought it blasphemy to say 'I am *Brahman*'. When Sri Ramakrishna wanted him to read the *Ashtavakra Samhita*, a treatise on extreme non-dualism, Naren objected that the ideas expressed in the book were atheistic and sinful. The Master smiled and said: 'Just read a little to me. You won't have to think that you are Brahman.'

One day at Dakshineswar, Naren and a friend were smoking and making fun of Advaita Vedanta. Naren said: 'How can it be that this jug is Brahman, this cup is Brahman, and we too are Brahman? Nothing could be more absurd!' Hearing them laugh, Sri Ramakrishna came out of his room and asked: 'What are you talking about?' Then he gave Naren a touch.

As a result, Naren had an experience which he later described as follows:

'That magic touch of the Master that day immediately brought a complete revolution over my mind. I was amazed to find that there really was nothing in the universe but Brahman.... For the whole day I lived in that consciousness. I returned home, but there too everything I saw appeared to be Brahman. When I sat down to eat, I found that the food, the plate, the server, and I myself were nothing but Brahman. I took one or two morsels of food and again was absorbed in that consciousness. ... All the while, whether eating or lying down or going to college, I had the same experience. I was constantly over-whelmed with an indescribable intoxication. While walking in the streets, I noticed horse carriages go by, but I did not feel inclined to move out of the way. I felt that the carriages and I myself were made of the same substance.... When this state abated a little, the world began to appear to me as a dream. ... When I returned to the normal plane, I realized that I had had a glimpse of the non-dual consciousness.... Since then I have never doubted the truth of non-dualism.'

Later, Swamiji himself had the power of transmitting spirituality by a touch. There was a professor of science in Madras, an avowed atheist. One day he had a long argument with Swamiji about the existence of God. Finally, Swamiji gave the professor a touch, saying: 'Kidi, don't you see God: don't you see God?' The man was completely transformed. He renounced the world and henceforth lived a meditative life in seclusion.

Sri Ramakrishna did not want any of his disciples to be one-sided. Through the Master's grace, Naren had had a glimpse of the impersonal Reality. Now Sri Ramakrishna wanted to teach him that God can also have form. But Naren was firmly opposed to image worship, and used to call the Master's visions of the Divine Mother Kali hallucinations.

Meanwhile, Naren's father had died, leaving his family poverty-stricken. As the eldest boy, it was Naren's duty to provide for his mother and two brothers. He looked for a job, but could not find one. Worried and sad, he came to Sri Ramakrishna and appealed to the Master to pray for the removal of his family's wants. Sri Ramakrishna said: 'I can't make such demands! Why don't you go and ask the Divine Mother yourself? You don't accept her; that's why you suffer so much.' Then the Master told Naren to go to the Kali temple. On the way, Naren was filled with divine intoxication; and when he saw the image, the Divine Mother appeared to him living and full of consciousness. When he returned to Sri Ramakrishna, the Master asked him if he had prayed to the Mother on behalf of his family. But Naren had forgotten all about it; he had asked the Mother only for pure knowledge and pure devotion.

Sri Ramakrishna again sent him back to the temple to pray to the Mother to provide for his family's needs. At the sight of the Divine Mother, Naren again went into ecstasy. All his problems vanished in her presence. The Master sent Naren to the temple once more; but for the third time the young disciple found himself unable to pray for anything material. He then understood the lesson the Master had wanted him to learn. He bowed before Mother Kali and her power. After returning to the Master's room, he begged Sri Ramakrishna again to pray to the Divine Mother on behalf of his people. And now the Master agreed, saying: 'All right, they will never be in want of plain food and clothing.' This actually proved true.

Naren had now realized God with form as well as without form. One day, he told Sri Ramakrishna that he wished to remain continually absorbed in the superconscious state, coming out of it only to eat a little in order to keep his body alive. The Master was displeased, and said: 'Shame on you! There is a much higher state than that.' Naren was born for the good of mankind. He was not meant to only taste the bliss of God for himself, but to share this bliss with others. And so the Master taught Naren the highest spiritual ideal—to realize God and live in the service of mankind.

How this service was to be performed, Naren learned in a unique manner. On one occasion Sri Ramakrishna was seated in his room, surrounded by his disciples. Naren was present. The Master was quoting the following teaching of a great saint: 'Utmost compassion should be shown to all creatures.' Sri Ramakrishna, in ecstasy, repeated the word 'compassion' and then remarked: 'Who am I to show compassion to others?

No, not compassion for man, but service to him as the manifestation of God.' On coming out of the room, Naren said: 'If the Lord grants me the opportunity, I will proclaim throughout the world the wonderful truth I have heard today.'

And he did proclaim this truth: See God in every being, and serve – not as philanthropy, but as a spiritual practice, as worship.

After the passing away of Sri Ramakrishna, his monastic disciples plunged themselves into spiritual disciplines. Why, it may be asked, did they find it necessary to practise austerities when they had already attained *samadhi* through Sri Ramakrishna's grace? When Maharaj (Swami Brahmananda) was questioned on this point one day, he answered: 'True, the Master did everything for us. But we wanted to make this state our own.' And on another occasion, Maharaj said to one of his disciples: 'Why do you want to practise austerities? We have done all that for you,' indicating that their spiritual disciplines had been performed not only for themselves but for others. And he said to this disciple, 'Just love me.'

Swamiji passed several years travelling through India as a wandering monk. He practised meditation intensively and depended entirely on the Lord for food and shelter. Seeing his people's poverty and suffering, he realized that the economic and educational standards of the masses needed to be raised. How could they be taught religion when their stomachs were empty! He received the inspiration to plan a voyage to America, to give there the message of Vedanta and to raise funds for his needy countrymen. Money was collected for his passage to the United States, but Swamiji gave it away to the poor. Another fund was collected. But Swamiji wanted to know the Lord's will before undertaking the journey. After praying to Sri Ramakrishna and the Holy Mother, he had a vision of the Master walking on the ocean and beckoning him to follow. Still not satisfied, Swamiji wrote to the Holy Mother, asking her advice. At first, the Holy Mother wanted to write him not to go to America; like a mother, she felt anxious at the thought of one of her spiritual sons travelling to such a distant land. But she then had a vision of Sri Ramakrishna which convinced her that Naren's journey was divinely ordained. And so she sent him her blessings.

It is interesting to note that Buddha preached his first sermon
in Benares, the seat of learning of his time, and that Vivekananda preached his first sermon in Chicago at the World's
Parliament of Religions, where the Western intellectuals of his
day had congregated. There is another similarity between these
two great teachers: both Buddha and Vivekananda had a message for their own time as well as for all ages. What was the
substance of Vivekananda's message? It was the message of
harmony and universality in religion. To quote from Vivekananda's Chicago Address:

'. . . if there is ever to be a universal religion, it must be one
which will have no location in place or time; which will be
infinite, like the God it will preach, and whose sun will shine
upon the followers of Krishna and of Christ, on saints and
sinners alike; which will not be Brahminic or Buddhistic,
Christian or Mohammedan, but the sum total of all these, and
still have infinite space for development; which in its catholicity
will embrace in its infinite arms, and find a place for every
human being, from the lowest grovelling savage not far removed from the brute, to the highest man towering by the
virtues of his head and heart almost above humanity, making
society stand in awe of him and doubt his human nature. It
will be a religion which will have no place for persecution or
intolerance in its polity, which will recognize divinity in every
man and woman, and whose whole scope, whose whole force,
will be centred in aiding humanity to realize its own true,
divine nature.'

This, in short, is the message of Vivekananda, and it is also
the message of Vedanta. Vivekananda had a dream. And his
dream was to harmonize the cultures of the East and the West.

If we go to the original teachings of Christianity, we find
there the one eternal truth of all religions. If we go to the
original teachings of Hinduism, we find there that same eternal
truth. Our concern, however, is what Christianity and
Hinduism preach today. And it is now that we must establish
harmony between the Eastern and Western cultures.

What has been the emphasis in the West? Humanistic and
scientific development. Yes, there exist God-fearing people.

But what is their objective? For the majority, enrichment of their life on earth. The idea of contemplation also exists in the West, but, generally speaking, only as a means for a temporal end. The religion taught by Christ – to know the truth, to pray unceasingly, to be perfect even as the Father in heaven is perfect – has become forgotten.

And what has been the emphasis in India? The spiritual life. Achievements in the external world were neglected because they were considered ephemeral. The result was that a few individuals devoted themselves to God and became saints, while the masses fell into inertia and idleness because they were not fit to devote themselves to a meditative life. That, of course, is not the true religion of the Hindus. But it is how Hinduism has been preached and misunderstood.

The industriousness of the West and contemplativeness of the East must be harmonized. If external achievements are made the goal of life and God the means to reach that goal, there will continue to be suffering and misery. But if God is known to be the supreme purpose of existence, and activity and outward achievements are made the means to fulfil this purpose, then the divinity within man will become manifest, and he will see this divinity everywhere. This is the essence of religion, which Vivekananda summed up as follows:

'Do not depend on doctrines, do not depend on dogmas, or sects, or churches or temples; they count for little compared with the essence of existence in man, which is divine; and the more this is developed in a man, the more powerful is he for good. Earn that first, acquire that, and criticize no one, for all doctrines and creeds have some good in them. Show by your lives that religion does not mean words, or names, or sects, but that it means spiritual realization. Only those can understand who have experienced it. Only those who have attained to spirituality can communicate it to others, can be great teachers of mankind. They alone are the powers of light.'

And Vivekananda was such a power of light.

25

SRI RAMAKRISHNA AND THE RELIGION OF TOMORROW

East is East, and West is West, but the time has now come when Swami Vivekananda's dream of a perfect civilization, by the merging of the East and West, should be realized.

Before we can understand what the nature of such a civilization would be, we must understand what the West has to contribute and what the East has to contribute. Then only can we see how they could meet for the benefit of all mankind.

What are the predominating characteristics of modern Western civilization? They can be summed up as a scientific spirit, rationalism, and secular humanism; these again can be traced back to classical antiquity.

It was the Greek mind that laid the foundation of natural science, which means that everything must be tested and proved by experiment and reason. That was the foundation of Greek civilization, and that is the basic principle of the modern West.

Also we find that the Greek mind concerned itself with the natural man, the man as he is known to himself, his bodily desires, and his mental powers. True it is that in such ancient Greek thinkers as Pythagoras and Plato, a certain mystic element is found; yet the Greek mind as a whole was never influenced by this mystic element.

In the mediaeval age we find that the two great religions, Judaism and Christianity, influenced the thought of the West. Their chief contribution was the insistence upon the insufficiency of the intellect and upon the importance of historic revelation. Both Judaism and Christianity took their stands on revelation: God reveals his will to his lawgivers and prophets.

Superficially this may seem very good, but when righteousness is practised – not for its own sake – but because of authority, there is bound to grow narrowness and fanaticism. Whenever a man bases his life on authority, in the name of religion, his reason is stifled. He becomes a fanatic. That is why we find that when fanaticism became rampant, most irreligious deeds were done. Down through the ages the name of religion has been marred by bloodshed, by killing, and by murder.

With the Renaissance came intellectual and scientific advancement, bringing new ideas in social living. But, with the growth of these new ideas, traditional religion was thrown aside, and morality declined. The object of all striving and action was to enrich the physical man, gratify his bodily desires and satisfy his intellect.

But now the present chaos of the world has brought us to a period of reconsideration. In every country thinkers are beginning to look with suspicion upon the past and present way of life. Are we travelling the right path? How can we live in peace and harmony? We have reached the peak of the old civilization – the scientific and rationalistic outlook of life – and we find ourselves standing on the brink of a volcano.

We have reached the point where we see only darkness, destruction and annihilation: we have come to a point when we must reconsider and readjust ourselves. Everywhere the cry is to return to religion. We must base our life on spirituality. That is the cry in the hearts of thinking people. That is the cry in the hearts of the masses.

Now let us see what India has contributed and what Sri Ramakrishna, the prophet of modern India, has contributed.

We have already mentioned the form of traditional religion of the West, based on revelation and authority. We have shown that if we give up our scientific and rationalistic attitude, religion becomes narrow fanaticism. Furthermore, it is not possible at this stage of growth of civilization to give up that spirit of rationalism. When we look to India, we find a reconciliation between revelation and rationalism. We shall come to this point later.

Religion has always been, and still is, the predominating influence on the mass mind of India. It is true that, as India came in touch with Western civilization, several of her countrymen fell under its influence. As a result they considered religion to be the cause of her degeneration, her slavery to a foreign nation, and wanted to 'throw out the baby with the bath water'. But they did not succeed, because religion has been the one deep-rooted, predominating influence in the cultural life of India.

It is interesting to note that there have been great politicians and great statesmen active in India during the past few years; but India, on the whole, did not respond to their pleadings and preachings. There was one man, Gandhi, who did exert the greatest influence over the people of India. Was it because he was a politician or a statesman, or was it because he was a *mahatma* – a religious man? Thus you can see, if you study and understand India, that howsoever degraded India may be, she responds only to religion and to a religious teacher.

Now let us see what type of religion India has. There we find religion based on revelation – as in Judaism and Christianity. But instead of acceptance of this revelation on authority alone, it is based fundamentally on experience. As one of her great teachers, Shankara, pointed out, 'In matters relating to Brahman, the scriptures are not the only authority. There must be a personal experience.' To state simply on authority of revelation that God *is*, to state simply on authority that we must practise such-and-such as good, and avoid such-and-such as evil, because that is the law – the command of God – is not sufficient; it does not work in the hearts of people. To know and believe that God is, means that there is a possibility of experiencing Him in one's own life. That must be the guiding principle in the life of a spiritual man. Why should I do that which is good and avoid that which is evil? Because by doing good we reach God, and by doing evil we go into greater darkness. Because this has always been the attitude regarding religion in India, there has never been a stifling of the rationalistic spirit.

Religion to the Hindu is the direct experience of God, union with the Godhead. It is not enough to believe that God is; the living presence of God must be felt. Next, faith in that living presence must be transformed into the vision of God; the words of the scriptures must be transformed into vision. You must come directly and immediately into union with God. That is the definition of religion given in the Indian scriptures.

There comes, however, a rise and fall to every civilization. Though religion has been truly defined in the scriptures, at times this truth becomes forgotten. Whenever this forgetfulness comes to India, we find in different ages great spiritual giants rising out of her very soil to revive that spirit. In this present age when India first came into contact with the Western world, as already stated, there was a real degeneration of religion. But fortunately for India, and fortunately for the world, there came one of the greatest prophets, one of the greatest illumined souls the world has ever produced. His name was Ramakrishna.

Ramakrishna lived near the city of Calcutta, a city engulfed by the greatest tide of Western civilization that ever swept over the people of India. At this period in the history of Bengal, there were born many great thinkers, great writers, but all were imbued with the spirit of the West, and along with them there grew youth movements which sought to inculcate the Western civilization. It was the fashion among the young men of Bengal of that time to think that to be Westernized meant to drink whisky and to eat beef.

Unknown and unrecognized for a time, Sri Ramakrishna lived in a temple nearby, practising his spiritual disciplines in the solitude of the temple. His one ideal, his one purpose of life, was to see God, to experience Him. He worshipped God as Mother. Although he did not go to any school or college, and hardly knew how to read and write, he had the scientific temper and rationalistic spirit of a true scientist. He would ask, 'Mother, are you real? Are you true? If you really exist, why don't you reveal yourself to me?' Thus he would pray from day to day, and when the temple bells would proclaim the approach of evening, he would cry out, 'Mother, another day has passed, and I have not seen you.' To him life was empty, life was a vanity, without the realization of God. He determined the value of all things by one standard: 'Does it help me to realize God?' He would take a piece of gold in one hand and a lump of dirt in the other, and say to himself: 'This is gold and this is dirt. People give their lives to find this piece of gold. Does it give me God? Yes, I can build a house, I can live comfortably with gold, but does it help me to realize God?' Then he would reply, 'Gold is dirt, and dirt is gold,' and throw both in the river.

Such was the man living in a temple in India at a time when India was madly chasing Western culture, and this was the man who, through his yearning, realized God the Mother. He saw Mother and he talked to Her. Following this first experience of God, he wanted to experiment with the other religions of the world. He followed the teachings of the different sects of India; he followed the religions taught by Christ and Mohammed; and by following each one of these religions he came to the realization of the same ultimate reality. Then was it that he proclaimed, with authority: 'The many religions are so many paths to God.'

Sri Ramakrishna used to say, 'When the lotus blooms, bees come to gather the honey.' The seekers after God began to gather around him, and to those who came to him with the earnest, sincere longing for God, he gave the vision of God. Their lives were transformed. However, Sri Ramakrishna did not limit the vision of God to his disciples or to the people of India. He said, 'I have many children in far-off countries whose language I do not know, and they will all come to me.' He had a vision wherein he saw himself in the centre and many people from foreign lands gathered around him, and they were all God-intoxicated. In this vision he saw the future of mankind; he saw that many a soul would be born who would drink of the love of God.

But this does not mean that all the people of the world will come to accept the personality of Ramakrishna. Sri Ramakrishna is only a symbol of a truth, an embodiment of certain spiritual principles. Let us see what those principles are.

God is not merely a hypothesis, He is. God can be realized and must be realized in this very life. Religion is eternal. It has no boundary. It is neither of the East nor of the West. It is neither Hinduism nor Christianity; neither Buddhism nor Judaism. The world is not saved and can never be saved by merely believing in creeds which accept a particular faith; it can be saved by wisdom only. It is not that any or all of the existing religions of the world will be wiped out and that there will be one world religion. Sri Ramakrishna experimented with the existing religions and found that they are all true, inasmuch as they are the ways, the paths, to realize the one God. He came to bring harmony; he came to fulfil and not to destroy.

Now, what about humanism, the prevalent religion of the West? The general welfare of the body and the mind cannot be ignored. You cannot ignore the physical and intellectual man. India, during the past few centuries – not the India of old – has ignored the external aspect of man, while the West has ignored the inner man through a preoccupation with humanistic ethics and a secular outlook on life. In the life and teachings of Sri Ramakrishna we find that, instead of ignoring humanism, he elevated it to the level of the spirit. In this connection I will mention one incident. One day Sri Ramakrishna was in a very high spiritual mood, and in that mood he was, as it were, talking to himself. There were many disciples present, and among them was young Narendra (Vivekananda). Sri Ramakrishna quoted a well-known teaching of Sri Chaitanya, repeating over and over again: 'Compassion for mankind!' Then he said: 'Compassion – compassion – no! no! no! Not compassion – but service!' Naren listened attentively to these words, and as he left the room he said: 'I have learned a great lesson today. If I live I shall some day give this truth to the world.' And what did Vivekananda preach? He preached the ideal of service to God in man. When we learn to see God within ourselves, we learn to see Him in all. We learn to see that our own good lies in the good of all mankind. Thus it is that humanism becomes spiritualized. The ignorant way is to strive to enrich our life on earth, and the spiritual way is to try to find out how best we can live on earth in order that we may reach God.

To sum up: the scientific temper and rationalistic spirit are not opposed to religion and revelation, if by religion we mean experimenting with the truth and experiencing the truth of God. Intellect when elevated and expanded becomes revelation. To accept religion and revelation without this spirit of experimenting and experiencing the truth of God, leads man to fanaticism. Intellectual culture and scientific temper, unless expanded into revelation, leads to its own destruction.

Intellect and revelation are to be harmonized, humanism is to be elevated to the spirit, morality or ethical life is to be spiritualized, external decorum is to be guided by inner restraint. In this way harmony can be established between the civilizations of the East and the West.

PART V

VITAL QUESTIONS ON RELIGION ANSWERED

VITAL QUESTIONS ON
RELIGION ANSWERED

Q.: What is the ultimate goal for a follower of the Hindu religion?

A.: The ultimate goal for a follower of the Hindu religion is the same as that for a follower of any religion – it is the attainment of perfection in Godhead. Whether you are a Hindu, a Christian, a Buddhist, a Jew, a Mohammedan, or a Zoroastrian, the ideal is the same – whether you call it the beatific vision, illumination, *samadhi*, or *nirvana*. Christ expressed it in these words: 'Be ye therefore perfect, even as your Father which is in heaven is perfect.' He didn't say that you have to die a physical death in order to attain that perfection. But your ego must die and you have to be reborn in Spirit in order to enter into the Kingdom of God. The goal, as both Hindus and Buddhists emphasize, is to be reached here and now, in this very life.

Q.: Gaining realization of God seems to me like swimming the English Channel – reserved for the very few. What can the rest of us get out of religion?

A.: It may seem that way, but you are absolutely wrong. You see, it is possible for every human being to realize God. And you don't have to have strong muscles. But one very important thing you must have: an earnest desire for that realization. Why do we see only a few illumined souls? Because only very few desire and seek that illumination. What trouble we go through in order to pass a college examination or even just to buy a hat! But we don't bring that interest when it comes to praying and meditating. So the main thing is to create the desire for God – by reading scriptures, praying to God, chanting his praises. Eventually there will come a time in your life when you feel that God alone is real, and you seek him and him only. Then you will find illumination.

Q.: Is a spiritual aspirant justified in taking a human life in defence of country, home or person?

A.: That is a very complex question, and it cannot be answered categorically. All I can say is this: It depends upon the spiritual growth of the individual. There are people who must protect other persons, who must defend their homes and their country; if they didn't, human society could not continue. But if a spiritual aspirant has reached a stage of unfoldment in which he is constantly absorbed in the thought of God, then it becomes impossible for him to take arms. He sees no enemy. So I would say that for some persons killing in defence is justified; for others, not.

Q.: Jesus said: 'No man cometh to the Father, but by me.' Does not this statement prove that Christ was a unique representative of God on earth and rule out other so-called divine incarnations?

A.: No. This statement does not rule out the advent of other divine incarnations. In the *Bhagavad-Gita* we find that Sri Krishna also says: 'Worship Me! Follow Me! I am the Way!' What does it mean? Are these two contradicting each other? No. When Jesus and Sri Krishna say 'Me' or 'Mine' or 'I', they do not speak as human beings; they speak as *Brahman*, as God. Both Christ and Sri Krishna are expressing the same truth. The same God which came as Sri Krishna came again as Christ – and as other divine incarnations; he only chose a different dress. Sri Krishna explains this in the *Gita*: 'In every age I come back to deliver the holy, to destroy the sin of the sinner, to establish righteousness.'

Q.: Please explain what is meant by purification of the heart, and the best way to attain it.

A.: From a negative standpoint, purity of heart is freedom from lust and greed, freedom from craving for the things of the world. But in its positive aspect, purity means that your heart is filled with divine consciousness.

Now the method to purify the heart is that of concentration and meditation. There are also other means – selfless service, for instance.

Q.: Does meat-eating lower spiritual vibrations? Is it wrong to eat meat?

A.: It all depends on you. One person can eat meat and become absorbed in God, and another can eat vegetables and be a rogue. If you consider vegetarianism from the standpoint of non-killing, remember that even potatoes have life. So I would say, eat what agrees with you and what you can digest.

Q.: How can a householder be detached from work he dislikes?

A.: Why do you dislike your work? Because you are not concentrated on it. Learn to attach your mind completely to your work while you are doing it, and you will find joy in it. But then, don't remain attached; learn to detach your mind from your work at a moment's notice. But this detachment is not indifference. My master said:

'Everyone wants to do the work he best likes to do, but that is not the secret of work. Whatever work you do, whether you like it or not, know that it is the Lord's work, and adjust yourself accordingly. Remember this, all work must be done as worship of God . . . It is easy to do great deeds, the deeds that bring name and fame. But it is by his small, everyday actions that a man's character is known. The true karma yogi does not work to gain publicity. No matter how insignificant his work may be, he throws himself wholeheartedly into the task, because, for him, his work has become worship of God.'

Q.: Suppose we want to do God's will? How can we be sure what that will is?

A.: Actually, we cannot know in any given situation what God's will is until we become spiritually illumined. Only he who has known God intimately – who lives in His consciousness all the time – can do His will, because his will has become merged in the divine will. And throughout the ages there have been a few rare souls who live in such a state of union with God.

But there are many people who do exactly what they want to do and proclaim that it is God's will. And so we must analyse ourselves: Are our thoughts and actions selfish or unselfish? All selfishness must be eliminated from our hearts before we can do God's will.

In our ignorance, what we can and should do is to follow the teachings of the scriptures and the examples of perfected souls. And we can pray: 'Lord, I don't know what your will is. Guide me! May I be a tool in your hand!'

Q.: Can anyone have the vision of God?
A.: Yes, if the following three conditions are fulfilled. These are human birth, longing for God, and the society of the holy. When the first two conditions are met, the third fulfils itself. It is the desire for God which is lacking in us and which we must develop.

Whenever Sri Ramakrishna was asked, 'What is the way to find God?' he used to answer, 'Yearn for Him with a longing heart.' Or he would say: 'People shed streams of tears because sons are not born to them; others eat away their hearts in sorrow because they cannot get riches. But how many weep for not having seen God? Very few indeed! Verily, he who seeks the Lord, who weeps for Him, attains Him.'

Q.: Is there any preservation of personality when one experiences *samadhi*, or transcendental consciousness?
A.: I will answer that question if you can tell me what personality is.

Q.: Well, anything that would be attributable to the uniqueness of an individual. Is there such a uniqueness?
A.: That's what I am questioning! No, what we normally call personality is not real. We are hugging a shadow. Take the personality of a thief – does he have to remain a thief in order to keep his personality? Everybody's personality is changing each moment. If one remained the same, it would be unfortunate. Where lies our real personality? In the *Atman*, in God. When we reach our union with God, we become true persons.

Q.: I should like to think of the personal aspect of God, but how is this done?

A.: All right. You know what the love of a father, or a mother, or a friend, or a sweetheart is. Any of these relationships may be established with God. On the human plane, these loves may fail you. But God is the one Person who will never fail you.

You see, all such questions arise as long as we are on the fringe of religion. But do something! Think of Christ or Krishna and see what happens! Nobody can love Christ or establish a relationship with him immediately; but think of him and go on thinking. Then you begin to realize what perfection means, what love means. It is an experimental process.

Q.: Would you comment on the part sex plays in religion? Are not many of our modern-day symbols really phallic signs for which a meaning is now lost?

A.: The sex energy, if it is not dissipated, plays a great part in religion. It becomes transmuted into spiritual energy when it is conserved. What does conservation mean? Overcoming lust. You see, there is one great obstacle to spiritual life; that is lust. He who has conquered lust has gained mastery over himself and the world. Now a wall has no lust; but that does not mean that this wall is a saint! But there is lust in man in order that he may overcome it and become a saint.

Now to the next part of your question. What the Western scholar considers a phallic symbol is not so regarded by the Hindu devotee. The word *lingam*, which has been translated as phallus, actually means symbol. A devotee who worships the *lingam* or the *yoni* is thinking of the fatherhood or motherhood of the universe, the source of creation, preservation, and dissolution. He does not think of these as symbols of sex. Oil and water do not mix; similarly, sex and religion don't mix. Remember that! If you feel lustful, admit your weakness. Don't try to cover the dirty spot with rose petals.

Q.: If everything about us is God, what of that harsh noise or unkind word that breaks in on our meditation? And what of the pains and base desires that distract us?

A.: Everything is God, that's very true. But it is a matter of

239

experience. If I consider this physical and mental universe as God, I will be mistaken. So first we must say: 'All is not, God is.' While we live in the domain of *maya*, of name and form, there are base desires and harsh words, good desires and sweet words. But as spiritual aspirants we must avoid the former. When we go to pray, we must try not to let any distractions arise. If they come, we have to avoid them.

Sri Ramakrishna once said to a young disciple: 'You may say, "There is no thorn," but put out your hand and it will prick you.' As long as the world is so real to us we cannot say: 'All is God.' But once we have been given divine sight we actually see God as the material and efficient cause of the universe. Then we see that he is everything. Then there are no more harsh words, no more base desires. But that is a high state of attainment.

Q.: I am discouraged about my spiritual life. I don't seem to be making any progress. What shall I do?

A.: Keep up the struggle! You see, there is no such thing as progress in a straight line. In spiritual life, too, there are ups and downs. But there is no failure as long as you make an effort.

Swami Brahmananda, my master, used to give the following illustration. The calf tries to get up on its feet within a very short time of its birth, but it falls down. For fifteen minutes, half an hour, or one hour the calf tries to get up, but it keeps falling down. Still it doesn't relinquish the struggle. Later, it not only stands but begins to run. It is the same in spiritual life. You make a resolution that you will do so much meditation. Then laziness gets hold of you: 'Oh, I'll skip it for today.' Or restlessness and passion distract you, and all your good intentions are forgotten for the time being. But if you have fallen, get up again. Struggle! Promise yourself: 'I will try to do better.' You see? You will fail many times, but don't give up. That's how we grow.

Q.: How would you define mysticism?

A.: Mysticism is the essence of religion. It is the conviction that God can be seen; that he can be directly known and realized; and that to have this realization is the only purpose of life.

Q.: Does Vedanta accept the Indian caste system or does it reject it as incompatible with religious ideals?

A.: Caste, as described in the *Gita*, is concerned with the division of work according to a man's temperament and capacity. In this sense, caste will always exist – not only in India but everywhere in the world. There will always be spiritual leaders and teachers, politicians and soldiers, traders and artisans, and labourers. The *Gita* says that, regardless of caste, all mankind is born for perfection; each shall attain it by following the duty of his own nature, if this duty is performed as worship of God.

What is usually thought of as the caste system – some castes being considered inferior to others and discriminated against – is a degeneration of the original idea. As you know, since India gained independence, caste has been practically abolished. But traditionally, monks have been regarded as beyond caste; and they have often been instrumental in teaching harmony and understanding to the prejudiced and intolerant. This reminds me of an incident which I will tell you.

It happened in our Ramakrishna monastery at Madras while Swami Ramakrishnananda was the abbot. On Sri Ramakrishna's birthday, a group of *brahmins* and a group of untouchables came to attend the special worship. The two groups stayed at opposite sides of the prayer hall. Then hymns were sung, and Swami Ramakrishnananda went into an ecstatic mood. He began to dance, first toward one group, then toward the other. An intense spiritual atmosphere was created. Responding to it, the *brahmins* and untouchables forgot themselves, and moved closer to one another. Finally, all were dancing together, united in the thought of God.

This is what happens when you give people true spirituality: ignorance and prejudice leave of themselves. Reform by legislation does little; we must begin reform at the roots.

Q.: I have come across the term *sahaja yoga* repeatedly in Vedantic literature. Would you please explain what it is?

A.: Literally, *sahaja yoga* means 'easy yoga', the easy way to union with God. It is the way of constant recollectedness. While you are sitting, or lying down, or walking, or working – think of the presence of God. Let a current toward God flow in your heart at all times. You don't have to close your eyes or ears to do this. Remember him always, while you are busy and while you are idle – and you will see him.

Q.: If God is all good, how do you explain the evil in this world?

A.: Both evil forces and good forces are working in this relative world. God, the Absolute, remains unaffected by them. If he were affected by evil, he would not be God. If he needed man to remove the world's evil, he would not be God. Evil and good both belong to him, but he is beyond them. God is playing, and in our ignorance we see his creation as evil or good. We are dreaming this dream of good and evil. When our dream breaks, when we have the wisdom of God, then we realize that he alone exists, then we realize that everything is his play.

This does not mean that we should do nothing. Shall we sit quietly and let the evil forces win out? As long as we see wickedness, it is our duty to struggle against it; and we must use the forces of good in order to overcome the evil we perceive. But let us not go and fight wickedness with the idea that we are helping God! We are worshipping him.

What is evil, after all? It is ignorance – nothing else. A veil of ignorance covers the truth of God. How to remove the veil? Pray that the ignorance may be removed from your sight and from the sight of all mankind, so that God within may shine forth. Pray that everyone may find peace and illumination in God. Work for that, and you will help yourself and everybody.

Q.: I have concentrated all my mental energy on overcoming asthma, but so far have had little success. What would be your advice?

A.: My advice is to go to a doctor.

Q.: Doesn't Vedanta believe in healing?

A.: It depends on what you mean by healing. Vedanta teaches how to overcome illness for eternity. By eternity I don't mean continuity in time, but absolute existence – beyond time, space, and relativity. If you use Vedanta philosophy in this sense, you will rise above all illness and death, although your body will pass through these modifications. You are not the body, the mind or the senses. You are the Self, the Spirit – one with God. When you realize this truth in transcendental vision, death won't frighten you. Dying will be like throwing away a worn-out garment, that's all. The *real* you won't be affected. Of course, if you wish, you may get health by praying for it – but suppose you are healed today? Tomorrow you may be sick again; and some day you will have to face death. So heal yourself in such a way as to gain eternal life. 'Lay not up for yourselves treasures upon earth, where moth and rust doth corrupt and where thieves break through and steal: but lay up for yourselves treasures in heaven. . . .'

Q.: Does vicarious atonement have a place in Vedanta?

A.: Yes. In every religion there are examples of saints who suffered vicariously. I will give you an instance from the life of the Holy Mother, Sri Ramakrishna's wife. Whenever she came to Calcutta, hundreds of people would line up at the Udbodhan Office, her residence, for the privilege of touching her feet. And she took upon herself the sins of those who prostrated before her. Afterwards her feet would burn, and she would have to bathe them in the cool water of the Ganges to get relief. One day a disciple said to her: 'Mother, we give you pain when we touch your feet. We should not do it any more, nor should we allow others to touch your feet.' Holy Mother's answer was wonderful. She said: 'What is this? Did the Lord come only to eat rasagollas?' Her meaning was that Sri Ramakrishna was born for the purpose of taking the sins of mankind on himself, and her mission was to help him in his work. They were not born to eat rasagollas, a kind of sweetmeat; in other words, they were not born for their own enjoyment.

But only great saints and divine incarnations can take the *karmas* of others upon themselves.

Q.: How does one get rid of spiritual pride?

A.: I will tell you a story. Radha, one of the shepherdesses whom Krishna loved best, became apparently very egotistical. The other shepherdesses complained to Krishna about her, so

Krishna suggested that they ask Radha about her ego. Radha told them: 'Certainly I have an ego. But whose ego is it? It is not mine, for everything I have belongs to Krishna.'

The way to overcome pride or any of the passions is to turn them over to God. If you must be vain, be vain that you are a child of God. But at the same time feel that everyone else is a child of God just as much as you are.

Q.: Should you tell anyone about your spiritual experiences?
A.: No, only your *guru*. In India we have a saying that a man should keep his spiritual experiences as secret as he would keep secret the fact that his mother was unchaste. Your experience may not be a spiritual experience at all. Now if you go and talk about some vision you have had to someone else, that person may feel he should have such an experience too. And so confusion will be created. One should never make a show of spiritual matters.

Your *guru* alone should hear of your spiritual experiences. He will tell you whether they are genuine or not. Of course, you may not always like what he tells you!

Q.: In order to progress in spiritual life, should I give up my comforts?
A.: It is possible to live in a most uncomfortable way and think lustful thoughts, and it is possible to live in comfort and think of God. You don't have to lie on a bed of nails in order to meditate; you may sit on a cushioned chair, if you wish. Externals are not important. The Lord looks into your mind and heart. If you are sincere in your desire for him, he will reveal himself to you. So don't worry about giving up your comforts; but learn to devote yourself to contemplation of God, and you will progress on the spiritual path.

Q.: What is grace?
A.: It is the divine power which operates in man to transform him, to make him attuned to God so that he can feel his unbounded love. Divine grace can be tangibly felt at a certain stage of spiritual unfoldment. Of course you have to struggle before you can feel it.

These two ideas of grace and of self-effort are not contradictory. Sri Ramakrishna used to say: 'The breeze of grace is always blowing, but you have to set your sail to catch that breeze of grace.' 'Setting sail' means that you have to put forth some effort. What effort? To keep your mind in God, to struggle to meditate, to pray earnestly for divine love. Then what happens? Suddenly, one day, you will feel a power striking you and drawing your mind to itself, as the magnet draws the needle. Then the vision of God will open before you. This experience cannot really be expressed in words. All I can say about it is that you will feel God's love overwhelming you and lifting you up.

Q.: If God is present in everyone, how does one explain people like Hitler?

A.: God dwells everywhere. God dwells in the heart of the tiger too, but that doesn't mean that you have to hug the tiger. It is like this: The self-luminous sun is shining, but rain clouds have gathered and it seems to us the sun has disappeared. Actually the clouds have not affected the luminosity of the sun; it continues to shine behind the clouds. Similarly, God dwells in a Hitler too and remains unaffected by the thoughts and deeds of the man. The man reaps the fruits of his *karmas* (the consequences of his thoughts and deeds), and suffers. But through such suffering his character will be purified, and in some life he will wake and realize his divinity.

Q.: How can we live successfully in the world but not be of it?

A.: Everybody has to live in the world. We monks also have to live in the world. I remember a disciple once asked Maharaj whether anybody can find God while living in the world. Maharaj answered: 'Where else would one live?' But remember, let not worldliness attach itself to you. How do you keep worldliness away? By attaching your mind to something greater, something higher. The only way to live in the world and not be attached to it is to attach yourself to God. Let your hands work, go about your business; but keep a part of your mind in God, knowing him to be the one reality, the eternal truth. He alone is your very own. We have to convince ourselves that there is one object of love, one being who

really loves us – and that is the Lord. He is your very own.
You belong to him. Have that awareness; then you can live
in the world and nothing will touch you.

Q.: Swami, how can we learn to distinguish between what
is the Lord's will and what is our will?
A.: There is just one way. Do you feel the presence of God
and remember him? If you do something and consider it God's
will and have forgotten God, then you may be sure it is your
own will.

Q.: How can we learn to keep the mind in God?
A.: Practice! Practice! Then one day you'll look at someone. Suddenly you'll think: There is the presence of God.
You'll look at the sky and feel: Oh, there is God! Someone
will be talking to you and you'll know: That's God's voice!
One can do this when one begins to fall in love with God.
Then recollection of him comes automatically, as when you
were young and had a sweetheart. It was no trouble then for
you to think of him or her. Your mind did it automatically.
In the same way, when your heart is filled with love for God
you think of him.

Q.: How can feelings of lust be controlled?
A.: Keep your mind engaged in chanting the name of the
Lord. If lust persists, go into your room and clap your hands
and chant the name of the Lord loudly. This will free you
from lust. Of course you have to have the desire to be free.
Prayer is answered, but you must be sincere.

Q.: Why is it easier to meditate at certain hours of the day?
A.: There are four times during the day and night which
are considered especially conducive to meditation: dawn,
midday, sunset, and midnight. At these hours, nature takes on
an attitude of calmness. Take advantage of these hours whenever you can.
But after all, where do we meditate? In our own minds.
Therefore, any time you meditate is beneficial. Later on you
will be successful in your meditation wherever and whenever
you meditate. But in order to reach the stage where you can

become absorbed in God regardless of external circumstances, it is very important that you practice the spiritual disciplines regularly at the same time every day.

Q.: How can fear be overcome?

A.: It is very difficult. We fear so many things for so many reasons, imaginary and real – and most of the time imaginary. We fear things that will never happen. A man becomes fearless when he has the love of God in his heart. We have a saying in India: 'Fear is fearful to approach Him.'

Q.: Are there any particular disciplines that can lessen fear?

A.: The only discipline I know is to keep the mind fixed in God. In order to fix your mind in God, chant his name as often as you can. When you think of God you are in the sanctuary. Nothing can touch you.

Q.: What constitutes the difference between thinking about God and meditating on him? Is it a degree of intensity?

A.: Thinking about God gradually leads one to meditation. Meditation is the state when the mind flows continuously toward God. There is a consciousness of the presence of God. Meditation, in fact, is next to *samadhi*. It is a state attained through practice of purity of heart and concentration upon God. To quote the *Bhagavad-Gita*: ' "The light of a lamp does not flicker in a windless place." That is the simile which describes a *yogi* of one-pointed mind, one who meditates on the *Atman*. When, through the practice of yoga, the mind ceases its restless movements and becomes still, the *Atman* is realized.'

Q.: I have read that one's thoughts at the time of death determine the road he is to travel in the hereafter; therefore, God-recollectedness is vitally important at this time. Yet, what of legitimate drugs or an intense pain that might keep one's mind from God at this moment?

A.: It is the thought *most prevalent* during a person's lifetime that comes to him at the moment of death, regardless of drugs, pain, or any other abnormal condition. That is why the *Gita* tells us to think of Him constantly.

'At the hour of death, when a man leaves his body, he must depart with his consciousness absorbed in me. Then he will be united with me. Be certain of that. Whatever a man remembers at the last, when he is leaving the body, will be realized by him in the hereafter; because that will be what his mind has most constantly dwelt on, during this life.'

Q.: What is the Vedantic attitude towards the use of LSD and other such drugs to induce a 'mystical' state? It seems that such use would run contrary to spiritual life.

A.: Mystical states can never be induced by drugs. If salvation could be produced chemically, Krishna, Christ, and Ramakrishna would have opened drugstores instead of preaching! Drugs may induce psychic visions, which, to a man ignorant of mystical visions, may appear as spiritual. Those who have had both drug-induced visions as well as genuine spiritual visions through the grace of God, know the two to be as different as night and day. We must also understand that it is not enough to have only mystical visions. They are only an index of spiritual growth. The ultimate is to be established in *Sat-chit-ananda* (existence-consciousness-bliss). This experience cannot be expressed in words.

Q.: We are so far from illumination. How can we maintain this long uphill climb to the final purification of our minds?

A.: You are not far from illumination. You are carrying *Brahman* within you all the time. 'Know ye not that ye are the temple of God and that the spirit of God dwelleth in you?' Your Christian scriptures tell you that! Why does God seem far away? Because you don't think of him. In reality, he is nearer than the nearest.

Q.: How do we become convinced that God loves us?

A.: It is very difficult. Let me give you an illustration. It is a hot day and you find yourself walking toward the ocean. Suddenly you feel a breeze, and you know it is from the ocean. It is a feeling, a sensation that comes to you before you arrive at the ocean. God is love, so we begin to feel his love as we approach nearer to him. Before we have seen him, we begin to feel his presence, we begin to receive the bliss of his grace. However, there must be a certain unfoldment within you before you feel this. Sometimes, too, as you practice the presence of God through meditation or by chanting his name, you begin to gain a little in concentration and start to feel his love. These are all experiences of spiritual aspirants.

Q.: How is it possible to love those who hate you?
A.: This is an ideal presented by all religions through their avatars and through all men of God. Christ, Buddha, Krishna, and Ramakrishna and many others exemplified it in their lives. Yes, you can love even those who hate you by seeing God in them – not their external expressions; know that they also are God. See God in a wicked person behind the mask of wickedness, and you can change that person. Love *does* conquer hatred. The changed lives of numerous individuals, through their association with the holy, attest to this truth.

Q.: When we are feeling spiritually 'dry', is this an indication that we are 'backsliding'?
A.: No. Spiritual growth doesn't develop along a straight line. When you travel in the mountains, you find yourself climbing up and down constantly – but you are steadily gaining in elevation. Remember that in spiritual life there is never any failure – so long as you keep up the struggle. Maharaj used to give the illustration of the newborn calf; though it keeps falling down in many attempts to walk, it eventually stands and runs. It is the same with spiritual aspirants. You may fall many times in the beginning – you may not be able to live up to your ideal for five minutes – but finally you arrive at the stage where you don't fall down. Don't be depressed if you fall from your ideal; but at the same time don't compromise. Continually tell yourself: 'I will never lower my ideal.'

Q.: What compels a person to move towards God? What makes him struggle for realization?
A.: Discrimination. He loves to think of God. In order for one to think of God and to love him, one must be discriminating. Try to understand that God alone is the Reality. Hold

on to God. Make your life God-centred. Think of him as often as you can, discriminate – then you will become dispassionate. That is, your attachment, your craving for things of the world will become less and less. You will realize God only when you become completely desireless. Holy Mother told us to pray for desirelessness in order that we may intensely desire the Lord. The more you think of God, the more will other desires begin to drop away. To desire anything else is vain, because it is like trying to bid the clouds to stay.

Q.: You mentioned that Swami Vivekananda said to 'accept' and not just 'tolerate' other points of view about religion. What did he mean?

A.: All roads lead to Rome if your destination is Rome. All roads and sects and denominations lead to God if your destination is God. But are they talking about realizing God through their particular sect or denomination? That is the crucial point.

One time I heard a Christian minister speak. He said, 'I don't like your ideas of renunciation and contemplation. What we believe in is doing good.' He believed only in humanism. He had forgotten what Christ taught. Remember the rich man who came to Christ seeking a better life? Christ told him to sell all he had and follow Him. But he couldn't do it. The main truth that Christianity has taught is to love the Lord thy God with all thy soul and all thy heart. If you love God that way you will be contemplating him. The goal is the important thing. If God is your goal, and you are on a path with that intention, it will lead you to Him. All religions, if properly understood, have that one goal – to realize God.

Now to come to the point of your question. Vivekananda believed in accepting the truth of all religions. To 'tolerate' means that I alone have the truth – I only endure your religion.

Q.: If we are divine, why then are we so weak and perverse? What is the matter with us?

A.: Yes, you are divine; but you are also ignorant. It is the nature of the diamond to shine, but it cannot if it is covered with dirt. However, as soon as the dirt is removed it will shine again. We are like that diamond. The blissfulness of the *Atman* is covered by ignorance. Whatever you think you become; so if you think you are a mortal human being and a sinner, you will stay that way. But, instead, if you tell yourself: 'I am free, perfect, and divine,' how then, can anything evil come from you? But this is very difficult because we have an ego. Let your *Atman* become your Lord, your chosen ideal, and keep your mind and heart concentrated on him. The simplest method given us is to chant the name of God – the *mantra*. The Name and his Being are identical. When you repeat your *mantra*, the Presence is there – immediately. That is because *Brahman* is everywhere. If you can't do anything else, chant the name of the Lord. Make it a habit. You will receive great benefit from it. But you must struggle.

Q.: It has been said that for us to see God we must 'go within'. If I decide to meditate twice a day, for say three years, what can I expect to happen? Will I get definite results?
A.: You don't have to wait three years. Do a half-hour of meditation a day, but true meditation – which is like the pouring of water from one vessel to another – with the current of your mind flowing toward God. If you can do that for half an hour, then you will attain *samadhi*. But to reach that state it might take three years or three lives, depending upon how much effort you put into it: Usually our minds run away somewhere else. We don't work hard enough to stop our mind in its wandering. It all depends on how much effort we employ. It's the quality that counts, not the quantity. If you think of God for even five seconds, those are five blessed moments in your life. The other moments are in vain – wasted moments. So make your life blessed every moment by thinking of the Lord every moment. We must have purity of heart. What is the sign of this purity? It is when the natural tendency of your mind is to flow toward God. When you attain this state, you will see God.

BIBLIOGRAPHY

Books Recommended for Further Study

Babbit, Irving (translator): *The Dhammapada*. New York: Oxford University Press, 1936.
One of the most important guides to Truth in Buddhism. An excellent essay, 'Buddha and the Occident', is appended to the work.

Huxley, Aldous: *The Perennial Philosophy*. Cleveland: World Publishing Co., 1962.
An anthology of first-hand accounts of mystical experience with a commentary by the author.

Isherwood, Christopher: *Ramakrishna and His Disciples*. New York: Simon and Schuster, 1965. London: Methuen and Co., 1965.
A graphic account of the life of Ramakrishna written by a well-known writer who is both a devotee of Ramakrishna and a student of Vedanta. Although based on existing works, it also incorporates new material.

Isherwood, Christopher (editor): *Vedanta for Modern Man*. New York: Collier Books, 1962.
Articles on Vedanta philosophy and practice selected from *Vedanta and the West* magazine from 1945 to 1951 by thirty-four writers. Many writers have contributed several articles.

Isherwood, Christopher (editor): *Vedanta for the Western World*. London: George Allen and Unwin, 1948.
Seventy articles on Vedanta (from *Vedanta and the West* magazine from 1938 to 1945) by Gerald Heard, Aldous Huxley, John van Druten, Swami Prabhavananda, and others.

'M': *The Gospel of Sri Ramakrishna*, translated by Swami Nikhilananda, New York: Ramakrishna-Vivekananda Center, 1942.
The first time in the world's history that the words of a great saint have been presented with almost stenographic accuracy. Features a biographical introduction by the translator. Foreword by Aldous Huxley.

Prabhavananda, Swami: *The Eternal Companion*. Hollywood: Vedanta Press, 1947.
Simple, direct and practical teachings regarding meditation and the contemplative life by Swami Brahmananda. Includes a biography by the author, who was a disciple of the Swami.

Prabhavananda, Swami: *The Sermon on the Mount according to Vedanta.* London: George Allen and Unwin, 1964.
In the form of a part-by-part commentary on the entire Sermon. Christ's teaching are compared with those of the Vedanta.

Prabhavananda, Swami (with the assistance of Frederick Manchester): *The Spiritual Heritage of India.* London: George Allen and Unwin, 1962. New York: Doubleday, 1964.
A comprehensive history of the philosophy of a country which has never separated philosophy from religion. It is a sourcebook of spiritual teachings as well as a scholarly textbook.

Prabhavananda, Swami, and Isherwood, Christopher (translators): *The Bhagavad-Gita, the Song of God.* New York: New American Library, 1951. London: Phoenix House.
A readable and poetic version of the 'Bible' of Hinduism. It expresses beliefs and attitudes underlying all religions and embodies psychological truths of permanent value in the language of simplicity and nobility.

Prabhavananda, Swami, and Isherwood, Christopher (translators and editors): *How to Know God: The Yoga Aphorisms of Patanjali.* Hollywood: Vedanta Press, 1966.
One of the most practical guides to the spiritual life. The accompanying commentary applies the ancient teaching to the spiritual seeker of today. A basic textbook on Hindu psychology: gives a full picture of what yoga is, its aims and its practice.

Prabhavananda, Swami, and Manchester, Frederick (translators): *The Upanishads.* New York: New American Library, 1957.
Simple, poetic translation of the twelve principal Upanishads, omitting a few less essential passages. The Upanishads are the basic Hindu scriptures.

Smith, Huston: *The Religions of Man.* New York: Harper and Row, 1958.
A fine and fair presentation of the world's religions. Each account is approved by a recognized exponent of that particular religion.

Vivekananda, Swami: *The Complete Works of Swami Vivekananda,* 8 vols. Calcutta: Advaita Ashrama, 1962 (U.S. agent: Vedanta Press, Hollywood).
All of the speeches, writings, interviews, sayings and letters in existence from one of the foremost interpreters and teachers of Vedanta.

INDEX

Index

Kapila: defines happiness, 79; on perfection, 87; on suffering and misery, 79

Karma, 212, 243; doctrine, 44ff; law of, 195; meaning of, 171, 172; Yoga, 92, 155, 174

Kingdom of God, 143; and tribulations, 181

Knowledge: as food, 166-7; three knots of, 83; three steps to, 116

Koran, 31, 38, 55

Krishna, Sri, 33, 50, 52, 53, 62, 66, 69, 72, 92, 98, 107, 110, 127, 162, 169, 174, 187, 243-4; on action, 174; instructs Arjuna, 96; on control of the mind, 137, 147; as form of God, 46; and Karmas, 212; on Maya, 124-5; on Tapas, 154; on worship, 213; and his worshippers, 182, 213, 214; and Yoga, 154

Lawrence, Brother, 84

Lethargy, 166

Liberation, 127, 135; desire for, 127-8; and erudition, 181; longing for, 117; ultimate, 200

Life: after death, 59, 147-8; and evil, 34; full of discord, harmony and suffering, 159; goals of, 59ff

Livelihood, right, 203

Mahayana Buddhism, 205; elements of, 206

Man, composition of, 33: and God, 38; illumined, 98f; mind of, 133; as Spirit, 33; will of, and Atman, 182

Mandukya Upanishad, 61, 91, 112

Mantra, 36, 157, 251. See also Mantram, name of God, 168, 169

Maya, 43f, 122, 123, 181, 200, 212; limits within, 124

Meditation, 74, 86, 137, 155, 156, 167, 178, 203, 239-40; degrees of, 247; described, 157; formal, 93; Gautama, 190; habit of, 139; practice of, 138; spread of in China, 207; times of, 246; the West and, 28

Mind: cleaning, 147; control of, 136f; freeing of thought and consciousness, 144f; powers and uses of, 133ff

Mindfulness, 203

Misery and suffering, 79

Mohammed, 72, 105; revelation of, 31

Mohammedanism, 47

Mohammedans and truth, 53

Moral conduct, 199

Moral laziness, 200

Mundaka Upanishad, 157, 170; and Self, 149

Mystical states and drugs, 248

Mysticism, 32; definition of, 240; and escapism, 34; and form of God, 40; objection against, 34; and perfection, 39; and reasoning, 34

Mystics: and form of God, 40; and seeing God, 41; and the superconscious, 90

Narada, Indian teacher, 97

Naren: abilities and interests of, 217-18; discovers Brahman, 220; and the Divine Mother, 221; and fancy wants, 220-1; and the ideal of Brahmo Samaj, 219; and image worship, 220; goes to Ramakrishna, 217. See also Vivekananda, Swamiji

Nature, man's real and apparent, 170

Nirvana, 33, 90, 133, 199, 235; attained, 197; of Buddhism, 198; Buddha, 194; Buddha gives meaning to, 196; eternal peace, 202; ideal of Buddhahood, 192; illumination, 195; supreme enlightenment and peace, 204

Nirvikalpa samadhi, 39, 110, 111, 112

Nityamukta, ever-free soul, 218

Non-dualism, 43, 194. See also Dualism

Obstacles: explained, 150-1; and fear of death, 153; meaning of differs, 150; how to overcome, 153-4; in spiritual life, 149

Opposites, pain of, 171

Pamada, greatest sin, 200

Patanjali, 61, 67, 69; on disciplines, 154; and distracting impressions, 68; on Ego, 172; on existence of Godhead, 88; on obstacles, 150-1, 156; and theory of evolution, 150; Yoga, 143

Path to follow, 35, 36

257

Index